MATCH ANNUAL 2001

D1134545

TAKEN FROM THE PAGES OF MATCH facts

MATCH ANNUAL 2001 MANAGING EDITOR Chris Hunt **ART DIRECTOR** Darryl Tooth **ASSISTANT EDITOR** Ian Foster **FEATURES EDITOR** Bev Ward **SENIOR SUB-EDITOR** James Bandy **SUB-EDITORS** Richard Adams, Kev Pettman **DESIGNERS** Becky Booth, Martin Barry, Leyton Edwards, Calum Booth, Ben Bates, David Houghton **STAFF PHOTOGRAPHER** Phil Bagnall **CONTRIBUTORS** Tim Street, Cassia Baldock **AND THE REST OF THE MATCH TEAM** Hugh Sleight, Kev Hughes, Phil Smith, Giles Milton, Katherine Hannah, Dawn Brown, Lloyd Rogers, Richard Ecclestone & Russ Carvell.

MATCH BRITAIN'S BIGGEST-SELLING FOOTBALL MAGAZINE

Bretton Court, Bretton, Peterborough PE3 8DZ ★ Tel: 01733 264666/260333
Fax: 01733 465206 ★ e-mail: match.magazine@ecm.emap.com

ROUTE ONE

SHEARER GOES BACK TO HIS ROOTS!

It's like having Shearer as your schoolteacher. Cool!

Alan Shearer tries to out-stare the Sunderland fan in the audience.

This is by far the most interesting story I have read on me in ages. How do you do it Route One? You know, you're by far the best!

Alan Shearer may have quit the international scene after Euro 2000, but he's still something of an ambassador for English football. And one of the things he likes best is going out and meeting his fans. He invited Route 1 along on one such occasion, when he let a class of pupils from his former school fired questions at him. The first question thrown at him by an eager fan was how he would cope with being a manager when he retires from playing? **"I think becoming a manager is becoming more and more difficult, but it does interest me,"** the Newcastle captain answered. **"Football is all I've done since I was 15 and I'd like to give management a shot. I've been fortunate enough to work with a lot of very good and experienced managers, but John Barnes has proved that experience doesn't help you become a good manager the first time around. He might go into his next job and do very well though. I would like to become a manager, but I've still got a few years to play so it's still early to be talking about it."** Too right, there's still that elusive trophy to win at Newcastle. But for someone so ambitious, Route 1 has always wondered why he didn't join Man. United. So we bribed one of the pupils to ask! **"I had to decide whether to stay at Blackburn, go to Man. United, go abroad or join Newcastle. It was a big decision,"** says Al, but we already knew that. **"I always wanted to play in front of these fans at St James' Park. I think it's part of growing up in Newcastle that your mums, and particularly your dads, want you to play for Newcastle – your home town club. It was a big decision, but I enjoyed it and I still do."** Oh, we see now. That old chestnut. Well, the pupils certainly liked it anyway.

The striker tried to escape, but the kids were having none of it.

Little did the boy know that Shearer was writing 'you stink' on his plaster cast.

NOT SO FOXY FOXES

Leicester may not spring to everyone's mind as a strong Premiership team, but they are the League Cup holders and have beaten Liverpool at Anfield on their last three visits there. Plus they have a great new manager in Peter Taylor, but what's the secret to why they do so well without spending much money? **"It's team spirit, down to earth players and no flash harry stars,"** explains 'keeper Tim Flowers. **"We just bond together and play well as a team. You don't have to be a brain surgeon to work out how we play. We're a 100 per cent in-your-face team and we work hard all season."** Now comes the hard part, making Stan Collymore work hard all season and be a little less flash.

F.R.I.E.N.D.S

match asks the stars who's their best mate in footy?

"Erik Meijer is a very good friend of mine. I played with Erik when we were at PSV Eindhoven in Holland and we still get on very well. I don't see him very often, but I have been to Liverpool to watch him play before."

· arthur numan · rangers ·

OWEN'S INSIGHT

Will David Thompson be an England regular?

Stevie G – an England captain in the making?

After the abysmal games England played at Euro 2000, it's no wonder that fans are talking of the England teams of the future. And it seems that Michael Owen's one player who's looking forward to it. **"If you look at the young players in the Under-21s, they will be great talents in five years' time,"** Michael told Route 1. **"I enjoyed coming through at a young age and it has helped me as a young player to learn a lot, which meant I developed well. There are some players in the senior side who are young as well, like Sol Campbell. The prospects of the England side in five years' time is just frightening. We have lads at Liverpool – Steven Gerrard, Jamie Carragher and David Thompson – who are all exceptional talents."** Five years' time, ready for the 2006 World Cup in Germany. But can England really wait that long?

SUPERSTITIONS

Footy stars reveal the things they do for luck.

WHAT DO YOU GET UP TO THEN SHAUN?
"I try to stick to the same routine. I wear the same suit, the same shirt, the same pants and socks."

SURELY YOU WASH THEM EACH WEEK?
"No, I don't wash them!"

YUK. ANY CLEAN SUPERSTITIONS?
"Yeah, I do the same preparation. I get rubbed before the game by the physio and eat the same food. I don't like to change."

NO, BUT CLEAN PANTS MIGHT HELP!

SHAUN NEWTON
CHARLTON

HODDLE'S DAN CLUB

Glenn Hoddle may have been public enemy No.1 at the end of his reign as England manager, but one player who will always love him is Chelsea's Dan Petrescu. **"I have played under a lot of managers, but the one I have learned most from is Glenn Hoddle,"** Dan tells Route 1. **"He has helped my career the most. I speak to him sometimes and when I become a manager, I will ask Glenn for help."** Quite!

The Contenders

After failing so badly at Euro 2000, **MATCH** picks 11 young stars to replace the current England team!

RICHARD WRIGHT
ipswich town

It's only a matter of time before Wright fills David Seaman's boots between the posts.

WES BROWN
manchester united

Will be aiming to put his injury nightmare behind him and get back to his very best.

JON HARLEY
chelsea

One of a rare breed of left-footed defenders. Will mature in time for the 2002 World Cup.

RIO FERDINAND
west ham

Reads the game well and is comfortable on the ball. The future of England's defence.

JONATHAN WOODGATE
leeds

Another defender who can bring the ball out of defence. Already an assured performer.

STEVEN GERRARD
liverpool

Should become an England regular with his tough tackling and accurate passing.

JOE COLE
west ham

Could be the answer to England's problems in midfield. Still has a lot to prove though.

KIERON DYER
newcastle

Causes havoc in opposition defences. Needs to improve his final ball into the box.

EMILE HESKEY
liverpool

The powerful forward has the potential to lead the line for both club and country.

MICHAEL BRIDGES
leeds

Lots of competition up front, but Bridges has an excellent record of scoring loads of goals.

LUKE CHADWICK
manchester united

The senior players at United all rave about Chadwick's skill. Is he the new Ryan Giggs?

POKEYMEN

#15 Giggsypuff
TYPE: Deceptive

Description

You may not have seen this one before. That's because Giggsypuff is a very rare Pokeyman and doesn't come along much more than once in a generation. Although he is cute and cuddly in appearance, he is deceptive and you should definitely watch out for him. When he attacks, even the toughest Pokeymen are sent to dreamland and their defences are rendered useless.

Last seen in Episode 74: Unleashing a quite spectacular attack on the Arsenal defence in the biggest battle of 1999.

Route 1's ongoing series. The FA's gotta charge 'em all!

THE WRIGHT STRIKERS!

Most goalkeepers fear reading the team sheets before the start of a game and finding out they're up against the likes of Alan Shearer, Dennis Bergkamp or Michael Owen. But not Richard Wright. **"I've always wanted to play in the Premiership against strikers like Alan Shearer and Michael Owen,"** the promising 'keeper told us. **"I've been involved with them in the England set-up. They got the ball early and had a lot of movement on the ball. It was just a good experience to see them both close-up."** Maybe, but wait until they score past you – you'll soon wish you were playing against Stockport's finest.

ROUTE 1 MOVIES GOLD

brings you a cinematic footy classic from the 20th century
STAN BY ME

STAR-STRUCK UNITED!

Meeting a football legend like Sir Bobby Charlton must be a bit terrifying, but it doesn't bother the United boys, according to Phil Neville. **"Sir Bobby is very modest about his achievements. He always asks how we are and congratulates all of us after a game,"** Phil told Route 1. So does he give the United team advice? **"I'm sure he would if we asked him, but he's not the type of person who preaches about his career."** Maybe he should, though. Route 1 reckons he should let the England squad into the secret of how to win a World Cup!

Keegan's policy on bringing in young players goes a bit far.

The ol' man still knows a trick or two.

It's just like talking to David Beckham.

Another player scores past Keegan's side.

"I taught Becks everything he knows about free-kicks."

Michael Chopra keeps his eye on the ball.

Keegan forgets to take the ball.

KEEPING THE HAMMERS

Stephen Bywater's West Ham debut was a baptism of fire. He came on for the injured Shaka Hislop against Bradford last season and conceded four goals. The Hammers still won 5-4, but Bywater is getting lots of help to ensure that game was a one-off. **"Les Sealey is an outstanding goalkeeping coach – he's always reminding us about all his medals!"** Stephen told Route 1, before dishing the dirt on his close rivals. **"Shaka Hislop is a top man. He and Craig Forrest have helped me tremendously. You have to learn from watching them in games. But their dress sense is poor – they're both stuck in the '60s!"**

Chopra puts his best foot forward.

IN DA COURT!

Leeds' new signing **Olivier Dacourt** is the new judge and jury for the Premiership, so who's in Da Court?

NAME: Chris Sutton

CHARGE: Failing to score for former club Chelsea last season after a huge £10 million transfer fee.

SENTENCE: "You may have moved young lad, but you must still face your responsibilities like a man. So you will be taken from Da Court and forced to wash-up in the Chelsea canteen until you have repaid the money."

FINAL PLEA: "I had injury problems your honour, and I've moved now, and it was such a big transfer. Don't make me do the dishes!"

Newcastle midfielder **Kieron Dyer** *strolls down memory lane with MATCH!*

...FOOTBALL BOOTS

"I was about seven years old at the time and I was bought a pair of football boots which were about two sizes too big for me. I think they were called something like Adidas L2000 and they had green stripes on them. I wore about ten pairs of thick socks with them so they'd fit!"

...FOOTBALL KIT

"Yeah, I remember it was one of Liverpool's old kits. The shirt was grey with flashes of red all over it. I was obviously a Liverpool fan at the time. I got it for Christmas when I was a kid and I was over the moon with it."

...GAME AS A PLAYER

"The first time I played football properly was for one of the teams at school. They put me in a team that was three years above my own age group. I think I scored the winner as well! We won 3-1 against one of the rival schools where I used to live, so that was especially good."

...GAME AS A FAN

"The first game I went to as a football fan was at Portman Road. Ipswich were playing Derby County at home and it was either 1986 or 1987. Derby won the game 2-0, unfortunately, so I didn't think it was a very good first match to watch. I wouldn't say I was a mad Ipswich supporter, but when they got promoted to the Premier League I went to quite a few games because all the big teams were coming to play at Portman Road."

...RECORD

"The first record I ever bought was a single by a group called New Edition. Their lead singer at the time was the great Bobby Brown. The song was called Candy Girl."

...KISS

"Yes, I can remember my first kiss. It was with a girl called Tanya and I was nine years old at the time. It was over quite quickly, though! Ha, ha, ha! I was very embarrassed by it all!"

...DRINK

"Erm, I can't really remember when I had my first drink. It was probably at home with my mum and dad, though."

KEEGAN & THE NEW SHEARER

"Give it your best shot Michael!" shouted Kevin Keegan, who was having target practice at an Adidas coaching day with Michael Chopra, the 16-year-old pro who's tipped to be the next Geordie goal-machine. **"I have never met Kevin before, even though I play for the England Under-16s,"** said Michael. **I'm a Newcastle fan and Kevin was a legend up here as a player. He made me have a free-kick competition with him, which showed the kids how to take free-kicks."** The youngsters at the coaching day want to follow the progress Michael's made, even if they don't get spotted. **"A couple will always slip though the net,"** said Keegan. **"I met a certain 13-year-old on this training ground called Alan Shearer when he came along to a Newcastle soccer day – we obviously didn't see his talent then. Much later when I was manager I ended up paying £15 million for him, that was a costly slip!"** Just a bit!

'Ere, Kev, can you hold your leg up like this for more than two minutes? My record is three days!

Young Michael Chopra is desperate to be the next Newcastle goal machine.

V-DUKA BOMBER

Former Croatia Zagreb striker Mark Viduka was named Scotland's Player Of The Year by his fellow professionals last season after scoring 25 goals for Celtic. But Viduka already had a reputation for goalscoring before he arrived in Scotland. **"The nickname that they gave to me in Croatia was the V-bomber,"** Mark told Route 1. **"I was called that because of the amount of goals I scored for my team in Croatia. I was a bit of a hero over there. I don't know what the secret is, though – you just have to be in the right place at the right time."** Yeah, Mark, or maybe you scored so many goals last season because some of the defences you came across weren't exactly world-class opponents.

LEBOEUF'S LE-LURVE

French footballers have a weird view of life. Eric Cantona would rant on about seagulls and trawler boats, while David Ginola spilled out his fair share of philosophical nonsense. Now it's the turn of everyone's favourite Frenchie, Chelsea's Frank Leboeuf. **"When you win your first trophy it is like losing your virginity,"** he tells Route 1. **"Once you have got it out of the way you can carry on with life, carry on with your football."** Understand that analogy? Right Frank, carry on. **"I was 28 years old when I won my first trophy – I didn't see myself finishing my career without winning anything."** Okay, thanks for that enlightenment.

WHO IS THE BEST... england striker?

Are they shouting for me or big Niall Quinn?

Sunderland striker **Kevin Phillips** selects four contenders.

MICHAEL OWEN
liverpool

"When he's fit and on top of his game, Michael's definitely a world-class striker. He's quick and he'll take on defenders. Those are great assets to any side."

EMILE HESKEY
liverpool

"At his best Emile's phenomenal. He's got such great pace and strength. He isn't a natural goalscorer but he creates loads of chances. He's unbelievable!"

ANDY COLE
manchester united

"He's just a natural goalscorer. Andy's quick and he scores lots of goals. He can take defences on, get in the box and score goals at the highest level for any side."

ROBBIE FOWLER
liverpool

"I've trained with Robbie and I think he's the best finisher in the country. He's instinctive, always hits the target and if he's fit it'll be great news for England."

KING FOR A DAY

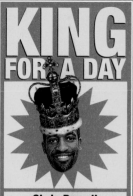

Chris Powell
Charlton

King Chris reveals to **Route 1** what he'd do if he ruled the nation!

Who would you knight?
"I'd have to knight Mark Bright! I'll do that to him in honour of his services to football! He's an ex team-mate of mine and I can honestly tell you that everyone loved him at Charlton. He did really well in his career and he's doing well in his new career in the media. He was a player that younger people could look up to and I would definitely make him a 'Sir'. He'd love it!"

Who would you behead?
"That would be Brighty as well! Ha, ha, ha. You say that I can behead anyone though? Then I'd behead any Arsenal player because I'm a Spurs fan!"

Who would be your Queen?
"Oh, now that's a tough one! I think I'd choose my daughter, that's a nice and safe option! My daughter's name is Morgan and I'm sure that she'd love to be a Queen for the day. She deserves it!"

What law would you change?
"I'd bring in a new law so that everything in life was free, so you wouldn't have to pay for anything! It may cause a lot of problems and there would be riots and stuff in shops, but it would be good to just have anything you ever wanted."

What would you eat?
"I get to choose anything I want to eat? You keep asking some tricky questions! Okay, I'd have a king-size Twix, or loads of them! They're by far the best food around – I'd be scoffing them all day at the feasts in my castle. I know that too much chocolate isn't very good for you, so I'd have to make sure that I kept up with my training routines to maintain my fitness. Mind you, I probably wouldn't have to do that much training if I was King. That sounds good!"

WAGE RISE FOR REFS!

Do you reckon match referees have been any better this season? Well they certainly should be, because they're being paid loads more money! The men in the middle had a 50 per cent pay rise in August and by March their wages will have doubled from last season, meaning they'll get paid £1,200 per game! That's not bad when you consider that the vast majority of referees have a day job as well. Maybe Route 1 should have a go at being a ref...

Rile Niall

Football's biggest bovver-boys queue up to try to wind-up Sunderland's genial Irishman.

This Week
NEIL RUDDOCK

NEIL RUDDOCK: "In PE lessons at school you were always the last one to be picked, you big kipper. Even your brothers chose you last, and when they did eventually pick you out, it was as a goalpost!"

NIALL: "You're right Neil, so you are. I'd just stand there waiting for the ball and nod it in whenever it came near me. It worked every time, so it did! And look where I am today."

BECKHAM the predator

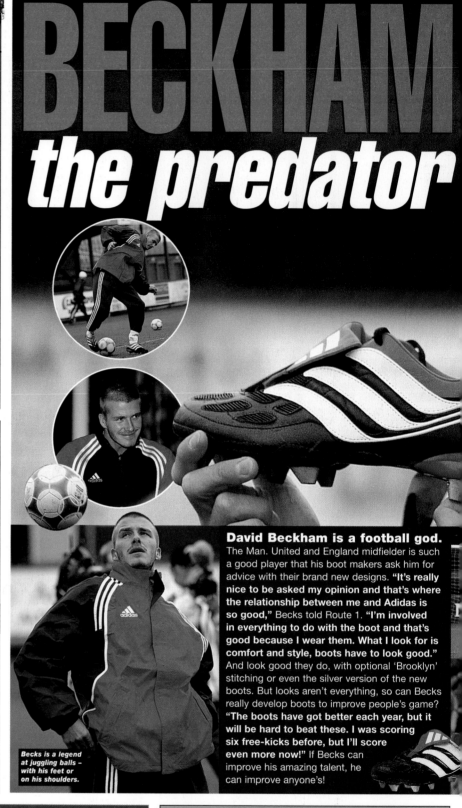

David Beckham is a football god. The Man. United and England midfielder is such a good player that his boot makers ask him for advice with their brand new designs. **"It's really nice to be asked my opinion and that's where the relationship between me and Adidas is so good,"** Becks told Route 1. **"I'm involved in everything to do with the boot and that's good because I wear them. What I look for is comfort and style, boots have to look good."** And look good they do, with optional 'Brooklyn' stitching or even the silver version of the new boots. But looks aren't everything, so can Becks really develop boots to improve people's game? **"The boots have got better each year, but it will be hard to beat these. I was scoring six free-kicks before, but I'll score even more now!"** If Becks can improve his amazing talent, he can improve anyone's!

Becks is a legend at juggling balls – with his feet or on his shoulders.

LOYAL BATIGOL

With all the comings and goings in modern-day football, it's refreshing to see a footballer being loyal – even if, erm, he's now being loyal to someone else! Argentina star striker Gabriel Batistuta stayed with Fiorentina when they were relegated to Serie B a few years back, but decided that after many years in Florence he would join another club – Roma. He hadn't been in Rome for five minutes when he declared he was ready to die for his new club. **"I will defend this shirt to the death,"** he proclaimed to the Roma faithful. **"My team-mates and I will give everything for this club. On seeing you I feel like playing and winning straight away."** What more do you want? The Serie A golden boot, perhaps?

GEORGIE G

The word on the street wiv de main man of de Spurs Massive!

"Booyakasha! Dis week I is finking what I is going to get me crew in de Spurs Massive for Christmas. Me mate Dave reckons he can sort me out with nuff videos off the back of a lorry. but I is still finking these ain't the sort of things I want me mates watching. Dave says the vids would be perfect for me main man Chris Armstrong. 'cos they'll tell him how to score from all different positions. I told Dave dis ain't a good idea. Me main man Chris Armstrong knows how to score. 'e just don't like showing everyone. Till next time. Keep it real."

Becks dons his Predator Precisions and tries to score all those extra free-kicks.

SHEARER'S REPLACEMENT

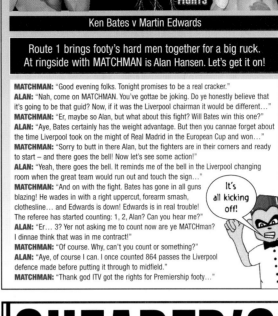

Paul Robinson may not have figured in Robby Bobson's plans much this year, but the Newcastle striker will never be forgotten for being selected ahead of Alan Shearer. Ruud Gullit picked Robinson rather than the £15 million man for last season's derby clash with Sunderland. **"It was complimentary that I was picked ahead of Alan Shearer for the Sunderland game,"** explained Paul. **"I used to room with Alan but he dumped me as soon as Rob Lee got back in the team! I don't room with anyone else now because the gaffer says I'm too hyper!"** Shearer obviously couldn't deal with the pace of his counterpart, but Robbo just loves his captain. **"It's unbelievable playing alongside Alan Shearer. Four years ago I was at school watching him on TV!"** And now it's from the bench!

BRADFORD'S STUART McOLD

Stuart McCall's little old legs don't carry him as far as they used to. In fact, when the Scot returned to Bradford for his second spell with The Bantams, he had to remind them that he was getting on a bit. **"I think a lot of people thought I'd be as good a player as I was previously, which put a lot of pressure on me,"** he told Route 1. **"Some people thought I came back to ease down my career and go into management, which wasn't the case. But things have gone really well, although obviously I'm not as mobile as I was ten years ago."** Exactly, that's why you've suddenly realised that management wasn't such a bad idea after all and taken up the offer of assistant boss at Bradford!"

TOP 10

Goalkeepers in the world still playing footy today.

1 **PETER SCHMEICHEL**
sporting lisbon

The Denmark stopper is still the world's No.1 'keeper. Rudolph has a trophy cabinet full of medals and a reputation for intimidating strikers.

2 **EDWIN VAN DER SAR**
juventus

The huge Dutch international is dominant in the air and has excellent all-round ability, a serious rival to Schmeichel's throne.

3 **GIANLUIGI BUFFON**
parma

The 22-year-old Italian No.1 is renowned for acrobatic saves and reacting superbly from close-range. Missed Euro 2000 with injury.

4 **FABIEN BARTHEZ**
man. united

The bald eagle is a lively 'keeper who loves to entertain the crowd, and was part of the France side that won Euro 2000.

5 **OLIVER KAHN**
bayern munich

Germany's finest says he felt humiliated after conceding two late goals in the 1999 European Cup Final, but he's still a solid 'keeper.

6 **DAVID SEAMAN**
arsenal

Nearing the end of his top-class career, but penalty king Seaman is still England's No.1 and difficult to beat, unless you try lobbing him!

7 **NIGEL MARTYN**
leeds

Unlucky not to get more chances for England, Martyn is an excellent shot-stopper and reliable performer. Has helped Leeds improve.

8 **JOSE LUIS CHILAVERT**
velez sarsfield

Eccentric Paraguayan 'keeper who has scored 35 goals from penalties and free-kicks in his career. Pretty useful between the sticks too!

9 **IKER CASILLAS**
real madrid

The 18-year-old started last season as only the third-choice 'keeper at Real, but he went on to be a revelation. Just ask Fergie and Man. United.

10 **JOSÉ RENÉ HIGUITA**
veracruz

He may not be the best 'keeper in the world, but after his scorpion kick save at Wembley, the mad Colombian has to get a mention!

NO SKY BLUES FOR KEANE

Robbie Keane, for many people one of the best young players of the new millennium, has spoken out about his first year at Coventry. Expectations were high when Gordon Strachan signed the Irish hitman and Keane was surprised the club didn't achieve more last season. "We really wanted to finish in the top ten," he said. "But I still think it was the best move I could have made. It's helped me to progress as a player, Gordon Strachan is a fantastic manager and definitely knows his football. If I had a doubt about the club's potential I would not have signed in the first place." Insist all you like Robbie. Route 1 knows you're only there 'cos Fergie refused to sign you for Man. United!

NOT TO BE CONFUSED...

> Football is my only religion!

Christian Ziege | **Christian leader**

GIO'S SCOTTISH LESSON

It's something of a running joke that Scottish football isn't the best in the world. The cliché is when players join a Scottish club, their international prospects are harmed and they don't develop. But it's certainly not a step down, says Rangers and Holland ace Giovanni van Bronckhorst. "Some people said this when I moved from Feyenoord but I think it is not true," he told Route 1. "Some people said I should go to England or Italy but I chose Scotland and the Scottish league has made me a better player. When I was at Feyenoord I thought I was a good player but in Holland the game is slower and you do not always have to do quite so much running as here. At Rangers I have learned to play good football, but at the same time always working hard for 90 minutes, so it has brought on other parts of my game that might not have been so strong." So there you go. Players can learn something from football in Scotland, so there!

KEEPER v KEEPER

This year saw the Clash of the Titans! No, not England v Germany, nor France v Italy, but the battle between two young upstarts who fancy their chances in the Premiership – Nicky Weaver v Richard Wright! Previously a friendly rivalry between the two former Division One 'keepers, they are both progressing at speed. Ipswich man Wright is hoping to become England's No.1, but Man. City's Nicky Weaver is having none of it. "Playing in the Premiership will definitely be vital for my own personal development," he said. "It's certainly better than being in the First Division and it will give us both a better chance of getting into the full England squad." And Wrighty agrees that the rivalry will intensify! Get in your corners boys!

HOME SWEET

Derby County's Malcolm Christie may have burst onto the Premiership scene from nowhere last season, but after being labelled one of the Premiership's top young strikers, he's unlikely to let the new stardom go to his head.

The Rams' striker prefers to just be flash on the pitch by scoring goals, and stays at home rather than splashing out on a plush pad of his own. That's why, after training and matches, Christie's straight back to his parents and his home town of Stamford in Lincolnshire.

"I think staying at home has helped me a lot to be honest," Christie told Route 1. "I was in digs at Derby for a couple of months when I first joined the club but I didn't really like it that much. You had one room to yourself and there wasn't much privacy, so I used to nip home now and again. It's a great pressure off me to come home and have my mum and dad sort things out for me. I think I'd struggle a bit if I lived on my own." But living with mum and dad doesn't mean Christie can't go out and live it up a bit – he still likes a night out on the town now and again! "I've got my friends here, my family's here and I can go out at night and everyone accepts me for who I am," he said. "You come across the odd person who's a bit jealous of what I've achieved, but you just have to ignore them because everyone else is delighted for me, I think everyone at home is happy for me." And they'll be even happier, Malcolm, if you manage to become an England Under-21 regular this season!

CHRISTIE 12

Christie's treble dent Whittlesey double bi

The man who frames anything – no need for wallpaper in his house!

OWEN'S NEW KID

For the last couple of years Michael Owen has been the new kid on the block and the hottest thing on Merseyside. Now he's having to relinquish that title to the new kid, his Liverpool team-mate Steven Gerrard. Still, he knew it would happen. "I've played with him since we were ten years old, right the way through the Liverpool ranks. You ask any of the players that were playing with him then – everyone knew he'd go right to the top, he is such a good player," Michael said. "I can't think of a fault in his game, apart from experience, but he's going to get that. He can tackle, head, pass; he has a good engine, makes forward runs – everything you could want." Well, everything except a date with Rachel from S-Club 7!

HOME FOR CHRISTIE

My name's Malcolm – gottle of geer, ha, ha!

Christie's treble dents Whittlesey double bid

Rangers' Christie

STAMFORD SOCCER STAR CHRISTIE: EXCLUSIVE

The striker's always made the headlines.

STARS IN THEIR EYES

This Week Matthew, Michael Gray is....

Macy Gray

GIVE US A CLUE!

"Right lads. It's one word. It starts with 'r' and sounds like jelegation."

GARY PALLISTER
MIDDLESBROUGH

BEST GAME

"United's 1991 Cup-Winners' Cup Final against Barcelona definitely stands out. It was just a fantastic night in Rotterdam, a fantastic result and a fantastic game, with fantastic celebrations afterwards. It couldn't have been managed any better and it was one of those days that you don't want to end."

BEST PLAYER

"If I had to pick one player – and I'm not creeping now because he's my manager – it would be Bryan Robson. I played with Eric Cantona, who was a world-class performer and gave United the dimension to go on to win titles with his vision and creativity, but a man who had everything was Bryan Robson. As a competitor he was second to none and he was a great motivator as captain. It was great to play with him."

BEST GROUND

"I would say the Nou Camp, but when I was at United we lost 4-0, so we didn't have a very good experience there! I would also say Old Trafford, because of all the experiences and fond memories I had there. It's something special on European nights, but it can be quiet in games against lower opposition. I'll always remember playing at that ground."

BEST STRIKER

"Ronaldo, when Man. United played Barcelona at The Nou Camp. The 4-0 scoreline says it all. He is the best striker I've ever played against because I just couldn't get anywhere near him. He was so alive and knew what was going on in the game around him. He could do anything with a ball, either when he was moving or standing still. He was a really intelligent player and a very elusive striker."

BEST TEAM

"Probably one of the best team performances I've seen is when we played against Arsenal a few years ago. We lost 6-0 and it was a very hard game. They were so much better than us that day and everything they did just went right. We couldn't stop them."

COTTEE'S OFF!

Don't be surprised if you don't see much of Tony Cottee again. The Leicester striker was so happy with his League Cup winner's medal last season, he's not that bothered about playing again! **"I'm really pleased with winning the cup and I can retire now that I have finally won a trophy,"** Tony says. Mind you, as he goes on, the medal becomes insignificant. **"It was one of the best moments in my career, although I don't know if it beats making my debut for England."** Well, why didn't you retire back then, Cottster?

OASIS CAN'T AFFORD CITY PRICES

Man. City and Indie rockers Oasis appear to be on opposite parallels – while one rises, the other one slumps. But while Oasis seem to steadily drop from the shoulders of giants, so their beloved City have risen from the depths of Division Two to the top flight. Once regarded as a possible future chairman of City, Noel Gallagher scoffs at the idea that he and Liam could take over the club. **"I don't have enough money to buy into the club,"** he ranted at Route 1. **"We never had enough money. The talk of us buying the club was all bulls***. The idea was only to put our names on the shirts, to have Oasis written on the shirts. There was never talk of buying, because if I had £10 million, I'd find better places to put it than a football club."** Like where, Noel? We dare not even imagine.

O'NEILL'S BLUNDER

Football managers are notoriously quote-worthy, especially when they've recently been appointed manager of a new team, but even more so when it's Martin O'Neill. When asked if Celtic was the only club he was prepared to leave Leicester for, O'Neill said: **"There is another club which springs to mind but there's no vacancy there at the moment because they have one of the best managers in the world."** Okay, let's work this one out. He was obviously not referring to Bradford or Sheffield Wednesday there folks! O'Neill removed his foot from his big mouth and continued: **"With 60,000 people coming to watch Celtic play every week, there's a real chance for me to restore this club's fortunes and I'll do everything I can to make that possible."** Second choice to Man. United? Bet the Celtic fans loved that! Still, it makes a change from coming second to neighbours and arch-rivals Rangers yet again!

ALAN SHEARER
Newcastle United

Every year the Newcastle skipper's supposedly past his best, but surely he's done some things right?

CHILD PRODIGY

Alan is spotted by a Southampton scout and joins The Saints at 15. He then scores 13 goals in one game at school! And it wasn't even against Sheffield Wednesday! **RATING 7**

STARTLING DEBUT

A hat-trick on his Saints debut makes Shearer an instant success and a household name. It's not long before a big-money move to Blackburn comes along. **RATING 10**

BREAKING RECORDS

Shearer breaks records the day he signs for Blackburn for £3.6 million and continues when he becomes the first player to score 30 goals three seasons in a row. **RATING 9**

TITLE WINNER

Shearer forms a lethal partnership with Chris Sutton at Blackburn and they shoot Rovers to the league title in 1995, pipping Man. United on the last day of the season. **RATING 10**

EURO '96 STAR

Although the Championship evades England, Shearer takes home the Golden Boot award as he finishes top scorer with five goals in as many games. **RATING 10**

HE'S COMING HOME

Soon after Euro '96 the Geordie boy fulfils a childhood dream by getting a record £15 million transfer to his boyhood heroes Newcastle and claims the No.9 jersey. **RATING 9**

BAD SEASON

His first season with The Magpies ends on a low. Despite finishing with the golden boot, Kevin Keegan departs and Newcastle finish second in the Premiership. **RATING 4**

LEADER OF THE PACK

Shearer becomes England captain in the absence of Tony Adams and leads the team into the World Cup in France. But England sadly bow out in the second round. **RATING 6**

DROPPED BY THE TOON

Shearer never sees eye to eye with new manager Ruud Gullit and, after an awful start to the 1999-2000 season, he gets dropped for the crucial Sunderland game. **RATING 3**

GOLDEN GOALS

In the 1999-2000 season, Shearer scores the 300th goal of his career against Arsenal, 199 of which were scored in the league. Not bad going by anyone's standards! **RATING 9**

EURO 2000

In his international swansong, Alan scores to give England their first tournament win against Germany in 34 years, but England go out in the first round. **RATING 5**

SHEARER RATING 8.2

SHEAR CLASS!

JAMMY GERMANY!

About the last person we need is a poncey ex-tennis player to tell us why Germany (whose ass England whupped 1-0 at Euro 2000) were successful in clinching the 2006 World Cup. But even Route 1 had to begrudgingly acknowledge that Boris Becker had put his finger on where England went wrong in the bid. **"You concentrated on the past. We talked about the future."** A good point well made. He added that success wouldn't have happened without football legend Franz Beckenbauer. **"Usually, when you think of German people, you think of people who are arrogant, self-conscious and strong-minded about what they can do."** Right again. **"But Beckenbauer is not a man who breaks down the door to get into a room. He's not loud, he's polite and dignified. You know with him leading the bid the Germans were more humble than anyone else."** And with that, he blew a raspberry and wandered off into the sunset.

> "If he was an inch taller he'd be the best centre-half in the whole of Britain."

Sir Alex Ferguson says Gary Neville needs to stretch a little bit more before games.

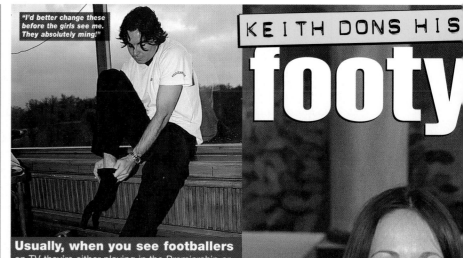

"I'd better change these before the girls see me. They absolutely ming!"

KEITH DONS HIS footy

Usually, when you see footballers on TV they're either playing in the Premiership or being interviewed, but not Middlesbrough's star midfielder Keith O'Neill. Oh no. Not content with appearing on the small screen as just a football star, he became a presenter for 'Footy Shorts', Channel 4's top footy show!

So the obvious question to ask was what was more nerve-wracking – playing in front of 35,000 Boro fans or performing in front of the cameras? **"I didn't have loads of lines and I didn't have to think about too many things, so it was quite easy really,"** he revealed when Route 1 popped down to see the programme being filmed at the end of last season. **"Sometimes it got a bit too easy and I didn't do it properly, so I needed to be careful of that."**

And with foxy co-presenters Sophie Blake and Sarah Cawood around, it was easy for anyone to get distracted. But the Boro ace looked like the consummate professional when we were casting our critical eye. Could this be the start of a brand new career after football – the next Alan Hansen perhaps? **"I don't know about that,"** he said. **"But I just like doing TV stuff. I once did a few children's shows in Ireland. I can make a bit of a show of myself at times, though!"**

So what did the rest of the Boro team make of the budding Des Lynam? **"Not all of the lads knew,"** he admitted. **"A few of them said that their kids had seen it. Now they've all seen the show and they think it's really good. They have given me a bit of stick, but it's been nothing too bad."** Now that's no good is it? The team not giving you stick? Gazza would turn in his grave.

Keith learns his lines – well he will, after he's read all his fan mail.

My life in pictures

Route 1 looks through the photo album of LIVERPOOL star striker ROBBIE FOWLER.

A FRESH-FACED LAD AT 'POOL WANTING TO MAKE HIS MARK.

I WAS ALWAYS WELL DRESSED, EVEN AS A YOUNG LAD!

EVEN I NEED A BIT OF HELP WITH MY LOOKS EVERY SO OFTEN!

IT'S NICE FOR ME TO MEET THE FANS AS OFTEN AS POSSIBLE!

THE EARS GIVE IT AWAY - ME AND THE GREAT GARY LINEKER!

IT'S ALWAYS NICE TO MEET UP WITH MY MATE RUSHIE, TOO.

HOW TIMES CHANGE!

Football has changed loads over the last 20 years. Players are now paid huge amounts in wages and they're worshipped like pop stars. So it's a good life for young footballers nowadays, driving around the town in their flashy motors, as Southampton and Wales 'keeper Paul Jones revealed to Route 1. **"James Beattie has a Porsche and Matty Oakley drives an Aston Martin DB7! They both got a fair amount of stick from the other players when they first bought their cars, but we've laid off them now. When I was that age and first starting out, I used to knock around in an old Vauxhall!"** And you probably still do old timer!

shorts

After a good old chuckle reading their favourite mag, the 'Footy Shorts' team are ready to film another episode!

"So then, how do you like your eggs done in the morning?"

Keith says the Boro lads give him some stick about the show.

KICKING UP A STINK!

Major tournaments are turning into graveyards nowadays, with a mass exodus of managers after the last World Cup and Euro 2000. It seems that if you don't perform – or even if you do in some cases – you're expected to quit or you get the sack. But does anyone really fancy taking over these positions to pick up the pieces? After Euro 2000, the Italian Coach, Dino Zoff, quit his job despite taking his side to the final and within a whisker of victory, but this time the successor might do a better job. The new Italian coach, former Fiorentina manager Giovanni Trapattoni, seems to have this management lark sussed. **"Coaches are like fish,"** the philosophical Italian boss explained. What? **"After a while they start to stink."** So the best advice to keep your job? Just take a shower like any ordinary person! Or keep yourself carefully wrapped up in the fridge. You decide.

HENRY WANTS THE MOON!

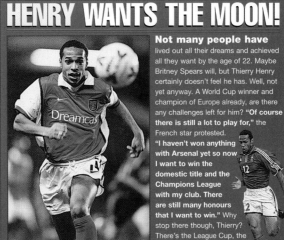

Not many people have lived out all their dreams and achieved all they want by the age of 22. Maybe Britney Spears will, but Thierry Henry certainly doesn't feel he has. Well, not yet anyway. A World Cup winner and champion of Europe already, are there any challenges left for him? **"Of course there is still a lot to play for,"** the French star protested. **"I haven't won anything with Arsenal yet so now I want to win the domestic title and the Champions League with my club. There are still many honours that I want to win."** Why stop there though, Thierry? There's the League Cup, the FA Vase and a whole load of other Mickey Mouse cups!

ROBBO WELCOMES Back UNITED

If you asked the vast majority of managers, they would probably be annoyed that Man. United are back in the FA Cup this season, but not Middlesbrough boss and ex-United hero Bryan Robson. **"I think it was disappointing for everyone to lose such a charismatic club in the FA Cup,"** the Boro boss said. **"I think United were the only ones who couldn't win in that situation, because people would have criticised them whatever decision they made. I think it was good that they were representing us on the world stage, but it's good to have them back in the competition, although I wasn't that happy about them knocking us out of the 1999 FA Cup."** Too right Bryan, and no doubt you'll change your mind if it happens again!

SUPERSTITIONS

Footy stars reveal the things they do for luck.

SO STEVIE, WHAT DO YOU DO?
"My rituals change every game. I'll have one match where I have to go down and have breakfast at a certain time, but then we'll get beaten so I'll change it!"

THAT'S HARDLY A SUPERSTITION THEN!
"Well, I don't believe in it that much."

SO WHY HAVE ONE?
"Because I think, 'Oh well I'll try this and see if it works'."

YOU KEEP ON LOOKING, STONEY!

STEVE STONE
ASTON VILLA

IAN'S WRIGHT!

Ian Wright may have quit footy at the end of last season to concentrate on his burgeoning TV career, but he still wants to play an active part in football. **"I want to stay involved in soccer schools, but it's been really hard to keep doing that while I've been doing this TV work,"** Wrighty said to Route 1, before going off on one. **"But I do think that footballers should try to give something back to the kids. Coaching benefits so many children out there and it gets them off the streets – the kids are genuinely enthusiastic about any professional footballer they meet, but not all footballers feel the same. Some of them just do their job, then they go home and that's the end of it. I think there should be more to it than that."** Too right Wrighty. You tell 'em son!

WHERE DID IT ALL GO WRONG?

Route 1 charts the tragic fall from grace of our beloved England.

ENGLAND

WHAT THEY WERE...

WORLD CUP WINNERS
Yes, we know everyone keeps going on about it, but we won a World Cup. It may have been back in 1966, but that's the only success we've had so we've got to keep going on about it.

PROUD TO BE ENGLISH
Under Terry Venables, players were proud to pull on the shirt and fight for the cause and the Three Lions were so close to the Euro '96 Final.

FIGHTERS
England could come back from a goal down. Remember the Argentina game at France '98? We lost on penalties, but played like we wanted to win.

LOSING ON PENALTIES
It's fair to say England have had their fair share of bad luck where penalties are concerned. We could have had great success with a bit more luck.

LOSING TO GERMANY
The Germans managed to beat us at the 1990 World Cup and at Euro '96 on penalties. It seemed like we'd never beat them in a tournament.

WHAT THEY ARE...

GERMANY BEATERS
We turned the tables with the 1-0 win over Germany at Euro 2000, but this was more a reflection of how rubbish the Germans have become, not how much England have improved.

COMPLACENT
With all Kevin Keegan's cheap talk of winning Euro 2000, the England boys thought they only had to turn up for the games to win. The result? England were knocked out at the first hurdle.

DISINTERESTED
It seems half of the players just aren't bothered about turning out for their country any more, like England should be doing them a favour!

SECOND-RATE TEAM
As France win every trophy in sight, England have slipped out of the top 20 FIFA-ranked teams. Teams don't fear England and with Wembley gone, the home record could get worse.

NOT EVEN BEST IN BRITAIN
Even Scotland came to Wembley and won last year in the second leg of the Euro 2000 play-off. What on earth is happening to the national team?

WHAT DOES THE FUTURE HOLD?

The players love Kevin Keegan, so why don't they ALL play their best for him? Let's all take some pride and get back to the top!

MATCH COVER

KEANE ★ SHEARER ★

STARS!

Hold the front page! Four of the most famous **MATCH** cover stars reveal the highs and lows of their sensational careers.

WHAT DOES IT TAKE TO APPEAR ON THE FRONT cover of Britain's best-selling footy mag? Well, the Premiership has many exciting players and they need bags of talent to play in one of the best leagues in the world, but that isn't always enough for a player to grace the cover of MATCH. They must be in irresistable form for club and country and they have to be making headlines for all the right reasons.

Cover stars need a sparkling charisma to help them stand out on and off the field. They must appeal to supporters all over Britain, not just fans of the team they play for. Most of the cover stars have gained this recognition from playing for their country as well as their club. It's one of the greatest honours in a player's career to be featured on the cover of MATCH. Wouldn't you like to see yourself on the front page of Britain's biggest-selling football magazine?

The very first cover in 1979 featured England international Kevin Keegan, who had reached the top of his game after moving to Germany to play for Hamburg. One of the greatest players of his generation, Keegan was the European Footballer Of The Year at the time and deserved to be our first ever cover star.

The greatest players have never been off the front cover of MATCH. In recent years, England superstars David Beckham and Michael Owen have enjoyed a lot of coverage because of their exciting talent and their incredible worldwide appeal. But other stars like Dennis Bergkamp, Ryan Giggs, Alan Shearer and Roy Keane have dominated the covers for a number of years now, because their talent is unrivalled in the British game and their achievements have rightly won them many admiring fans.

MATCH looks back at four of the most famous covers stars to pay tribute to their sensational careers. Bergkamp, Giggs, Shearer and Keane reveal how they were feeling during the good times, when the trophies were flowing in, and also during the bad times, when nothing seemed to be going right for the superstars.

BERGKAMP ★ GIGGS

BERGKAMP

"I realise more than most that without my team-mates, I wouldn't have won anything and the highlight for me is being part of a successful team."

WITH ALL THE ARGUMENTS ABOUT THE INFLUX OF FOREIGN players into the Premiership, critics should remember the impact Dennis Bergkamp has made on English football. The Dutch striker came to England in 1995 and he's made a stunning contribution to the game ever since, scoring some fantastic goals and showing the kind of sportsmanship that has earnt him the respect of his team-mates and peers.

Bergkamp arrived at Arsenal boasting a UEFA Cup winner's medal from his previous club Inter Milan. He had an unhappy spell with the Italian club, but it wasn't long before he formed a deadly striking partnership with Ian Wright. The goals started to flow at Highbury and awards followed. Bergkamp was named the PFA and Football Writers' Player Of The Year in 1998. In the same season he collected two more awards as The Gunners beat Man. United to the Premier League and FA Cup double.

A fans' favourite, Bergkamp always gives 100 per cent to the team, even if it means travelling hundreds of miles by ferry, car and train to play in Europe. His fear of flying rarely stands in his way. But it's not just fans of The Gunners who have come to love the Dutch striker, because Bergkamp is a legend in his home country. It is a great shame that he has now retired from the international scene having never won a trophy with the Oranje after playing nearly 80 games over ten years for his country.

During his long international career Bergkamp broke Holland's goalscoring record as the Dutch came close to victory on several occasions. In 1992 Holland lost the European Championship semi-final to Denmark on penalties. They bowed out of USA '94 at the quarter-final stage and were knocked out of Euro '96, the 1998 World Cup and Euro 2000 on penalties.

The latter tournament was held in his home country and it was the biggest blow to Bergkamp as the Dutch side lost in the semi-final to Italy. He has now retired from the international game as his fear of flying will stop him travelling to the 2002 World Cup in Japan and South Korea.

Incredibly, although he is regarded as one of the best strikers in the world, Bergkamp is often criticised for his failure to score goals, but if the Dutchman is on fire, the team around him will also be playing well. He's at his best in a settled team, displaying the vision, creativity and skill that has won him thousands of neutral admirers across the world.

The Dutch star has exerted almost as much influence on the Premiership as Eric Cantona did with Man. United and he may even decide to end his career in north London with Arsenal. That'll certainly please the fans, who rate the striker as a Gunners legend.

MATCH charts Bergkamp's career over the past five years, looking at the the high points and the low points that he's endured with both Arsenal and Holland.

July 1995
RECORD GUNNERS SIGNING

Arsenal manager Bruce Rioch made a transfer coup to sign Bergkamp from Inter Milan for £7.5 million. Recognised as one of the world's finest strikers, the fans were excited about seeing his talent up front with Ian Wright.

DENNIS SAYS: "I was excited at the prospect of playing for Arsenal. I came to Arsenal with an open mind, but I believed I could show people the real Dennis Bergkamp. It was a quick decision once I decided to leave Inter Milan. I wanted to go to England and as soon as I heard the name Arsenal, that was it. I've always made decisions like that, it's a feeling. I thought of London, I thought of the club – a very successful club – and it was a logical choice for me to come here to play. The timing of the move was right and it was the right decision."

September 1995
UNDER PRESSURE

Bergkamp failed to score in his first seven games for Arsenal and was criticised by the Press. He soon silenced his doubters though with a double strike in the 4-2 victory against Southampton on September 23.

DENNIS SAYS: "It was great to get my first goal for Arsenal under my belt in that game against Southampton. I hoped the newspapers would finally have something else to talk about, rather than counting down the hours until I scored my next goal. I hoped they would have to leave me alone after that. I never felt like I was playing badly for Arsenal, but scoring goals does ease the pressure on you. The fact that I was happy, settled and part of the English way of life was reflected in the kind of football that I was playing."

June 1996
PENALTY KNOCK-OUT

Holland had problems off the field at Euro '96. A goal from Bergkamp sealed a win against Switzerland, but the Dutch were thrashed 4-1 by England and headed home after losing to France on penalties in the quarter-finals.

DENNIS SAYS: "Until someone discovers a better way to decide the winner of a match, the penalty competition will remain part of the game in the big tournaments. I don't like the golden goal rule because, in my opinion, it's not the natural way to win a game. There were signs of problems before Euro '96, but afterwards the team was only thinking about one thing – qualifying for the next World Cup. We had a team of 11 good players with equally good players waiting for their chance and I knew it would be possibly my last World Cup."

May 1997
SUCCESSFUL SEASON

Bergkamp inspired Arsenal to third spot in the league and was named Arsenal's MATCHman Of The Season for 1996-97. He scored one of the best goals ever seen in a north London derby to take his tally for the season to 12.

DENNIS SAYS: "In England every game is played with such passion, you have to be 100 per cent motivated and committed to get three points in the Premiership and you really have to concentrate. While I have been happy with the way I've been playing there will always be room for improvement in my game. I always strive to do better and I think that's normal for a footballer. I've been happy with the way things have gone during my time so far at Arsenal, but it would obviously be better if the team was winning more trophies."

January 1998
FANS' FAVOURITE

In the 1997 MATCH Readers' Poll, Bergkamp picked up the Undisputed Player Of The Year award, beating David Beckham, Ronaldo, Paul Ince and Ryan Giggs by gaining almost 50 per cent of the vote.

DENNIS SAYS: "I was extremely pleased with the MATCH award, particularly as it was voted for by the younger football supporters. I have said that playing in England has been one of the happiest periods of my career. It's great to be popular with the fans of your own club, but the award came from supporters all over the country. It's obviously nice to be appreciated and I will always cherish the Player Of The Year award. I have won several honours and nominations from supporters' clubs, but that was the first award I'd won from a weekly magazine."

April 1998
HONOURED BY HIS PEERS

Bergkamp's consistent form in 1997-98 was rewarded when he was named Player Of The Season by his peers. A few days later, the striker was awarded the same honour by the football writers of England.

DENNIS SAYS: "The highlight of my season had been playing in a successful team, a united side. Obviously I enjoyed some of the personal glory, like scoring goals and collecting the award from the Professional Footballers' Association, but I have always preferred team success. What would please me most is if I justified my own awards through the achievements of the whole team. If Arsenal were always winning I would be happy. I realise more than most that without my team-mates, I wouldn't have won anything."

May 1998
ARSENAL WIN CHAMPIONSHIP

After a tense fight with Man. United, Arsenal wrap up the Premiership title just one point ahead of their rivals. A depleted Gunners side can even afford to lose their final two games against Liverpool and Aston Villa.

DENNIS SAYS: "I think Arsenal were very lucky to be in the situation they were in. We had a very difficult period at one stage of the season and we lost a lot of ground on the leaders. But we came through that difficult spell and other teams who could have challenged for the title dropped points. You wouldn't expect teams like Manchester United to drop points against sides they would normally beat. I achieved a lot when I was at Ajax and I won the UEFA Cup at Inter Milan, but winning the league with Arsenal was something truly special."

May 1998
INJURY DESTROYS CUP DREAM

It was Bergkamp's childhood dream to play in an FA Cup Final, but his hopes were shattered in 1998 when his hamstring injury forced him to watch Arsenal's final against Newcastle from the sidelines.

DENNIS SAYS: "It was terrible because I was so desperate to make the final. I felt that I had made a great contribution to the other games in the competition but I wasn't there at the end. It didn't really bother me not playing in the last league game because I still felt involved, but I was concerned about the FA Cup Final. It's a game on its own and I wanted to be playing. You don't have the same feelings as the other players. They were coming off the field tired and thinking, 'Yeah, we won this,' while I was on the sidelines watching."

June 1998
WORLD CUP DESPAIR

At the 1998 World Cup in France, Holland won their group and Bergkamp set a record with his 36th international goal in Holland's victory over Argentina. But the Dutch team went on to lose to Brazil in the semi-finals.

DENNIS SAYS: "I think Holland got very, very close to winning it. Our semi-final against Brazil was one of the most heartbreaking matches I have ever played in. It was the way we lost the game which hurt us most. We had the chance to beat Brazil in normal time. Pierre Van Hooijdonk was fouled in the dying seconds and every player in our team knew it was a penalty, but we went out on penalties after extra-time, which was very frustrating. We got lots of flattering comments. Holland and France were the only teams who tried to play attacking football."

April 1999
PENALTY MISS KILLS DREAM

Bergkamp was desperate to get to the FA Cup Final in 1999 after missing out the year before, but Man. United stood in the way. With the score at 1-1, Bergkamp missed a penalty and a wondergoal from Ryan Giggs won the cup.

DENNIS SAYS: "I was desperate to get to the final after missing out on the last one. I knew it would be very tough against Manchester United, but we had a good chance. For the club, the league is probably more important because of the prestige of being the champions and because it gives you a place in the Champions League, but for me the FA Cup is very important. It has always been a dream for me to play in the FA Cup Final at Wembley. I used to watch the finals on television when I was young. I hoped to lift the trophy, but it didn't happen."

"I ALWAYS STRIVE TO BE BETTER AND THAT'S NORMAL FOR A PLAYER."

November 1999
CHAMPIONS LEAGUE DISMAY

Arsenal are knocked out of the Champions League at the group stage for the second year running after their defeats at home to Barcelona and Fiorentina. But, under the new system, The Gunners enter the UEFA Cup.

DENNIS SAYS: *"It was one of the worst days of my career. I was devastated because I was sure we would do well in the competition. I felt as bad as I did when Holland lost in the World Cup semi-final. We had strengthened the squad and there was no excuse for not qualifying. I cannot begin to explain what went wrong against Barcelona, but they got the breaks. Even so, going into the Fiorentina game we felt we had a good chance to qualify, so it was a big disappointment. The open space of Wembley played into the opposition's hands too often."*

MAY 2000
UEFA CUP FINAL DEFEAT

Bergkamp suffered more pain in Europe after The Gunners sadly lost the UEFA Cup Final on penalties to Galatasaray. Rumours suggested he was unhappy at Highbury and there was mounting speculation about his future.

DENNIS SAYS: *"I haven't signed a new contract at Arsenal and we haven't even spoken about it. I still have a contract at the club which doesn't expire until the season after next, but it's difficult to decide what to do in the long-term. I want to see out my contract, but beyond that I don't know. I've always maintained that I won't step down from this level and I intend to stick by that. In the past I've been too eager to sign a three or four-year contract, but I must think about the future – the implications of signing the deal of my career."*

July 2000
EURO 2000 HEARTBREAK

Dennis said he would retire from international football after Euro 2000, making success vital. Holland looked impressive in a superb 6-1 win over Yugoslavia but it was heartbreak again as they lost to Italy on penalties in the semis.

DENNIS SAYS: *"I think it was important for the supporters and for the tournament that we got to the next stage, and we had a bit of luck in the first couple of games so that helped us as well. But it's tough to accept that we finished the semi-final as losers and it was a bad ending to the tournament. I think people expected a lot from us. Sometimes it's difficult to live up to that kind of expectation. The teams we played against weren't stupid. They knew how the Holland side played and they knew how to play against us."*

M 19

DREAM TEAM

Nikos Dabizas Newcastle, Greece

"I think I would play the 4-4-2 formation, because that is the system we use at Newcastle. My fantasy team would have a very good goalkeeper in Fiorentina and Italy stopper Francesco Toldo. It would also have a good defence. I would like to play in the midfield in this team, but I could also play in the defence if I needed to. I think Gabriel Batistuta and Alan Shearer would play very well together up front. Shearer's my team-mate at Newcastle so I would have to talk to him about his retirement!"

Lilian Thuram Parma
Position Defender
Country France

Jaap Stam Manchester United
Position Defender
Country Holland

Francesco Toldo Fiorentina
Position Goalkeeper
Country Italy

Marcel Desailly Chelsea
Position Defender
Country France

Roberto Carlos Real Madrid
Position Defender
Country Brazil

David Beckham Manchester United
Position Midfielder
Country England

Roy Keane Manchester United
Position Midfielder
Country Rep Of Ireland

Gabriel Batistuta Roma
Position Striker
Country Argentina

Alan Shearer Newcastle
Position Striker
Country England

Redondo Real Madrid
Position Midfielder
Country Argentina

Nikos Dabizas Newcastle
Position Midfielder
Country Greece

TOP 10

Ten of the best English left-sided players.

ROBBO'S BAD REPORT

Bryan Robson certainly got a lot of stick last season from Middlesbrough fans up in the north-east. They were unhappy after there were no additions to the Boro trophy cabinet, despite the arrival of several big money signings. Still, Robbo probably missed most of the criticism because he wasn't even reading Boro's match reports! "When I lived in Manchester, I used to travel back there after the game," Robbo told Route 1. "I read the Manchester newspapers because there wasn't much about us in the Press there – it was all about clubs in the North-West." Mind you, if pick up any national newspaper and it'll be the same – north-west clubs are just far more successful!

VIALLI'S SCARE TACTICS

In the Chelsea dressing room the players regularly get beaten by a large stick if they don't play to the best of their ability. Or that's what manager Gianluca Vialli would have you believe. "I expect my team to produce the same performances that I was capable of, to train and play with the same mentality," said Luca. "I have got the player out of myself, but having been a good player, I am very demanding. The standards I set have perhaps been too demanding. There must be times when I am more understanding." Yep, but you can't treat players with kid gloves all the time, hence selling the goal-shy Chris Sutton to Celtic.

HARRY KEWELL
Leeds United

EURO 2000

DIARY OF A TOURNAMENT

MATCH looks back at the 11th European Championships and relives the magic moments.

PHIL NEVILLE'S LEFT-FOOT MIGHT HAVE ENDED every England fan's dreams of glory, but Euro 2000 was undoubtedly the greatest European Football Championships ever. And following on from the spectacle of Euro '96, that was no mean feat! From the colour of the Dutch and the flair of the French to the erratic brilliance of the Portuguese and the aggression of the Yugoslavs, the tournament was a mouth-watering gala of goals from start to finish. Whether it was Spain's dramatic 4-3 victory over Yugoslavia or Holland's heartbreaking penalty exit at the hands of the Italians, Euro 2000 had it all!

It was a tournament of extremes, with good guys like Figo and Zidane fighting for headlines with bad boys Mihajlovic and Hagi. The third-choice Italian 'keeper, Toldo, made a late break into the side and surprised everybody with his penalty-saving antics, while Raul's spot-kick nightmare stole the limelight for all the wrong reasons as Spain crashed out.

Brought to life in print and on the telly by some 1800 journalists, Euro 2000 proved a circulation and ratings booster from Preston to Prague! As the UK's biggest-selling football magazine, MATCH played its part, too. With four journalists and one photographer based in Belgium and Holland for the entire tournament, we covered all 31 matches, drove some 11,000 miles and filled 250 pages with the hottest happenings from the competition. We talked to the biggest stars of European football and chronicled the experiences of over 100 fans!

MATCH was there to document the full story of Euro 2000. We witnessed the highs and the lows, the heartache and the histrionics, the guts and the glory, the happiness of the Oranje fans and the horror of mindless English hooligans in Brussels. Here, the MATCH ANNUAL relives those heady days of June and July 2000 – when hearts were broken all over Europe and the Premiership stars of France went home as all-conquering winners once again.

Shearer celebrates his goal, but England just didn't get the luck they needed.

Amsterdam was a sea of orange for Holland's opener against the Czech Republic.

THE FINE TASTE OF THE ORANJE!

BEFORE THE TOURNAMENT HAD EVEN STARTED, THE DUTCH WERE WELL INTO THE SWING OF things. Nearly every restaurant, bar and shop in Amsterdam was covered in orange banners and balloons wishing the Oranje good luck. Locals counted down the days until the first game, when thousands of fans packed out the Amsterdam Arena to see their heroes play. The players couldn't help but be impressed by the atmosphere. **"It's just been Oranje from day one,"** said Jaap Stam. **"Everyone in Holland is very excited and all of our fans want us to do well. But we know as a team that it's not going to be easy, especially playing in our home country."**

Inside the grounds, the Dutch fans impressed with their passionate chants and swaying, and in the host towns they showed everyone else how to party as they took the tournament one step further from Euro '96. The cities welcomed supporters from the 16 nations and those from even further afield who had come to join the fun. Some fans played spontaneous matches in the streets, while others arrived with musical instruments and, bizarrely, chickens!

Eindhoven held an 'Abba' day when the Swedish team came to town and there was even a football comedy play at a Dutch theatre, which meant everybody got into the spirit. Only one colour dominated the streets, though. **"I've driven through Holland and seen it's orange,"** said 'keeper Sander Westerveld. **"We're used to this happening in Holland. Every time the country has a championship, everyone buys orange clothes and they wear them during the matches. It's just something they always do – it was the same when I was a kid. I had carrots on my head and everything!"**

Orange boiler suits were a popular item with fans in Holland.

Many of the shops and houses in Amsterdam were adorned with orange banners.

June 10-11 Opening Weekend

The opening ceremony, with its story of an ideal football match doesn't quite capture anyone's imagination, so co-hosts Belgium do their best to impress their fans with a 2-1 victory over Sweden, thanks to a fantastic winning goal from their talented young frontman Emile Mpenza. The next day, Turkey feel aggrieved in Arnhem when the referee awards a harsh penalty after Ogun connects with Filippo Inzaghi, and the striker scores from the spot for Italy's winner. Dino Zoff's side are left to rue several missed chances but still win 2-1. France make the most of their opportunities in Bruges and show their potential with a 3-0 win over Denmark. **"It's the first time I've played for a team that, every time the two strikers have the ball, you feel the fear from the opposition team,"** says Frank Leboeuf. **"Every time Thierry Henry or Nicolas Anelka got the ball they scared the Danish defence. It's good for the future of French football."**

The tournament is well underway when Holland, supported by a packed stadium of Oranje in Amsterdam, get a last-minute penalty to beat the plucky Czechs. **"There is more pressure at home, especially when you start,"** explains Dennis Bergkamp after the game. **"People expect you to walk over the opposition. France won 3-0 in their opening game, so a lot of people thought we would do the same. But it's difficult to find space. You have to realise it takes a lot of hard work before you can show your game."**

June 12 England Kick-off

The big day arrives for thousands of England fans who pack into the Philips Stadium in Eindhoven to watch Kevin Keegan's side take on much-fancied Portugal. Outside the stadium there's a real party atmosphere with fans dressed up as St George and the Three Lions. The game kicks-off with a bang as England race to a 2-0 lead, but Luis Figo inspires a Portuguese comeback to steal the game 3-2. **"It was a brilliant start,"** explains Michael Owen. **"At 2-0 up you don't expect to lose and you don't even expect to draw when you score two goals. But we conceded three and that really killed us."** England are left bottom of Group A after Germany fight out a 1-1 draw with Romania.

June 13-15 Element Of Surprise

Norway provide the first big surprise of Euro 2000 when they snatch a win against one of the favourites, Spain. Despite the firepower of Raul, the Norwegian side shut up shop and score the only goal of the game through Steffen Iversen after a long kick upfield from the 'keeper. **"Our strength is that we are very, very hard to score against,"** says Chelsea striker Tore Andre Flo. **"We have succeeded with our tactics and we are very happy."** The other game in Group C is far more exciting as Slovenia go 3-0 in front against Yugoslavia, before the ten-man Yugoslavs make an epic comeback to bring the game level to 3-3. Italy show they're a force to be reckoned with in the finals with a 2-0 win over co-hosts Belgium. **"We played a great game,"** says Italy coach Dino Zoff. **"We are delighted with the result. We are now a team and we have found our best shape."**

June 16-17 France Storm On

In Bruges, France continue their winning ways thanks to Thierry Henry's goal in a 2-1 win against the Czech Republic, sentencing the unlucky Czechs to an early flight home. Meanwhile, Denmark are dealt the same fate in Group D after losing 3-0 to Holland. Portugal seal a quarter-final place with a 90th-minute winner against

The England base in Spa was well-guarded during the championships.

Shearer waves goodbye to international football.

Becks tries out his yoga during a training session.

ENGLAND LIVE IN LUXURY!

KEVIN KEEGAN WANTED ENGLAND'S BASE IN BELGIUM TO BE perfect, so he visited the area four times before the tournament started. Keegan finally chose the Alfa Balmoral Hotel – a small, friendly hotel set in the picturesque Ardennes area of Belgium. As well as a golf course and tennis courts, the players had the use of a gym, swimming pool, jacuzzi and beauty parlour, which kept Becks looking his best! One of the conference rooms was turned into a mini-cinema, while each player had a king-size bed and a colour TV in their room so they could relax on their own. **"You have plenty of time to think about the games, but there are other times when you just need to get away so you can relax,"** explained Nigel Martyn. **"In my room I'll phone home to see what's happening or just read a book or a magazine."** England's training area was just a short trip down the road to a practice pitch, which was surrounded by fencing. Kids from the local schools were invited to meet the players and they seemed delighted to get some famous autographs. The training sessions usually lasted 90 minutes, before the players broke for lunch and went to the on-site media centre to hold press conferences.

STARS OF EURO 2000

LUIS FIGO Portugal

Tipped to be one of the real stars of the tournament, Portugal midfielder Luis Figo lived up to his reputation from the first ball that he kicked in Portugal's opening game against England. He saw his side fall two goals behind, but then orchestrated an incredible comeback by simply running at the England defence. Figo soon dominated the match from the midfield and sealed his performance with a spectacular 25-yard strike which helped Portugal to a 3-2 win. MATCH just couldn't stop Abel Xavier from going on about how good his team-mate was. **"Figo is unbelievable. In my view he can become the World Player Of The Year, because Portugal are finally playing well. To have everyone's admiration in Europe you must play well in all the international tournaments, and he has done well."**

Luis Figo was inspirational in Portugal's exciting side.

France's bus driver, Gard, with his beloved bus.

ON THE BUSES!

As Holland and Belgium went football crazy, so did everything surrounding the football teams. Hotels cheered for the teams they hosted and supporters flocked to games in a sea of colours. But players also arrived at the games in style. The team buses were recognisable by more than just the name on the front, as they were decked out in the colours of the teams and had fans painted on the sides to add more colour to the tournament! The World Cup holders, France, were given a team coach when they arrived, but they still took their trusty driver, Gard – and his good luck charm – along with them. **"After the World Cup we all went to this fancy restaurant to celebrate,"** said Gard, bragging. **"They served wine in plastic bottles shaped like the World Cup. I kept one of them and I always carry it on my bus."** It must have been lucky then!

GERRARD IS ENGLAND'S GREATEST HOPE!

Steven Gerrard was one of the only players in the England squad to come away from Euro 2000 with his head held high. The young Liverpool midfielder was a late entrant to the 22-man squad, having made his senior debut just ten days before the championships began in a friendly against Ukraine at Wembley. But he came on in the second half of England's Euro 2000 showdown against Germany to show why he's rated so highly by fans and peers alike. Gerrard talked to MATCH about how he felt during the tournament.

HOW WOULD YOU SUM UP YOUR EURO 2000 EXPERIENCE?

"It was a great experience for me, it was just a shame we couldn't have stayed in the competition for longer because I was enjoying being out in Belgium. I wish we could have stayed to the end, but it just wasn't to be."

HOW PROUD ARE YOU OF YOUR PERFORMANCE AGAINST GERMANY?

"Dead proud. My family are too. At the start of the season we would never have expected that I'd be talking about playing at Euro 2000 and being in a team that beats Germany, so it was just unbelievable. Now I've had a taste of it, I want more."

WAS IT UNNERVING PLAYING AGAINST LEGENDS LIKE LOTHAR MATTHÄUS?

"I was excited more than nervous. I was thinking while I was on the bench, 'If I get on, I'll be playing against great players', but once I was on the pitch, all those thoughts had disappeared from my mind. I was just concentrating on doing what Kevin Keegan had asked me to do and listening to Paul Ince, Martin Keown and Alan Shearer. They were great and helped me through the match. I just concentrated on playing my game."

DID YOU WATCH ROMANIA'S PENALTY AGAINST ENGLAND IN THE LAST GAME?

"I watched the fans really. Where we were, the Romanian fans were to the right and the English fans were to the left behind the goal where the penalty was being taken. So I just listened for the reaction, that's how we knew, the sound. It was really quick, you heard the noise coming from your right and silence at the other end, so you knew they'd scored."

DO YOU THINK ENGLAND CAN GET BACK TO THE TOP IN WORLD FOOTBALL?

"I think we can, but it'll take time. We all know it won't happen overnight, but it will happen. I believe we have the right people in terms of staff and players, but we've really got to believe in ourselves and look to the future. It won't happen in weeks or months, we've got to be patient."

WILL WE EVER SEE YOU CAPTAINING ENGLAND TO GLORY?

"When I was a kid, I had dreams about playing for England and dreams about playing for Liverpool. I've done both of those now, so I must have other dreams and it's one of those dreams to captain my country. I hope it happens one day, and it would be great to win something with England."

Romania, and defender Abel Xavier is delighted once again. **"I think we have surprised all the people here, but maybe we have also surprised 12 million people at home as well because they surely don't expect us to be performing the way that we're performing. We'll stay the same, prepare well for the next game and you never know what could happen after that!"** In Charleroi, England set about breaking records. After 34 years of losing to Germany in major tournaments, it's payback time. It's a far from entertaining match, but Alan Shearer scores with a winning header in his last tournament before retiring from the international scene. Steven Gerrard also makes an impressive showing, after coming off the subs' bench, but nobody is happier than skipper Shearer. **"You could see the elation on my face when I scored, but that was nothing compared to what I felt at the final whistle. I was only minus four-years-old when we last beat them in 1966!"**

June 19-20 Crunch Time

Holland and France can sit back and relax in their last group game having already qualified, but most of the other teams still have a lot to play for. In Group B, Italy and Turkey win their last two games to go through to the next round, while one place is still up for grabs in the final match in Group A. Before their game against Romania, England are told they may be kicked out of the tournament after English fans are arrested for rioting. Keegan pleas for calm, but the team are soon going home anyway. After coming back from a goal down against Romania to lead 2-1, England concede an equaliser. The 2-2 scoreline is enough to send them through to the next stage, but Phil Neville concedes a late penalty to put England out of the competition. **"We don't blame Phil,"** says Sol Campbell. **"We're in this together, you can't blame anyone, but we're not happy at all. We haven't qualified for the next stage. You want to at least get through the group, then who knows? It's unlucky, we were hit by a sucker blow."**

June 21 Late Deciders

It's tight in Group C going into the last game, and any of three teams could go through. Norway play Slovenia in Arnhem while Spain kick-off against Yugoslavia at the same time in Bruges. The game finishes 0-0 in Bruges, so Norway wait to hear confirmation that they are through. It's 3-2 to Yugoslavia after 90 minutes, but Spain strike twice in injury-time to seal an unbelievable win and go through to the quarter-finals with France. **"We haven't won the title,"** says Spain's Ivan Helguera. **"We celebrated at the hotel, but Spain have only reached the quarter-finals. I really can't remember living too many experiences like the Yugoslavia game. When we got back to the hotel and watched the game, we realised how close it was. The goal didn't seem like it was going to arrive. Now we have to concentrate on France in the quarter-final, but it's up to our coach to sort out the tactics for that."**

June 25 It's A Knockout

After Holland's victory over a depleted French side in their last group game, the Oranje are fired up and Yugoslavia are on the receiving end. The Yugoslavs have the audacity to have two early shots on goal, but are soon taught a footballing lesson from the Dutch masters. Patrick Kluivert's 24th-minute goal opens the floodgates – he finishes with a hat-trick and Marc Overmars gets a brace in the 6-1 win. **"It was a very good result,"** says Jaap Stam. **"We deserved it because we all worked very hard for it. The Press are always on our**

Italy were just as defensive in training as on the pitch, so no-one scored any goals!

Francesco Toldo shows the players how to dive after the ball properly.

Alessandro del Piero was always followed by the Press.

There was a lot of competition to get in the starting line-up.

ITALY CAME, SCORED AND CONQUERED

EVEN BEFORE EURO 2000 HAD STARTED, ITALY'S CHANCES OF WINNING THE TOURNAMENT had been written off. After some poor results in pre-tournament friendlies, like suffering defeats against Spain and Belgium – as well as losing Christian Vieri and No. 1 'keeper Gianluigi Buffon to injury – things didn't look good for the Azzurri. But the Italians came, scored and conquered, and with a typically tight defence they only let in four goals in six games!

In training they looked just as disciplined as they were on the pitch, but on one occasion there were several more distractions for one of Italy's defenders at the training camp in Geel, 30 miles from Antwerp in Belgium. Alessandro Nesta proved popular with some female fans who turned up to see the Azzurri close-up. They shouted to him from one of the goals and he waved back, but dying of embarrassment. It was certainly a laughing point for some of his team-mates. It must have been the tight lycra shirts they were wearing – they're a hit with the ladies!

After the training was over, coach Dino Zoff headed to a press conference with loads of very serious-looking Italian journalists in a building near the camp. While some of the players headed to the bus, Luigi Di Biagio and Francesco Totti decided to do some extra training and work on their ball control – basketball that is! They took a break from their normal routine and looked pretty good at it – basketball is a popular sport in Italy so they have an alternative if the football ever goes wrong!

Patrik Berger teaches his team-mates how to fly.

AN EARLY CZECH OUT!

Had it not been for a difficult draw, the Czech Republic would have made more of an impact at Euro 2000. The Czechs had already shown what they could do by narrowly losing the final of Euro '96 to Germany on a golden goal. Then, in qualifying for Euro 2000, they won all of their ten games and only conceded five goals, lifting them to second place in FIFA's world rankings. However, despite boasting the excellent Pavel Nedved in their midfield, the Czechs bowed out of the tournament after just two games – losing to hosts Holland and World champions France. **"The game against Holland was the first time that I'd ever played a match in such style, yet lost,"** said a gutted Nedved. **"We prepared for two years for these championships and we have seen the result."** The Czech team got to restore some national pride in their final Group D match, with Patrik Berger playing his first game in the tournament. They beat Denmark 2-0, with two goals from Vladimir Smicer, before flying home.

STARS OF EURO 2000

ZINEDINE ZIDANE France

The sheer brilliance of the French playmaker Zinedine Zidane even overshadowed Luis Figo as he led France to another major championship triumph. To perform against some of the best players in the world is a sign of true genius and Zizou did not disappoint. **"Zidane is a fantastic player because he is a great influence on the team with his skill and technique,"** said his team-mate Bixente Lizarazu. **"It is clear with the way that he plays that he is a great team player, even though he is a talented individual."** Zidane's skill and deft turns were almost too quick for the eye, and his performances were always a joy to watch. Although there were many special players on display in Holland and Belgium, it was Zidane who impressed the most for the majority of the watching fans and media.

Zidane displayed more of his amazing skills at Euro 2000.

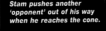

Holland take a break from their gruelling training schedule.

Stam pushes another 'opponent' out of his way when he reaches the cone.

Patrick Kluivert enjoys a joke with his team-mates in training.

Sander Westerveld practises his superman impression in training – see how he flies!

Edgar Davids frightens his team-mates with his incredible skills.

THE DUTCH TEAM IN GREAT SPIRITS!

IT WAS NO WONDER THAT HOLLAND WERE FIRMLY PLACED AS favourites to win Euro 2000. They may have faced a huge threat from France, the World champions, but after the French side had struggled in the qualifiers, everyone looked to Holland as the new favourites. Boasting a magnificent squad of famous names – even their two reserve 'keepers were two of the Premiership's finest stoppers – and a new-found harmony, the time seemed right.

At Euro '96, Holland possessed a similar set of fine players, but there had several problems behind the scenes and Edgar Davids went home halfway through the tournament. This coincided with the team's surprise 4-1 defeat to England, even though they made it to the quarter-final stage before being knocked out by France on penalties. It was a different story four years on. The confidence and the team spirit was evident at their team hotel in Hoenderloo, nicknamed 'Oranjeloo' by the fanatical locals during Holland's stay in the town. The Dutch team took over a secluded hotel during the tournament and were the only team to be afforded the luxury of having a training ground at their hotel.

Although some teams allowed their fans in to watch, Dutch coach Frank Rijkaard preferred closed sessions. **"These sessions let us work privately on set pieces, such as penalties, corner** kicks and free-kicks. We have very few secrets for the outside world, but I prefer to work behind closed doors."

While training every day was serious for Frank Rijkaard's side, the players still found time to have a joke together. One drill, which Holland often practised, involved the players separating into two teams and lining up next to each other. The first player from each team would race each other to a cone 100 metres away and, without clashing, would try to beat the other one back to the line – where the next two players would then start.

When Jaap Stam and Philip Cocu set off, the other players screamed their encouragement, but big Jaap made his own luck – by pushing Cocu out of the way at the cone and racing back to win the contest! When their next turn came around, Stam sprinted ahead while Cocu just gave up and walked to the back of the line, to the amusement of his team-mates who cracked up laughing!

The invitation to take Kluivert on didn't see many volunteers.

back in Holland because they are never quite satisfied with the way we play. Everybody playing in this Dutch squad wants to prove that we have a good team and that we're capable of playing good football, and that's exactly what we did today!"

Spain may have had all the luck against Yugoslavia, but they can't summon up a miracle in the dying moments of their quarter-final against France. After an impressive performance, Raul misses a penalty in the 89th-minute to end Spain's hopes, losing 2-1. Youri Djorkaeff, who scored France's winning goal with a superb volley, is thrilled to make the semi-final. **"It was a very, very difficult game, but the most important thing is for us to win, which we have done. I have scored, but I am not happy for me, I'm happy for the team. I thought God saw the game and made something for us."** As expected, Italy beat Romania, and Portugal overcome Turkey 2-0 to reach the last four of the competition.

June 28 France Go Through

World Champions France are afforded some luck in their semi-final against Portugal. After fighting out a 1-1 stalemate in normal time, the referee awards a penalty in golden goal extra-time after Abel Xavier is adjudged to have handled the ball on the goal-line. Portugal are furious – knowing that the decision could end their tournament – and Zinedine Zidane coolly converts the spot-kick. The Portuguese continue to protest after the golden goal and Nuno Gomes is shown the red card. It's a sad end to the tournament for one of its most entertaining teams and coach Humberto Coelho surprises everyone when he quits his post immediately after the game. **"The reaction of the players was natural,"** says France coach Roger Lemerre. **"Football can be very cruel, but there was a fault and if we had committed the fault we would have been upset, too."** There is a very different atmosphere in the two camps after the game, as France head back to their team hotel to prepare for Sunday's final, while the Portuguese team drive to the airport to catch a flight back to Lisbon.

June 29 Holland Bow Out

Next up, Holland take to the field to play Italy at the Amsterdam Arena, which is again awash with orange. **"We knew from the start that our people are incredible in how they experience a tournament, how they do it,"** explains Dennis Bergkamp. **"There are so many orange streets in Holland at the moment, it's amazing. We'd like to keep it up and stay here."**

But Italy have other ideas. Italy have performed far better than the rest of Europe expected, but with a tough semi-final draw against Holland, even the Italian people think the tournament is over for the Azzurri. **"Holland are the favourites and that suits us,"** admits coach Dino Zoff in his pre-match press conference ahead of the semi-final. **"For the first time in the tournament, the pressure is not on us. We meet a very strong team on their own soil. Of course it will be difficult , we will have to play one of our best matches ever."**

It turns out to be a sad end for the hosts in the other semi, but they have enough chances to win the match and progress to the final. Italy play their usual defensive game, but the home fans think the game is wrapped up when Italy's Gianluca Zambrotta is sent-off. Minutes later, Frank de Boer has a chance to score from the spot, but Italy 'keeper Toldo makes a great save. Another penalty is awarded in Holland's favour but Kluivert agonisingly hits the post. The Dutch feel the game slipping away from them in golden goal extra-time and throw away a place in the final after going 3-1 down in the penalty shoot-out. The fairytale just wasn't to be.

Anelka wasn't happy after being made to sleep in the luggage compartment!

"Oi, Thierry – up here. Take your headphones out!"

Zidane arrives with a washbag under his arm.

"Anyone need a tracksuit for the bench tonight?"

Fans film their fingers outside training.

Zidane plays on his own cos he's too good.

Are your headphones still in Thierry?

FRENCH FANCY A TROPHY

CAN YOU IMAGINE WHAT IT WOULD BE LIKE TO HAVE FRANCE training at your local stadium? You'd get yourself down there as quickly as possible to marvel at the skills of the World Champions, and that's exactly what the good people of Wavre, in Belgium, did. The small town is the home of Racing Jet Wavre, a Belgian Third Division side who would be the equivalent of Doncaster Rovers. Yeah, exactly. One minute the locals were watching Racing finish another dull season in a dull league – the next they were watching Zinedine Zidane, Thierry Henry and Marcel Desailly strutting their stuff on the field. They didn't even know that footballers could control a ball with just one touch, let alone do all sorts of fancy tricks!

Zidane certainly put on a display for the Belgians. Before and after the fitness work and drills, he would just play with the ball like it was stuck to his feet with glue. He was performing tricks you've never even seen him do on the pitch, as well as some of the spectacular ones he gets away with in matches. If the French looked impressive in training, they certainly transferred it on to the field as they won over numerous fans who argued that their World Cup win was just a one-off.

"He's great ain't he, Zinedine, like?"

STARS OF EURO 2000

PATRICK KLUIVERT Holland

When Holland started their Euro 2000 adventure, they had the kind of squad that most countries could only dream about. But while players like Bergkamp, Davids and Overmars all had blinding competitions, one star made everyone sit up and take notice, Patrick Kluivert. His skill, pace and strength bamboozled defenders in every match, and he just got better as the tournament progressed, as his superb hat-trick against Yugoslavia showed. **"When you're playing international football, especially in tournaments, you only get around two chances in one game,"** explained Sander Westerveld. **"If you want to be a European Champion or a World Champion you have to score with every chance you get. Patrick showed everybody that he is in great form and he is very, very important to us."**

Kluivert was the tournament's joint-top scorer after netting five goals, but he was also a vital member of the Dutch team, always making himself available for a pass and running his heart out for his team-mates.

Kluivert scores another goal en route to the golden boot.

Abel Xavier protests his innocence to the official.

XAVIER MORE THAN ABEL

It was the Romanians at the last World Cup in 1998, but this time around it was Portugal star Abel Xavier who got his hands on the hair dye. Xavier shocked everyone when he walked onto the pitch for the Portugal game against England after dying his hair and his beard blonde! And the fans thought it brought luck to the team. **"Maybe it gives a little talisman to Portugal, maybe it brings a little luck,"** said Abel. **"It was a personal thing for me to start with. It was nothing to do with wanting to be different or to stand apart from the other players, I did it to bring a little bit of a laughter to the dressing room, to make my team-mates laugh! I like to make people laugh!"** Xavier's hair may have helped to lift Portugal's spirits early on, but it didn't bring him any luck in the semi-final against France. He handled the ball in golden goal extra-time and France scored from the penalty to reach the final. Xavier's protests got him in trouble with UEFA and it was a sad end to his tournament.

France celebrate another win, but this time it's on foreign soil.

When they see the cameras the young strikers steal the cup away from the oldies.

Henry celebrates with golden goalscorer David Trezeguet.

FRANCE WIN TITLE TO SET A NEW RECORD!

WHEN FRANCE WON THE WORLD CUP BACK IN 1998, IT WAS a result that few people expected. The team seemed good on paper and the defence was playing magnificently, but they just couldn't score. Euro 2000 was a totally different proposition. With the red-hot Thierry Henry, the improved Christophe Dugarry and the frightening pace of Nicolas Anelka, France were many pundits' favourites to clinch the trophy as soon as the tournament began. The team even had strikers like David Trezeguet and Sylvain Wiltord on the bench, and they both had a dramatic impact on the final. Trezeguet grabbed the golden goal after stretching to send a crashing shot into the Italy net.

France made history by winning the Euro 2000 crown, becoming the first country to hold the World and European trophies at the same time. On the field, the French team joined hands in celebration and partied along with the supporters of Les Bleus in the stands as the whole of Rotterdam resonated to the sound of the French national anthem. They had provided the perfect finale to a magical tournament of football.

Back home in Paris there were equally jubilant scenes as the Arc de Triomphe and the Champs Elysées became one big sea of celebrations as people tried to comprehend what their country had done. 'Place Zinedine Zidane' was projected onto the walls in honour of their inspirational hero, along with messages thanking the team for their remarkable achievement.

The team deserved a great deal of credit for making history and never giving up against the superb Italian defence. **"I'm extremely happy,"** beamed French coach Roger Lemerre. **"It was down to the extreme will of the team that they became European champions, as Dino Zoff's team created many problems for us. With one minute to go I was hoping for a miracle, but perhaps we even helped this miracle along."**

July 1 Looking Ahead

While Holland is in mourning, two other sets of fans look forward to what many people think will be a rather boring final. "We know it will be a tough game," says Marcel Desailly. "But we were happy when we saw that Italy had beaten Holland because the Dutch are much better than Italy. We know that we can do something good against Italy if we are all strong." Italy progressed through the tournament with a typically defensive style of play and are expected to defend in numbers and strike on deadly counter-attacks in the final. According to Alessandro del Piero, they can do it. "After beating Holland we feel good. Now it is the final and we know we are just one game away from a memorable triumph. All the players in the team believe that we can beat France."

July 2 Arriving At The Ground

The teams arrive at De Kuip Stadium in Rotterdam and have a walk around to familiarise themselves with the pitch. As the fans begin to fill the stadium, the two team line-ups are announced to the crowd. To everyone's surprise, Alessandro del Piero and Filippo Inzaghi are left on the substitutes' bench by Dino Zoff, who prefers to use Marco Delvecchio up front. There are changes in the France line-up as well, with Nicolas Anelka being relegated to the bench and Emmanuel Petit failing to recover from the injury which has stopped him training for the last two days. "I am injured," explains Petit as he surveys the pitch with his team-mates before the final. "I have to take some medical examinations when we get back to Paris because I don't know what it is. I have irritation in my stomach and bad pain down my leg. I don't know what's going on."

Final Kick-off

The game is exciting from the moment the referee blows his whistle. France go all-out for an early goal, with the impressive Henry spearheading the attack – his first shot in the opening minutes hits the outside of the post. Italy clear up every other ball and look threatening on the counter-attack, but neither side creates a dangerous shot on target until after the break. Marco Delvecchio receives a cross from Pessotto in the box and slots the ball past Fabien Barthez to put Italy 1-0 ahead. France are shocked and Italy go mad but, just as it looks over for France, substitute Sylvain Wiltord pops up in the 90th minute to control a throughball and volley into the net.

The Italy bench, who were ready to run onto the pitch to celebrate at the final whistle, are stunned as the referee blows for extra-time. With the threat of losing the final on the golden goal rule, both sides begin to shore up their defences, but somehow David Trezeguet finds a way through Italy's rearguard. Robert Pires swings in a teasing cross from the right-wing and Trezeguet finishes in style, crashing the ball into the roof of the net for France's winning goal. The French camp go wild, while Italy sink to the ground. "We're totally down," says Demetrio Albertini after the game. "It feels like the whole world has fallen apart. We played so well, but after the equaliser we felt very tired. We had the game under control, but after the equaliser it got much harder psychologically."

Didier Deschamps holds aloft the Henri Delaunay trophy, to the thunderous cheers of thousands of French fans. "We are the first team to hold both the World Cup and the European Championships, so today was amazing," roars Man Of The Match Thierry Henry. "Having that record is important to me. I have seen the pictures of the Champs Elysées tonight in Paris and it is madness there, just like at the World Cup."

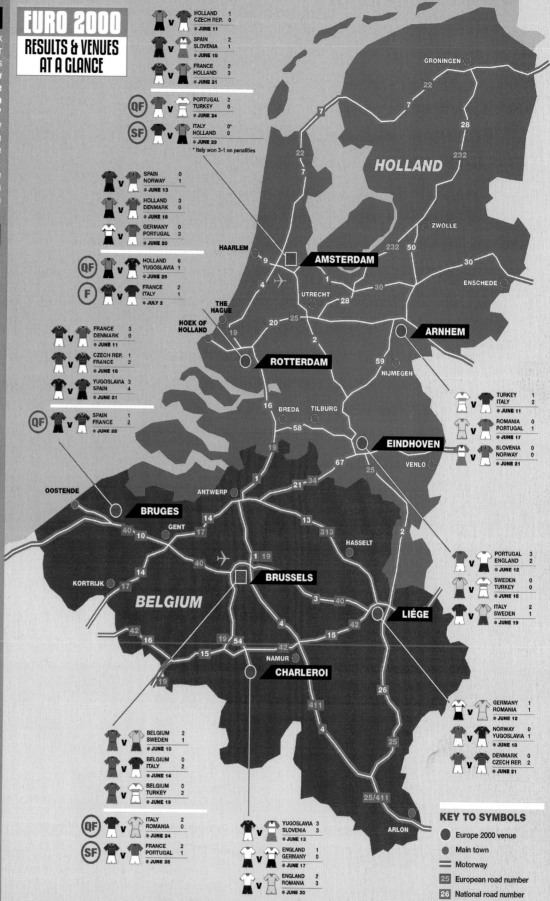

EURO 2000 RESULTS & VENUES AT A GLANCE

HOLLAND v CZECH REP.	1 - 0	JUNE 11	
HOLLAND v SPAIN	2 - 1	JUNE 18	
FRANCE v HOLLAND	2 - 3	JUNE 21	
QF PORTUGAL v TURKEY	2 - 0	JUNE 24	
SF ITALY v HOLLAND	0* - 0	JUNE 29	* Italy won 3-1 on penalties

SPAIN v NORWAY	0 - 1	JUNE 13
HOLLAND v DENMARK	3 - 0	JUNE 16
GERMANY v PORTUGAL	0 - 3	JUNE 20
QF HOLLAND v YUGOSLAVIA	6 - 1	JUNE 25
F FRANCE v ITALY	2 - 1	JULY 2

FRANCE v DENMARK	3 - 0	JUNE 11
CZECH REP. v FRANCE	1 - 2	JUNE 16
YUGOSLAVIA v SPAIN	3 - 4	JUNE 21
QF SPAIN v FRANCE	1 - 2	JUNE 25

TURKEY v ITALY	1 - 2	JUNE 11
ROMANIA v PORTUGAL	0 - 1	JUNE 17
SLOVENIA v NORWAY	0 - 0	JUNE 21

PORTUGAL v ENGLAND	3 - 2	JUNE 12
SWEDEN v TURKEY	0 - 0	JUNE 15
ITALY v SWEDEN	2 - 1	JUNE 19

GERMANY v ROMANIA	1 - 1	JUNE 12
NORWAY v YUGOSLAVIA	0 - 1	JUNE 18
DENMARK v CZECH REP.	0 - 2	JUNE 21

BELGIUM v SWEDEN	2 - 1	JUNE 10
BELGIUM v ITALY	0 - 2	JUNE 14
BELGIUM v TURKEY	0 - 2	JUNE 19
QF ITALY v ROMANIA	2 - 0	JUNE 24
SF FRANCE v PORTUGAL	2 - 1	JUNE 28

YUGOSLAVIA v SLOVENIA	3 - 3	JUNE 13
ENGLAND v GERMANY	1 - 0	JUNE 17
ENGLAND v ROMANIA	2 - 3	JUNE 20

KEY TO SYMBOLS
- ● Europe 2000 venue
- ● Main town
- ═ Motorway
- 25 European road number
- 26 National road number

THE FINAL WHISTLE

HOW DID YOU SCORE?
Think you're a footy nut? Check out the questions over the course of the annual and record your answers in the chart on page 108. There's a point for each answer.

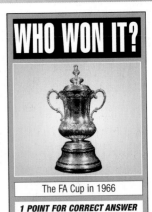

How much do you know about the Premiership?

first XI

The Premiership is now in its ninth season. How much do you know about one of the best leagues in the world?

1 Only three players have scored 30 or more goals in one Premiership season. Can you name them?

2 Leeds were the first team to win the championship in the first Premier League season. True or false?

3 Which team holds the record for the lowest number of goals scored in a Premiership season?

4 Can you name the team that won the league title in the 1997-98 season?

5 How many teams have lasted just one season in the Premier League before being relegated back down to Division One?

6 Which former Swedish international played for two Premier League clubs between 1995 and 1998?

7 How many English-born managers have managed a team to the Premier League championship?

8 Which Italian superstar joined Crystal Palace for the 1997-98 campaign, only to see them relegated to the First Division in that season?

9 Which veteran midfielder is the only person to have played for four Premiership clubs in his enduring career in English football?

10 On December 28, 1999, what unenviable record did Chelsea break when they played away to Southampton at The Dell?

11 Several team captains have had the honour of lifting the Premier League trophies so far. But can you rack your brains to work out how many of them were English players?

THE MEGA WORD SPOT

Can you spot the following Premiership young guns in the grid below?

T	C	P	G	R	I	F	F	I	N	K	K	E	W	E	L	L	L	J
Z	A	J	D	F	T	F	K	E	A	N	E	F	B	K	N	E	Y	W
M	R	S	K	X	C	A	R	R	A	G	H	E	R	J	Q	T	R	V
H	R	R	K	S	E	G	D	I	R	B	Y	Q	Z	Y	I	H	R	V
V	D	H	F	B	J	I	W	Q	L	Z	E	B	I	Z	Q	E	A	L
W	R	I	G	H	T	I	T	D	G	O	R	K	M	X	R	R	B	A
H	Y	E	L	R	A	H	F	S	P	D	F	M	R	T	E	I	S	M
S	M	I	T	H	U	X	Y	X	I	A	F	E	O	H	T	N	R	P
B	S	I	M	O	N	S	E	N	R	R	E	T	B	O	A	G	E	A
Y	D	O	A	M	K	C	I	W	D	A	H	C	I	M	W	T	F	R
E	W	U	C	R	E	K	R	A	P	Y	S	C	N	P	Y	O	F	D
K	E	Y	N	A	D	L	H	E	H	Q	c	E	S	S	B	N	E	F
S	A	R	P	N	R	W	C	B	L	G	M	N	O	O	C	K	J	J
E	V	R	R	Z	E	R	L	H	E	O	S	G	N	N	Q	N	L	J
H	E	N	D	R	I	E	I	R	I	R	C	A	M	P	B	E	L	L
S	R	M	Z	C	S	J	R	C	A	O	Q	J	X	O	P	J	H	F
K	I	N	G	S	J	A	M	H	K	Y	T	Y	E	L	K	A	O	S
L	V	M	V	Q	R	D	A	D	W	P	D	Y	E	R	Q	G	A	V
Y	Y	M	G	D	O	P	K	V	K	E	T	A	G	D	O	O	W	B

- BARRY
- BRIDGES
- BYWATER
- CAMPBELL
- CARR
- CARRAGHER
- CARRICK
- CHADWICK
- CHRISTIE
- COLE
- DUNNE
- DYER
- ETHERINGTON
- GERRARD
- GRIFFIN
- HENDRIE
- HESKEY
- KEWELL
- HARLEY
- JEFFERS
- KEANE
- KING
- LAMPARD
- McSHEFFREY
- MELCHIOT
- OAKLEY
- PAHARS
- PARKER
- ROBINSON
- SIMONSEN
- SMITH
- THOMPSON
- WEAVER
- WOODGATE
- WRIGHT

WHO WON IT?

The FA Cup in 1966

1 POINT FOR CORRECT ANSWER

MATCHfacts CODE BREAKER

Can you decode this to find a Premiership star?

CRACK THE CODE!

| 15 | 16 | 1 | 18 | 1 | 10 |
| 3 | 1 | 14 | 14 | 23 | 14 | 26 |

1-0 ONE-NIL

All these games ended 1-0 last season, but who got the goal?

1 September 1999 — Chelsea v Newcastle

2 October 1999 — Leeds v West Ham

3 February 2000 — Leicester v Aston Villa

4 March 2000 — Coventry v Everton

5 April 2000 — Leicester v Tottenham

CIVVY STREET

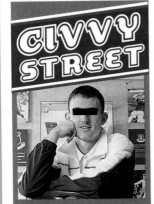

Can you name this top footy star without his kit on?

NAME THE CLUB!

Which team does this recent league record belong to?

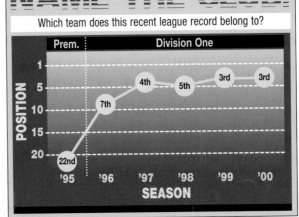

connections...

What connects Jamie Redknapp and Darren Ferguson, other than their shirt sponsors!

JON HARLEY
Chelsea

MATCH
YOUNG GUNS

WHO I SUPPO

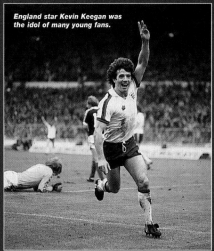

England star Kevin Keegan was the idol of many young fans.

THE MOST IMPORTANT THING ABOUT BEING a football supporter is allegiance. Every fan of the beautiful game has a favourite team which they follow every week, through the good times and especially through the bad.

Most fans support the team near to the place they were born, others choose their allegiance and then stick to it for life! Some people don't even get a choice – if their relatives support one team, they're made to follow the same side. The club that you choose to support can cause problems as well! Imagine being a Manchester United fan in a family of Man. City supporters or an Arsenal fan with a family tradition of supporting Tottenham!

But don't forget that the top Premiership stars were once fascinated fans dreaming of being like their idols. They also stood for hours to get match tickets and watched their favourite team in the pouring rain, just as thousands of people do every week.

Many of the top players still follow the teams that they supported when they were growing up, even if they've signed lucrative contracts for different clubs. It can be a bit difficult for some players – Liverpool's star striker Michael Owen was an avid Everton fan as a boy! While some players have been lucky, like Alan Shearer – who's now the captain of the club he supported when he was growing up – Newcastle.

MATCH asked a host of top Premiership stars about the teams they supported when they were younger and the players that they pretended to be in the park after school!

ALAN SHEARER

CLUB: NEWCASTLE UNITED
TEAM SUPPORTED: NEWCASTLE UNITED
FAVE PLAYER: KEVIN KEEGAN

WHO DID YOU SUPPORT AS A KID?
"I was a big Newcastle fan when I was a lad and I went to all of their games at home. I was quite lucky because my dad managed to scrape together a few quid for me to stand in the Gallowgate End. I didn't miss a home game when I was watching back then."

WHAT WAS THE BEST GAME YOU SAW?
"The match that sticks out in my mind is Kevin Keegan's debut game for the club. I started queueing at about nine o'clock in the morning and it was absolutely packed at about 12.30pm waiting for the gates to open at 1.30pm. I got in alright but we all got pretty squashed when we were in the ground! Kevin scored on his debut and we won the game, so all of the Newcastle fans left the ground with great big smiles on their faces."

WHO WAS YOUR FAVE PLAYER?
"Kevin Keegan was my idol. I used to go in the Gallowgate End at St James' Park to watch him play. He was brilliant and all the fans loved him. Then of course I was lucky enough to play under Kevin when he signed me from Blackburn Rovers and again when he became the manager of the England team in 1999."

GARETH BARRY

CLUB: ASTON VILLA
TEAM SUPPORTED: TOTTENHAM HOTSPUR
FAVE PLAYER: PAUL GASCOIGNE

WHO DID YOU SUPPORT AS A KID?
"I supported Tottenham Hotspur when I was younger. I enjoyed the way they played back then and they had some great players in those days as well."

WHAT WAS THE BEST GAME YOU SAW?
"I guess it has to be the FA Cup semi-final in 1991 when Tottenham beat Arsenal 3-2. I remember watching the game and I was really excited because it was against our biggest rivals. Paul Gascoigne scored with a fantastic free-kick and that is the best memory I have from watching the match. I didn't manage to actually go to Wembley though, I just watched it at home on the TV with my family."

WHO WAS YOUR FAVE PLAYER?
"Paul Gascoigne, definitely. I think he was probably everyone's favourite player in the early '90s when he was playing for Spurs and before he had all those troubles with injuries which really hampered his career. He was a really skilful player and his vision and passing could change any game in an instant. I think he played the best football of his career at White Hart Lane. I also remember what he did for England in the 1990 World Cup and that really launched his career."

NIALL QUINN

CLUB: **SUNDERLAND**
TEAM SUPPORTED: **LEEDS UNITED**
FAVE PLAYER: **JOHN GILES**

WHO DID YOU SUPPORT AS A KID?
"I supported Leeds, with the great team they had in the '70s, but then I moved to Arsenal. Leeds dominated English football then, but when they began to slip a bit I suppose I jumped ship to Arsenal!"

WHAT WAS THE BEST GAME YOU SAW?
"The best game was the European Cup Final in 1975. But as a tournament, the 1978 World Cup in Argentina made a big impression on me, because the hosts had a really great team to watch."

WHO WAS YOUR FAVE PLAYER?
"It was the Leeds midfielder John Giles. He was excellent and ran the show with Billy Bremner. He was only a small guy but he was great for Leeds and the Republic Of Ireland. He could pass, tackle, he was tough and he could run for 90 minutes. He's a real legend in Ireland after playing for and managing his country."

NICKY WEAVER

CLUB: **MANCHESTER CITY**
TEAM SUPPORTED: **SHEFFIELD WEDNESDAY**
FAVE PLAYER: **CHRIS WADDLE**

WHO DID YOU SUPPORT AS A KID?
"I was a Sheffield Wednesday fan. I was born in Sheffield and my dad took me to my first game when I was about five years old and it just carried on from there really."

WHAT WAS THE BEST GAME YOU SAW?
"I went to the League Cup Final in 1991 at Wembley, when we beat Man. United 1-0 and John Sheridan scored. We were in the old Second Division then and we had only just won promotion, so that was special. I must have been about 12 years old then, but it's a game I'll never forget."

WHO WAS YOUR FAVE PLAYER?
"It was Chris Waddle I think, when we'd just signed him from Marseille. Every time he got the ball all the fans used to stand up expecting him to do something, and he is probably the best player I've ever seen at Sheffield Wednesday. He was really unbelievable at his peak."

TREVOR SINCLAIR

CLUB: **WEST HAM**
TEAM SUPPORTED: **MANCHESTER CITY**
FAVE PLAYER: **JOHN BARNES**

WHO DID YOU SUPPORT AS A KID?
"Coming from Manchester, I was going to choose one of two teams. All of my mates supported City so I had to follow the boys in blue didn't I? I started going regularly to their matches when they got back into the old First Division. It was in the late '80s."

WHAT WAS THE BEST GAME YOU SAW?
"I clearly remember when we thrashed Manchester United 5-1 in our first season back in the top flight! I was standing on The Kippax and we all went mental. I still believe that City have more passionate fans than United!"

WHO WAS YOUR FAVE PLAYER?
"I didn't support Liverpool as a young lad, but there was no better winger than John Barnes when I was growing up. He was blessed with pace, skill and great passing ability – he had the lot and really made an impression on me."

Steve Froggatt worshipped the Liverpool team of the late '80s.

WAYNE BRIDGE

CLUB: **SOUTHAMPTON**
TEAM SUPPORTED: **SOUTHAMPTON**
FAVE PLAYER: **MATT LE TISSIER**

WHO DID YOU SUPPORT AS A KID?
"I'm from Southampton and I've always supported The Saints. I first started going to watch them when I was about ten years old – I had a season ticket for a few years. Back then the Wallace brothers, Rod and Ray, were playing and we had Matt Le Tissier, Neil Ruddock and Tim Flowers. Alan Shearer had started to make a name for himself too. Not a bad side at all."

WHAT WAS THE BEST GAME YOU SAW?
"When we beat Liverpool 4-1. It was in 1989. That was brilliant."

WHO WAS YOUR FAVE PLAYER?
"I've got two favourites – Matt Le Tissier and Rod Wallace. I always wanted to play for Southampton, so to get the chance to play alongside Matt Le Tissier was just fantastic. It's a bit of a strange feeling to play in the same side as someone you watched as a fan, but it's brilliant as well."

NEIL COX

CLUB: **WATFORD**
TEAM SUPPORTED: **SCUNTHORPE UNITED**
FAVE PLAYER: **BRYAN ROBSON**

WHO DID YOU SUPPORT AS A KID?
"I supported Scunthorpe United, because I lived about a minute from the ground and I was almost able to jump over my parents' wall and into the ground. It was better than having to pay. They're still sending me bills for it!"

WHAT WAS THE BEST GAME YOU SAW?
"The best game that I ever watched was Scunthorpe against Millwall. I can't really remember when it was, but it was about 18 years ago now! Scunthorpe were 2-0 down with just three minutes to go and they ended up winning 3-2. That was in the old Division Three."

WHO WAS YOUR FAVE PLAYER?
"My favourite player when I was a kid was Bryan Robson. He was just coming into the West Brom team and then he moved on to Old Trafford. Next time you see him MATCH, send him my regards."

KEVIN HORLOCK

CLUB: MANCHESTER CITY
TEAM SUPPORTED: WEST HAM
FAVE PLAYER: JULIAN DICKS

WHO DID YOU SUPPORT AS A KID?
"As a youngster, my dad used to take me to Charlton Athletic because that was our local team, but then once I had a choice I was quite close to West Ham. I used to travel to Upton Park with a few friends to watch them play."

WHAT WAS THE BEST GAME YOU SAW?
"I can't remember now, but West Ham had a great game against Manchester United a few years back, when Paul Ince scored a couple of goals just before he moved to Old Trafford. One of my biggest memories is the semi-final of the FA Cup when West Ham lost 4-0 to Nottingham Forest, which was a big disappointment to the fans."

WHO WAS YOUR FAVE PLAYER?
"For West Ham, I always used to look up to Julian Dicks. He played in my position at that time and obviously he was a very good player for the club."

JASON DODD

CLUB: SOUTHAMPTON
TEAM SUPPORTED: MANCHESTER UNITED
FAVE PLAYER: BRYAN ROBSON

WHO DID YOU SUPPORT AS A KID?
"Manchester United. Liverpool were flying at the time and hardly anybody supported United, so I used to get quite a lot of stick because Liverpool used to win everything. Times have changed now though!"

WHAT WAS THE BEST GAME YOU SAW?
"Good question. I can't remember that far back! But in recent times, probably when they won the Champions League Final. My main allegiance is with Southampton, obviously, but when Manchester United won the European Cup in 1999 it was just a great game to watch."

WHO WAS YOUR FAVE PLAYER?
"Bryan Robson. I used to pretend to be him in the playground. He was definitely my favourite. He gave 100 per cent for whoever he played for, including England, and that's the sort of style I relate to. He was one of the best players in Europe."

IAN TAYLOR

CLUB: ASTON VILLA
TEAM SUPPORTED: ASTON VILLA
FAVE PLAYER: GORDON COWANS

WHO DID YOU SUPPORT AS A KID?
"I was a big fan of Villa, of course, doesn't everyone know that? I was mad on them when I was young and now it's great to be able to play for them."

WHAT WAS THE BEST GAME YOU SAW?
"It's got to be Villa versus Barcelona in the 1982 European Super Cup. As a match it had everything – it was tense, it was such a huge occasion and there was a cracking atmosphere. But the best thing about it was Villa won! I really enjoyed that match and I can still remember everything about watching it, even now!"

WHO WAS YOUR FAVE PLAYER?
"My favourite Aston Villa player ever has to be Gordon Cowans, without any doubt. He even scored against Barcelona in that Super Cup Final! Everyone used to love him at the time and he's a big Villa legend even to this day."

STEVE FROGGATT

CLUB: COVENTRY CITY
TEAM SUPPORTED: LIVERPOOL
FAVE PLAYER: KENNY DALGLISH

WHO DID YOU SUPPORT AS A KID?
"Liverpool. Why? Well, I'm not really from Liverpool, I'm from Lincoln, but my dad was a Liverpool fan so I supported them too. I didn't manage get to many games when I was a kid – we couldn't afford it because it meant travelling to the other side of the country. But I used to go and watch my local side Lincoln with my dad."

WHAT WAS THE BEST GAME YOU SAW?
"It has to be one of the cup finals, or the time we played Nottingham Forest in the 1987-88 season. We won 5-0 and Peter Beardsley and John Barnes were great."

WHO WAS YOUR FAVE PLAYER?
"It was Kenny Dalglish. Although I could have picked anyone who was playing for them when I was growing up – Ian Rush, John Barnes, John Aldridge and Peter Beardsley – they were all brilliant. They were a great side when I was young."

MATT CLARKE

CLUB: BRADFORD CITY
TEAM SUPPORTED: SHEFFIELD WEDNESDAY
FAVE PLAYER: MARTIN HODGE

WHO DID YOU SUPPORT AS A KID?
"Sheffield Wednesday. I used to watch them in the days when Mel Sterland and Imre Varadi were there. It was great when I was at the club, but I never got involved in the team unfortunately. I'm at Bradford now, but I'm still a big Wednesday fan and I was gutted when they went down."

WHAT WAS THE BEST GAME YOU SAW?
"It was a semi-final I think, or something like that. If I remember rightly, we were 3-0 up at half-time and in the second-half a player called Paul Canoville scored a hat-trick. I think it ended up 4-4 with Mel Sterland getting a late penalty."

WHO WAS YOUR FAVE PLAYER?
"Here's one for you, Martin Hodge. When I moved over to Wednesday he was the goalkeeping coach there, so I worked with him and he taught me a lot. He's good to work with and really knows his stuff."

CAN YOU SEE YOURSELF

Matthew Etherington
Tottenham Hotspur

...becoming a manager?
"Yeah, I would like to become a manager of a team one day, although obviously that would be a long way off as I'm only 19 and I need to concentrate on my playing career with Tottenham first!"

...answering back to the gaffer?
"Would I answer back to my manager? I don't think so, no! I know about George Graham's reputation as a disciplinarian and I don't think I would want to talk back to him. I'm not that sort of player anyway – I don't like answering back to anyone to be honest."

...playing abroad?
"Yes, I would like to try playing abroad one day, although I'd obviously like to play for quite a few years and make a name for myself in England first. I like the football in the Italian and Spanish leagues, and to play for a big club like Real Madrid, Barcelona or Juventus would be amazing."

...ending your career in the non-league?
"I wouldn't want to finish my playing days in the non-league, even though I'm sure that it is a good league. I think I would like to finish my career in the same way Alan Shearer ended his England career – and that's finishing at the top."

...becoming a football journalist?
"There's no way that I would like to do that – I'd have to ask questions like this! No, but seriously, I wouldn't like to do that sort of thing. I know a lot of players do it while they are still playing, but I would rather concentrate on playing and I would like to stay in the game when I eventually finish my playing career."

THE Numbers GAME

ALBERTZ 11

SUBJECT: IBROX STADIUM

18,000	1,902	1,929	118,567
The number of fans who turned up for the first ever match at Ibrox against Preston. The game was abandoned after 70 minutes when fans spilled on to the pitch, with Rangers losing 8-1.	The year of the first Ibrox disaster, where 26 people were tragically killed when wooden terracing collapsed during the first England versus Scotland game to be held at the ground.	The year in which the grandstand, currently the front facade of the ground, was opened. This part of the ground is home to a marble staircase, the trophy room, the dressing rooms and offices.	This number was the British record attendance for a league game. It was set on January 2, 1939 during the Old Firm derby at Ibrox. Rangers ran out winners, beating city rivals Celtic 2-1.

JON THE TEDDY BEAR CLUB Phone 041-427 8844 MATCHDAY HOSPITA

13	1,200	2	49
The number of the staircase on which 66 people lost their lives in the second Ibrox disaster in 1971. After the tragedy, plans were made to turn Ibrox into an all-seater stadium to prevent a repeat.	The number of people that Ibrox can cater for on a matchday in the executive suites and lounges. The famous Rangers stadium is capable of seating around 49,200 people in the normal seats!	The number of giant TV screens in the corners of the stadium. These provide pre-match entertainment, replays and the scoreline during the match. They also screen action from away games.	The number of Scottish League crowns that Rangers have won during their illustrious history. Every one of those trophies have been won while Rangers were playing at Ibrox Stadium.

GERRARD: THERE'S MORE TO COME

Steven Gerrard is one of the most exciting players to hit English football in a long time. He's already played for England after only one full season, but the midfield star says there's more young talent to come out of Anfield. **"The Liverpool academy is a superb set-up. I spent a while down there before moving to Melwood,"** Steven told Route 1. **"We have Ian Armstrong, who plays for England Under-18s, Chris O'Brien and Steve Warnock – they're all young and great players. If they keep learning and progressing, they'll definitely make it to the top stage."** More young stars to come? Watch out Man. United!

GARETH LEARNS FROM GARETH

Gareth Barry has had a brilliant start to the new millennium. He may have been on the losing side in last season's FA Cup Final, but he's now a regular at the back for Aston Villa and made Kevin Keegan's squad for Euro 2000. Barry has put his success down to fellow England defender Gareth Southgate. **"I've learned a lot from Gareth in the last couple of years. He's a very experienced player at club and international level, and he's helped my game,"** Barry told Route 1. **"When I've made mistakes he's let me know where I'm going wrong and how to put it right."**

'KEEPING FIT'

Route 1 doesn't believe 'keepers have to train that hard – all they do is practice set pieces and head to the canteen for dinner. But Fulham No.1 Maik Taylor says it's all down to hard work. **"If you practice things on the training ground they'll come naturally to you on a Saturday,"** said Taylor. **"I haven't been in the game a long time, but even people like David Seaman will tell you they're still learning."**

high 5ive

RICHARD JOHNSON
watford

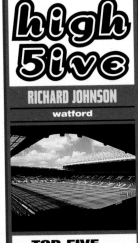

TOP FIVE... PREMIERSHIP GROUNDS

1. Old Trafford
2. Stamford Bridge
3. Anfield
4. St James' Park
5. Villa Park

FILA

Dr.
Martens

GIGGS

"I felt we were unbeatable with the team that we had in 1994. But to go on after that and build another successful team is a credit to the manager."

RYAN GIGGS IS ONE OF THE MOST EXCITING PLAYERS THAT Britain has ever produced. He first arrived on the professional scene as an enthusiastic 17-year-old in 1991. Even in those days, the slightly-built Giggs began to weave his magic down the left-wing and his exciting displays soon forced him into the star-studded Manchester United first-team. The Welsh wizard has never looked back, becoming a vital part of his team's domination of the Premiership in the '90s and one of the first names on the teamsheet. His trophy cabinet now boasts six Premiership titles, three FA Cups, one League Cup, three Charity Shields and a European Cup. Not bad for someone who's just turned 27, eh?

Giggs first came to prominence at Manchester United after signing professional forms in 1990. Sir Alex Ferguson wanted to protect him from the glare of the media spotlight, knowing he had a superstar and that fame and fortune might go to his head. The inevitable comparisons to another Old Trafford legend, George Best, were highly flattering but never an exaggeration. Giggs wasn't allowed to give interviews, although he always had time for MATCH, and this allowed the winger to concentrate on his football, rather than get carried away with a star footballer's lifestyle.

It certainly worked as Giggs scooped the PFA Young Player of the Year award in both 1992 and 1993, and has worked on improving his all-round game to become one of the best players in the world in his position. His speed and skill allow him to beat defenders with ease and deliver pin-point crosses to the likes of Andy Cole and Dwight Yorke and he's capable of scoring spectacular goals. One of the defining moments of his career so far was his extra-time wondergoal against Arsenal in the 1999 FA Cup semi-final. Giggs received the ball in his own half and went on a mazy dribble past four players before unleashing an unstoppable shot past David Seaman for United's winner. It was a truly sublime ten seconds of football.

Giggs has also grown to become an adaptable player. His manager at Man. United has used him on the left-wing, in a deep midfield role, behind the two strikers or even out on the right-wing – as he did when The Red Devils won the 1999 Champions League Final.

Despite captaining the England schoolboys as a teenager, Giggs chose to play for Wales, the country he was born in. He won his first full cap at the age of 17 years and 321 days, which was a record at the time. But Wales have failed to qualify for the major tournaments so Giggsy has been unable to put his skills to the test at either the European Championships or the World Cup finals. However, with his former United team-mate Mark Hughes now in the Wales hotseat, Giggs will be hoping that his country can do enough to make it to the 2002 World Cup in Japan and South Korea. MATCH charts Giggsy's highly-successful career, looking at the high and low points he's faced with Man. United and Wales.

May 1991
DEBUT GOAL

Giggsy picked a good game to score his first goal for United – it was against arch-rivals Manchester City. It was his first start for the club, playing against the club that he nearly signed for instead of The Red Devils.

GIGGSY SAYS: "My first goal was surrounded in controversy. I scored in the home derby game against Manchester City, which was my first full match for United. I got a touch on the winning goal but there was a debate over whether the defender had actually put the ball in, but they gave it to me. I'm working just as hard now as I was when I was first breaking into the United side."

May 1992
LOSING THE TITLE TO LEEDS

Man. United were struggling to score goals in the league and that meant they dropped out of the title race in 1992. That meant Leeds, with Eric Cantona, took the last Division One title before it became the Premier League.

GIGGSY SAYS: "For me, the lowest point in my career was probably losing out in the league to Leeds in 1992. It was my first full season at United and I remember that summer was the longest of my life. We had loads of fans coming up to us all summer saying, 'Are we ever going to win the title?' It was awful. We just couldn't wait for the next season to come around."

May 1993
TITLE WINNER

United won the new Premiership title in 1993 as Aston Villa lost 1-0 to Oldham, but they sealed the championship when Blackburn Rovers came to Old Trafford. Giggs scored with a 30-yard free-kick as United won 3-0.

GIGGSY SAYS: "Everyone had been waiting for that day to come. We'd just missed out the year before and all the lads were determined to make sure we won the title the next season. That free-kick against Blackburn was one of my favourite goals. I've scored a few that people thought were good goals, but the Blackburn one was special. The feeling of winning the title is just indescribable."

October 1993
WALES OUT

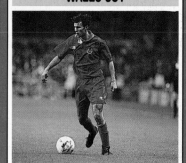

Any hopes that the Welsh had of making the 1994 World Cup in the USA were ended when they lost 2-1 to Romania. Giggs was upset, as he still dreams of playing at the highest level for Wales, and loves his home town of Cardiff.

GIGGSY SAYS: "The thought of never playing in either a World Cup or a European Championship is disappointing to say the least. To play in the World Cup would be the icing on the cake. But the day will never come when I regret playing for Wales and I've always realised that my country doesn't have the same resources as England. It's always nice to get back and see family and friends in Cardiff."

May 1994
DOUBLE SUCCESS

Manchester United secured the second of their Premiership titles and they went on to complete The Double by beating Chelsea 4-0 at Wembley in the FA Cup Final. Giggs knew it was one of the best United sides of all time.

GIGGSY SAYS: "We felt we were unbeatable with the team that we had in 1994, but even after that, to go on and build another team capable of continuing the success was a credit to our manager. I think the one key signing was Eric Cantona. When he came from Leeds he helped us to win the league in 1993 and from then on the team just went from strength to strength really."

November 1994
EURO EXIT

It was European hell for Giggs when the flying winger was substituted in the game against Barcelona, who knocked The Red Devils out of Europe. Giggs was frustrated that United weren't allowed to field their first-choice 11.

GIGGSY SAYS: "It's always disappointing going out of Europe. It was difficult with the foreign-player rule then, because it meant we couldn't play the same team that was playing well in the Premiership. The teams we played in Europe were able to more or less keep the same team, but we had to bring in some very young players and it was hard for them playing against the best sides in Europe."

May 1995
MISSING OUT

Giggsy struggled with injuries and United also struggled, gifting the title to Blackburn Rovers on the final day of the season by drawing at West Ham. They also lost the FA Cup Final 1-0 to Everton and crashed out of Europe.

GIGGSY SAYS: "Most teams would call what we have achieved a success, but everyone knows that success at Manchester United is judged by what is in the trophy cabinet at the end of the season and we didn't win anything that year. It was frustrating but I knew the best of Ryan Giggs was still to come, I was certain of that. I still don't want to go to Italy and I could stay at United for the rest of my career."

1996
A SECOND DOUBLE

United picked up the title on the last day of the season after a tough fight with Newcastle. Then, in the FA Cup Final at Wembley, Eric Cantona scored with only minutes to go to beat Liverpool and claim another double.

GIGGSY SAYS: "That was a very significant title for us because a lot of the players from 1994 had left and the youngsters came in – the Nevilles, Nicky Butt, David Beckham and Paul Scholes. The FA Cup Final was not a great game and I can't pretend otherwise, but the most important thing for us was that Eric came up with the winner just before the end and we won our second double."

May 1998
LEAGUE LOSERS

Arsenal walked away with the league title with two games left to be played, while United won away to Barnsley in the final game to lessen the gap to one point. But everyone at United was left gutted by a trophy-less season.

GIGGSY SAYS: "Seeing another team lifting the trophy that you could have won is always difficult. You want to be the ones lifting that trophy. It's hard defending the league title because everyone wants to win it, but that makes you even more determined for the next season. But we let the championship slip through our fingers and that made it hard to come to terms with."

April 1999
WONDERGOAL

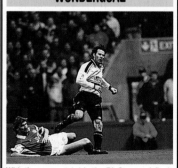

With the score at 1-1 in the FA Cup semi-final replay against Arsenal, Giggsy picked up the ball in his own half in extra-time and dribbled past four defenders before crashing a superb winner past a helpless David Seaman.

GIGGSY SAYS: "Once I started the run towards their goal, I just couldn't stop. I don't remember much, except sticking my head down and going for goal. As I got closer to the Arsenal penalty area I just kept thinking to myself 'You can go all the way here'. When it went past David Seaman I was off! It's only afterwards when you see the goal again that you think to yourself, 'Did I really do that?'"

"EVERYONE HAD BEEN WAITING FOR THAT DAY. WINNING THE TITLE IS JUST INDESCRIBABLE."

May 1999
UNITED CLINCH THE TREBLE

It was an historic, treble-winning season for Man. United, clinching the league, FA Cup and European Cup. They faced Bayern Munich in the final of the Champions League and two dramatic late goals clinched the trophy.

GIGGSY SAYS: *"It was a scrappy game, but great teams never give up and we kept going. The goals in injury-time were unbelievable. I knew we'd win after Teddy grabbed the equaliser. The German players were exhausted, they thought they'd won. We scored with the next kick, then they kicked off and the final whistle blew. Our success belonged to everyone, but particularly to our fans."*

April 2000
REAL LOSS

As champions of Europe, United found the next European campaign much harder, and their hopes were ended in the quarter-finals against Real Madrid. A 0-0 away draw and a 3-2 loss at Old Trafford put them out.

GIGGSY SAYS: *"We didn't perform out in Madrid. We just didn't reach the standards that we've set ourselves over the last few years when we've gone to places like Milan and Juventus and scored. Getting an away goal was the most important thing for us and we didn't get it. We still had a great chance at Old Trafford but we were chasing the game after Keano scored that unlucky own goal."*

April 2000
CHAMPIONS AGAIN

A few days after they crashed out of Europe, United travelled to Southampton in the league and turned on the style, with Giggs and his jubilant team-mates securing the Premiership title with four games still left to play.

GIGGSY SAYS: *"There are times when teams just get good runs towards the end of the season and we just got ourselves going on a good run. If you can do that as a team then it's going to be difficult for other sides to be up there challenging for the championship – if they lose a game that's it. We had a healthy lead and some of the other teams started to lose their way."*

FOOTY MAD!

THEY SAID WHAT!

MATCH looks back at the funny things we heard at Euro 2000 last summer.

"This is a great gift for Turkey. This is the best answer to give the Press. They thought our tickets home were booked, but it was an open ticket."
Proud Turkey coach Mustapha Denizli talks about his team reaching the quarter-finals.

"Germany played the worst game I've ever seen them play – it was chaos in defence and midfield. It was sad."
UEFA technical delegate Rinus Michels on Germany's 3-0 loss to Portugal. Sad, eh?

"I still maintain that we are on a very good path and, in a few months, we will be at the same level as the Dutch and the French teams."
Czech Republic coach Jozef Chovanec on the future, despite being knocked out of Group D.

"The Dutch were simply excellent, but I have to say they were lucky. Every shot on goal went in and when that happens there is nothing you can do."
Yugoslavia coach Vujadin Boskov is a sore loser after the 6-1 quarter-final defeat to Holland.

"It was probably the finest hour of my career. Perfect is the only word to describe it. When I say perfect, I am talking about the team and not myself."
Holland striker Patrick Kluivert gets carried away after his hat-trick against Yugoslavia.

"I don't have a preference who we meet next, but I am married to a French woman, so I would really like to meet them."
Portugal Coach Humberto Coelho obviously doesn't like his wife!

"We are like the German team was 15 years ago. Gary Lineker once said: 'If you play 11 v 11 it's always the Germans who win'. Now we are the same. We think we are dead – we think we are in hell, but we come back from hell and we win."
Frank Leboeuf in heaven after France win the final of Euro 2000 against Italy.

In the David Beckham thong debate these fans show their preference.

"A-ga-doo-doo-doo, push pineapple, shake the tree."

Who said the Germans don't express their love for each other?

Think this is good? You should see them do it on a motorbike!

Nuno Gomes suggests that the wall turns to face the free-kick.

The players try to work out who blew off in the tunnel.

"The gaffer going? No, I don't believe it! You're pulling my leg!"

"Hey there little fella. Wanna big hug?"

They couldn't afford fireworks in Holland.

United's prices had become so expensive that this was the only way for some to see the game.

Paolo di Canio liked to change the rules so that he could beat the other boys.

"You're on the straight and narrow? Ha, ha. That's a good one!"

"Okay, first one to blink has to leave the pitch."

After a whopping Friday night on the town, Barton crawls in.

"And, and, and... your mother's got a beard!"
Francis Jeffers plays dirty.

There was no truth in the rumour that Zola's eyes were going.

"Oi! Zola! Stop hugging that post and get on with the game." Old timer Jim Smith has a word.

Charlton's John Robinson celebrates promotion, then realises they won't win so often in the Premiership.

West Ham's youth policy was getting ridiculous.

Lee Hendrie won't get away with this dive.

As Liverpool continued to improve, the fight was on to get a move to Anfield.

"Sshh," whispers Henry. "The linesman can't see I'm offside from here."

Ever since he quit England, Shearer has found football boring.

KIERON DYER
Newcastle United

MATCH
YOUNG GUNS

1

The **MATCH** computer finds the most prolific British striker in Premier League history.

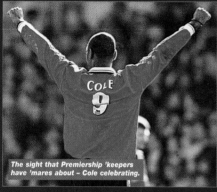

The sight that Premiership 'keepers have 'mares about – Cole celebrating.

SOME STRIKERS HAVE BUNDLES OF SKILL, others rely on their electric pace and the big men use their power in the air. But whatever their individual qualities, every striker is judged on the amount of goals they score.

We've seen some phenomenal frontmen in the Premier Leagues of England and Scotland over the last eight seasons (since England finally caught up with Scotland by forming a Premier League), but who's got the most prolific goalscoring record? To find out, the statistics of every striker in the English and Scottish Premier Leagues were put into the MATCH computer. The results are based on strike ratios – the percentage of goals the stars have scored compared to the amount of games they've played.

Kevin Phillips, Thierry Henry and Michael Owen all made the grade, but they'll have to keep scoring consistently over the next few seasons to reach Alan Shearer's record.

Who said the England legend was past his brilliant best? Shearer is currently the most successful striker in Britain, scoring 176 goals in 253 games, but Kevin Phillips may be the man to catch him if his first season is anything to go by. MATCH counts down the 15 most prolific British strikers in Premier League history, examining their strengths, weaknesses and scoring records.

RULES & REGULATIONS!

MATCH WENT BACK TO THE 1992-1993 season, when England moved in line with Scotland to form a new-style Premier League, to compile these strike rates. The MATCH computer used eight seasons of goalscoring data from 1992 right up to 2000 (last season) to find Britain's top striker. All these rules and regulations mean that any goals that were scored by players before the 1992-1993 season, or in any divisions outside English and Scottish Premier Leagues, were not included!

KEVIN PHILLIPS

Even the experts said Kevin Phillips would struggle to reproduce his scoring feats after Sunderland were promoted from Division One in 1999, and to be honest, who could blame them? Only five years earlier Phillips was playing non-league football for Baldock Town after failing to get a pro contract at Southampton. But what the critics didn't bet on was the striker's supreme confidence and the formidable partnership he has formed with Niall Quinn. Last season Phillips won the Premiership golden boot, joining a very exclusive club.

STRENGTHS: Phillips has the confidence a centre-forward needs to be successful in front of goal. He shoots at every opportunity and the ball often ends up in the back of the net. He's strong on the ball, surprisingly good in the air and has a good range of shooting, from tap-ins to sweetly-struck strikes.

WEAKNESSES: He's looked a bit out of his league at international level, with man-markers and without Niall Quinn, but he'll get better if given the chance to learn. Looks less effective without the big Irishman to lead the line.

CONSISTENCY: No striker was as consistent as 'Super Kev' last season, who had set himself a target of just 20 goals. His desire to score every game should serve him well over the next few years at The Stadium Of Light.

PREMIERSHIP CLUBS: Sunderland (1999-present)

PREMIERSHIP SEASONS: 1

GAMES/GOALS: 36/30 (2000)

LAST SEASON'S STRIKE RATE: 83%

BEST SEASON: 83% (1999-2000)

TOTAL GAMES/GOALS: 36/30 (83%)

STRIKE RATE 83%

THE CRITICS SAID PHILLIPS WOULD STRUGGLE TO SCORE IN THE PREMIERSHIP.

2

MARK VIDUKA

After scoring 25 goals last season, Viduka was bound to attract interest from the top sides in Europe and a £7 million bid from Leeds showed how highly he is rated. He was also named Player Of The Year last season in Scotland.

STRENGTHS: Viduka uses his powerful frame to get into good positions up front and he holds the ball up well, helping to bring others into the game. Also has a good awareness of space around him, making him a team player as well as a deadly finisher in front of goal with either his boot or head.

WEAKNESSES: His temperament has let him down on occasions and is yet to be tested at the very highest level. He also lacked a top quality striking partner last season and Celtic would have provided a better challenge to Rangers if he had top Swedish striker Henrik Larsson for company in attack.

CONSISTENCY: Made an impressive start to his Celtic career after joining the club late in the 1998-99 season, scoring five goals in just nine games. Continued his form in style last season and it was no surprise when Celtic started receiving multi-million pound bids for the Australian's signature.

PREMIER LEAGUE CLUBS:	Celtic (1999-2000)
PREMIER LEAGUE SEASONS:	2
GAMES/GOALS:	28/25 (2000), 9/5 (1999)
LAST SEASON'S STRIKE RATE:	89%
BEST SEASON:	89% Celtic (1999-2000)
TOTAL GAMES/GOALS:	37/30 (81%)

STRIKE RATE 81%

ALAN SHEARER

3

Shearer's last few seasons have been blighted by injury, but he came back with a bang in 1999-2000, dismissing claims that he was well past his best. After being relegated to the bench during Ruud Gullit's reign, he finished the season under Bobby Robson as the second highest scorer in the Premiership.

STRENGTHS: Shearer's still got enough stamina to terrorise defenders with his running off the ball. He's dangerous in the air and hits a thunderous shot from anywhere in the 18-yard box. Never gives up and hates losing.

WEAKNESSES: He's lost some pace after serious injury, which means he can be contained if defenders push him away from goal. Leads from the front, but needs a good striker beside him and service from the wings.

CONSISTENCY: No other British striker compares with Shearer over eight seasons in the Premiership. His record is phenomenal and he managed to score 23 goals last season in what was only an average Newcastle side.

PREMIERSHIP CLUBS:	Blackburn Rovers (1992-96), Newcastle United (1996-present)
PREMIERSHIP SEASONS:	8
GAMES/GOALS:	37/23 (2000), 30/14 (1999), 17/2 (1998), 31/25 (1997), 35/31 (1996), 42/34 (1995), 40/31 (1994), 21/16 (1993)
LAST SEASON'S STRIKE RATE:	62%
BEST SEASON:	89% Blackburn Rovers (1995-1996)
TOTAL GAMES/GOALS:	253/176 (70%)

STRIKE RATE 70%

HENRIK LARSSON

4

Henrik Larsson has been a revelation since his move from the Dutch league. His first two years in Scotland were explosive, scoring 44 goals in 70 games, but he suffered an agonising leg break early on last season. But an amazing recovery saw the dreadlocked striker make a surprising comeback for Euro 2000, but he couldn't fire Sweden past the group stages.

STRENGTHS: Close to the prototype striker, Larsson has bags of pace, power and skill. He is difficult to mark, unpredictable on the ball and a master at beating the offside trap. He is also a dangerous opponent in the air from corners and set-pieces, and displays clever running off the ball to gain space.

WEAKNESSES: Martin O'Neill will be wanting even more goals from his No. 1 striker if Celtic are going to beat Rangers to the title this season. Needs to keep going for 90 minutes to win as many games as possible for Celtic.

CONSISTENCY: Larsson has improved every season since moving to Glasgow in 1997. Celtic fans will be wondering if he has fully recovered from his injury and whether he can get back to his goalscoring best this season.

PREMIER LEAGUE CLUBS:	Celtic (1997-present)
PREMIER LEAGUE SEASONS:	3
GAMES/GOALS:	9/7 (2000), 35/28 (1999), 35/16 (1998)
LAST SEASON'S STRIKE RATE:	78%
BEST SEASON:	78% Celtic (1999-2000)
TOTAL GAMES/GOALS:	79/51 (65%)

STRIKE RATE 65%

ANDY COLE

5

STRENGTHS: Cole is the perfect foil for Man. United's counter-attacking. He has pace and scores with both feet, his head and from the odd overhead kick. At his best, he shoots instinctively and accurately, giving the 'keeper no chance.

WEAKNESSES: His main weakness is missing chances when he has too much time to think about his options. He is far more dangerous when he uses his predatory instincts and shoots before the ball gets caught under his feet.

CONSISTENCY: Some say he has improved as a team player since joining Man. United, but Cole was at his goalscoring best at Newcastle, where he netted a record-breaking 34 goals in the 1993-94 season. He's still breaking the net regularly for The Red Devils but has to share the goals with his team-mates.

PREMIERSHIP CLUBS: Newcastle (1992-95), Man. United (1995-present)

PREMIERSHIP SEASONS: 8

GAMES/GOALS: 28/19 (2000), 32/17 (1999), 33/16 (1998), 20/7 (1997), 34/11 (1996), 36/21 (1995), 40/34 (1994), 12/12 (1993)

LAST SEASON'S STRIKE RATE: 68%

BEST SEASON: 100% Newcastle (1992-1993)

TOTAL GAMES/GOALS: 235/137 (58%)

STRIKE RATE **58%**

ROBBIE FOWLER

6

STRENGTHS: Regarded as the best finisher in Britain, Fowler is difficult to knock off the ball, good in the air and scores plenty of goals with both feet. Has the instinct a good striker needs to get into goalscoring positions and has the ability to place the ball into the net rather than going for power every time.

WEAKNESSES: He's been in trouble for a series of incidents including the altercation with Graeme Le Saux and his line-sniffing goal celebration. Doesn't have blistering pace, but in a team with Michael Owen it isn't really a problem.

CONSISTENCY: Had a superb first three seasons for The Reds, but injury problems have hindered his progress and many of his appearances during the last two seasons were as a substitute. Moves ahead of Henry on goals scored.

PREMIERSHIP CLUBS: Liverpool (1993-present)

PREMIERSHIP SEASONS: 7

GAMES/GOALS: 14/3 (2000), 25/14 (1999), 20/9 (1998), 32/18 (1997), 38/28 (1996), 42/25 (1995), 28/12 (1994)

LAST SEASON'S STRIKE RATE: 21%

BEST SEASON: 74% (1995-1996)

TOTAL GAMES/GOALS: 199/109 (55%)

STRIKE RATE **55%**

THIERRY HENRY

7

STRENGTHS: Henry has phenomenal pace, which he uses to spin away from his marker and run on to cultured passes from midfield. The French striker relishes one-on-one situations and can hit the back of the net from every angle. He also seems to be getting better with every game – a frightening prospect.

WEAKNESSES: He's still adapting to the physical side of Premiership, so he's better at receiving the ball in front of him and running at goal rather than receiving it at his feet with a defender in close attendance ready to pounce.

CONSISTENCY: Scored 17 goals in 31 games in his first season at Arsenal and could do even better as he matures in his new centre-forward role. Went seven games without a goal at the beginning of last season, but Henry never stopped hitting the net after scoring his first Arsenal goal against Southampton.

PREMIERSHIP CLUBS: Arsenal (1999-present)

PREMIERSHIP SEASONS: 1

GAMES/GOALS: 31/17 (2000)

LAST SEASON'S STRIKE RATE: 55%

BEST SEASON: 55% (1999-2000)

TOTAL GAMES/GOALS: 31/17 (55%)

STRIKE RATE **55%**

MICHAEL OWEN

8

STRENGTHS: Owen beats defenders with his extraordinary pace, his subtle skill and his mazy dribbling. He is strong on the ball for his size and controls the ball superbly while running, allowing him to terrify any defender who attempts to keep up with him. He sometimes runs out of ideas, but he's still learning.

WEAKNESSES: Usually beaten in the air and over-dependent on his right foot when shooting, but has plenty of time to improve on his technique. Admits he still has a lot to learn, but Owen is still an unbelievable talent for his age.

CONSISTENCY: After scoring on his Liverpool debut at the end of 1996-97, Owen scored more than a goal every other game in the next two seasons, but the England star has been blighted by injury since then. Made 27 appearances last season but rarely for 90 minutes, so this is a big season for the young star.

PREMIERSHIP CLUBS: Liverpool 1996-present

PREMIERSHIP SEASONS: 4

GAMES/GOALS: 27/11 (2000), 30/18 (1999), 36/18 (1998), 2/1 (1997)

LAST SEASON'S STRIKE RATE: 41%

BEST SEASON: 78% (1998-1999)

TOTAL GAMES/GOALS: 95/48 (51%)

STRIKE RATE **51%**

LES FERDINAND

9

STRENGTHS: Leads the line superbly, using his power and bursts of pace to beat defenders. Always a threat in the air, Ferdinand is a good foil for other strikers and was at his best up front with Alan Shearer at Newcastle United.

WEAKNESSES: Has lost the ability to score 20 goals a season because of the many injury problems he has suffered since arriving at Tottenham Hotspur and he's proving to be less effective against the Premiership's faster defenders.

CONSISTENCY: First caught the eye as a powerful striker for QPR, but was most successful at Newcastle in 1995-96. Has failed to play a full season since moving to Spurs because of injury. Moves ahead of McCoist on goals scored.

PREMIERSHIP CLUBS: QPR (1992-95), Newcastle United (1995-97), Tottenham Hotspur (1997-present)

PREMIERSHIP SEASONS: 8

GAMES/GOALS: 9/2 (2000), 24/5 (1999), 21/5 (1998), 31/16 (1997), 37/25 (1996), 37/24 (1995), 36/16 (1994), 37/20 (1993)

LAST SEASON'S STRIKE RATE: 43%

BEST SEASON: 68% Newcastle (1996-1997)

TOTAL GAMES/GOALS: 232/113 (49%)

STRIKE RATE **49%**

ALLY McCOIST

10

STRENGTHS: 'Super Ally' has been so successful because of his ability to get into great goalscoring positions and gain that vital yard ahead of his marker. Has a natural instinct in front of goal so he's still an effective striker in Scotland, even though he's nearing the end of his career at the grand old age of 38.

WEAKNESSES: Has never been blessed with an abundance of pace but his age hasn't stopped him cracking in the goals in the Scottish Premier League, even though most strikers swap their boots for slippers when they approach 40.

CONSISTENCY: McCoist has been the most consistent striker in Scotland over an incredible 20 seasons of top-flight football and he has an extraordinary record of scoring a goal every other game since the 1992/93 season.

PREMIERSHIP CLUBS: Rangers (1992-98), Kilmarnock (1998-present)

PREMIERSHIP SEASONS: 8

GAMES/GOALS: 9/1 (2000), 26/7 (1999), 15/5 (1998), 25/10 (1997), 25/16 (1996), 9/1 (1995), 21/7 (1994), 34/34 (1993)

LAST SEASON'S STRIKE RATE: 11%

BEST SEASON: 100% Rangers (1992-1993)

TOTAL GAMES/GOALS: 164/81 (49%)

STRIKE RATE **49%**

OLE GUNNAR SOLSKJAER

 **11**

STRENGTHS: Solskjaer immediately adjusts to the pace of a game when he comes off the bench. It's not a situation he enjoys, but he scores goals for fun by making the 'keeper work and shooting whenever an opportunity comes his way. Gets into good goalscoring positions and will have a crack from anywhere.

WEAKNESSES: No matter how many goals he scores, the Norwegian striker just can't break up the successful pairing of Dwight Yorke and Andy Cole, who have a proven ability to play to each others' strengths for 90 minutes.

CONSISTENCY: Solskjaer has an excellent record considering that many of his appearances for Man. United have been from the bench since arriving from Molde in July 1996. His best season for The Red Devils was in 1998-99, even though Dwight Yorke arrived at Old Trafford from Aston Villa that season.

PREMIERSHIP CLUBS: Man. United (1996-present)

PREMIERSHIP SEASONS: 4

GAMES/GOALS: 28/12 (2000), 19/12 (1999), 22/6 (1998), 33/18 (1997)

LAST SEASON'S STRIKE RATE: 43%

BEST SEASON: 63% (1998-1999)

TOTAL GAMES/GOALS: 102/48 (47%)

STRIKE RATE 47%

PAOLO DI CANIO

 **12**

STRENGTHS: Di Canio is a difficult player to mark, as he is willing to move into deeper positions to collect the ball and feed his team-mates with precision passes. Defenders try to get near him but he dazzles them with breathtaking skill to gain that extra yard he needs for shooting.

WEAKNESSES: His fiery temper is well documented, especially when things aren't going well. He's let his colleagues down in the past by getting sent-off in games or being disciplined by the FA, leading to long suspensions.

CONSISTENCY: The Italian-born striker had his most successful season in 1999-2000 when he scored 16 goals – many of which were spectacular finishes – even though he had a variety of strike partners last season at Upton Park.

PREMIERSHIP CLUBS: Celtic (1996-97), Sheffield Wednesday (1997-99), West Ham (1999-present)

PREMIERSHIP SEASONS: 4

GAMES/GOALS: 30/16 (2000), 19/7 (1999), 35/12 (1998), 26/12 (1997)

LAST SEASON'S STRIKE RATE: 53%

BEST SEASON: 53% West Ham (1999-2000)

TOTAL GAMES/GOALS: 110/47 (43%)

STRIKE RATE 43%

DION DUBLIN

 **13**

STRENGTHS: Dublin is far more than just a big striker who likes the ball played to him in the air all the time. He holds the ball up well for other strikers and is prolific in the air, but he also scores his fair share of goals with his rocket right-foot shot. Always gives opposing defenders a hard, physical game.

WEAKNESSES: He'll never dribble past a defence and lacks real pace, but his manager at Villa has always complimented Dublin's aerial dominance with strike partners that have pace in abundance – like Carbone and Joachim.

CONSISTENCY: Hasn't cracked 20 goals in a season yet, but he remains a consistent striker when fit and provides plenty of assists for his team-mates.

PREMIERSHIP CLUBS: Man. United (1992-94), Coventry City (1994-98), Aston Villa (1998-present)

PREMIERSHIP SEASONS: 8

GAMES/GOALS: 26/12 (2000), 24/11 (1999), 36/18 (19998), 34/13 (1997), 34/14 (1996), 31/13 (1995), 5/1 (1994), 7/1 (1993)

LAST SEASON'S STRIKE RATE: 46%

BEST SEASON: 50% (Coventry 1997-1998)

TOTAL GAMES/GOALS: 197/83 (42%)

STRIKE RATE 42%

MARIAN PAHARS

 **14**

STRENGTHS: Pahars has a beautiful touch on the ball and sublime control, meaning he's capable of taking on any defender and beating them. The Latvian has supreme confidence and is difficult to mark because of his movement up front and in midfield. He thinks on his feet to make the best out of any situation.

WEAKNESSES: He has an obvious lack of height and the drifting that he does around the pitch can leave gaps in Southampton's attack. With Le Tissier failing to hold down a first-team place, the lack of a midfield playmaker in the team means he often turns provider rather than doing his job as a goalscorer.

CONSISTENCY: The Saints fans got a glimpse of what was to come at the end of the 1998-99 campaign, when he scored three goals in six games. He did well last season, but Glenn Hoddle will want more goals from him this season.

PREMIERSHIP CLUBS: Southampton (1998-present)

PREMIERSHIP SEASONS: 2

GAMES/GOALS: 33/13 (2000), 6/3 (1999)

LAST SEASON'S STRIKE RATE: 39%

BEST SEASON: 50% (1999-2000)

TOTAL GAMES/GOALS: 39/16 (41%)

STRIKE RATE 41%

DWIGHT YORKE

 **15**

STRENGTHS: Yorke is deadly around the box. He has two trademark goals, either spinning away from his marker before finishing low past the goalkeeper or rising to meet a pinpoint cross from Beckham or Giggs on the wing. He has awesome close control and an impressive understanding with Andy Cole.

WEAKNESSES: Relies on his skill rather than speed and he can play too deep for United, becoming separated from his strike partner. Alex Ferguson would probably prefer him to score more tap-ins than spectacular goals.

CONSISTENCY: In a Man. United team full of goals, Yorkie still managed to score 20 times last season, his best return ever. He's now a consistent scorer in the Premiership after only scoring 14 goals in three seasons at Aston Villa.

PREMIERSHIP CLUBS: Aston Villa (1992-98) Man. United (1998-present)

PREMIERSHIP SEASONS: 6

GAMES/GOALS: 20/32 (2000), 18/33 (1999), 12/30 (1998), 17/37 (1997), 17/35 (1996), 6/37 (1995), 2/12 (1994), 6/27 (1993)

LAST SEASON'S STRIKE RATE: 63%

BEST SEASON: Man United 63% (1999-2000)

TOTAL GAMES/GOALS: 243/98 (40%)

STRIKE RATE 40%

THE BEST OF THE REST...

The MATCH computer threw up some big surprises. There was no place in the top 15 for Michael Bridges, who had a slow start to his Premiership career as Sunderland were relegated in 1997. Leicester City's Stan Collymore was closer to the top 15 than most people would have predicted, just missing out as Dwight Yorke has scored more career goals. The best of the rest will all want to improve their strike rates this season so they make the top 15 next year!

TEAM	PLAYER	GAMES/GOALS
Leicester City	Stan Collymore	149/59 (40%)
Rangers	Billy Dodds	285/110 (39%)
Coventry City	Robbie Keane	31/12 (39%)
Leeds United	Michael Bridges	59/22 (37%)
Chelsea	Tore Andre Flo	98/31 (32%)
Everton	Kevin Campbell	169/52 (31%)
Bradford City	Dean Windass	38/10 (26%)
Derby County	Malcolm Christie	23/6 (26%)
Middlesbrough	Hamilton Ricard	79/29 (24%)

THE FINAL WHISTLE

HOW DID YOU SCORE?
Remember to fill in your answers to the following quiz questions in the space provided on page 108 and then flick through to the third XI on page 64!

Real Madrid lift the 2000 Champions League trophy.

second XI

The Champions League is no doubt Europe's premier club competition, but just how much do you know about it?

1 The European Cup has been running for a few decades now, but do you know when the first ever European Cup competition took place?

2 Can you name the giants of Spanish football who won the inaugural European Cup trophy?

3 Which team entered the record books in 1967 when they became the first ever British team to lift the European Cup after beating Inter Milan in the final?

4 In the following year, Manchester United were the first English side to win the coveted trophy, but who did they beat in the final?

5 What was the score when Red Star Belgrade and Marseille met in the 1991 final, which was held in Bari?

6 The 1994 final was officiated by an English referee. Can you name him?

7 In what year were Dutch giants Ajax last crowned champions of Europe, after their final against AC Milan?

8 Two Italian teams reached three European Cup finals in a row during the '90s. Can you name them?

9 Can you name the two Italian sides who were beaten by Manchester United in the latter stages of the 1998-99 competition?

10 Can you remember which striker scored Manchester United's winning goal against Bayern Munich in that final of 1999?

11 Name the player who scored Real Madrid's third and final goal against Valencia, as the Spaniards won 3-0 in the 2000 final.

CROSSWORD

Use your footy knowledge to solve the crossword below!

ACROSS
1. Scottish midfield star, John, formerly with Monaco (7)
4. Dave, manager who steered Darlington into the play-offs (7)
7. Joe-Max, American forward in the Everton squad (5)
9. The national side of Premiership stars Babayaro and Kanu (7)
11. Managers (6)
12. Tore, Norwegian defender with relegated Wimbledon (8)
14. Title by which a referee's assistant is commonly known (8)
16. Ex-Forest man Steve, who helped Villa to the FA Cup Final (5)
20. Roy, ex-Reds boss who was made Riedle's temporary assistant at Fulham last season (5)
21. Charlton and Republic Of Ireland midfield star, Mark (8)
23. Mario, Chelsea's little-used, ex-Ajax man given a cup final start (8)
25. West Brom's former Rams defender, Matt (6)
28. David, Harrow official who refereed the 1994 FA Cup Final (7)
29. Roy, midfielder voted Footballer Of The Year last season (5)
30. Scot, Graeme, in charge at Ewood Park (7)
31. The 1999-2000 Scottish Premier League champions (7)

DOWN
1. Tottenham defender, Sol, an England regular (8)
2. Millwall's club nickname (5)
3. Cameroon defender, Rigobert, who lifted the 2000 African Cup (4)
4. Ex-Arsenal midfielder, Stephen, transferred to Goodison Park (6)
5. Gordon, ex-Rangers and Chelsea striker playing in Australia (5)
6. Bradford and Northern Ireland full-back, Ian (5)
8. ...... Thome, Brazilian sold to Chelsea for a bargain fee (7)
10. 2000 UEFA Cup finalists from England (7)
13. Sunderland's volatile ex-Millwall Scot, Alex (3)
15. Full-back, Phil, in Man. United's title-winning squad (7)
17. John, ex-Wales boss who took McManaman to Real Madrid (7)
18. ... Ferdinand, West Ham and England centre-back (3)
19. Veteran Welshman, Dean, in Bradford's battling side (8)
22. Jody, Englishman at Stamford Bridge (6)
23. One-time Addicks full-back, Danny, now at Leeds (5)
24. Gunnar, former Elland Road Norwegian at Valley Parade (5)
26. Wales striker, Nathan, on Blackburn's transfer list (5)
27. Newcastle's ex-Ipswich England international, Kieron (4)

WHO AM I?
Can you guess the name of the player from these statements?

1 I am a Premier League player at long last.
2 I have played for Jamaica.
3 I nearly played for Scotland.
4 I am only 5ft 6ins tall.

1 POINT FOR CORRECT ANSWER

MATCHfacts CODE BREAKER
Can you decode this to find a Premiership star?

CRACK THE CODE!
9 26 18
7 12 9 12 2

former clubs
Who did these stars play for before their current club?

1 Carl Cort
Newcastle

2 Dennis Wise
Chelsea

3 Matt Elliott
Leicester

4 Kieron Dyer
Newcastle

WHO WON IT?

The European Cup in 1975

1 POINT FOR CORRECT ANSWER

DATING AGENCY
Can you guess this player from his personal information?

Nationality: English
Birthplace: Huyton
Age: 20
Lives: North-West
Height: 6ft 2ins
Hair: Short, brown
Interests: Cars, catching the bus

1 POINT FOR CORRECT ANSWER

what position?
match these First Division players with their positions

1 DEAN HOLDSWORTH
2 SEAN GREGAN
3 IAN BENNETT
4 NEIL ARDLEY
5 KENNY IRONS

A Goalkeeper
B Striker
C Winger
D Centre-back
E Midfielder

GARETH BARRY

Aston Villa

MATCH
YOUNG GUNS

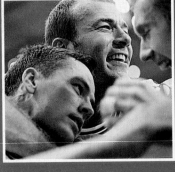

SHEARER

"To be the most expensive player isn't always easy to live with. I see it as a privilege and it gives me an extra incentive to show I give value for money."

THE PREMIER LEAGUE HAS BEEN HOST TO MANY AWESOME strikers since its inaugural season in 1992-93, but none more so than Alan Shearer. Born only a few miles away from St James' Park, the Newcastle star's career has been nothing short of explosive as the prolific striker has smashed records wherever he has played. As a boy he would watch Kevin Keegan from the terraces of St James' Park hoping to one day not only reach those heights, but to also emulate Keegan's achievements. Shearer achieved his childhood dream when he signed for his hometown club four years ago and he did it by signing for his idol, Kevin Keegan. But it could so easily have been a very different path to the top. At his Newcastle trial, his talent wasn't spotted by the coaches because he was made to play in goal and it was left to Jack Hixon, then Southampton's scout, to take him down to the south coast on an apprenticeship.

Since he moved away from Tyneside his rise has been nothing short of astronomical. A hat-trick on his league debut, a championship winners' medal, and two British transfer records to his name have made Shearer a household name.

But despite his predatory instinct in front of goal and his many goalscoring records, Shearer has had several problems. Plagued by a number of serious injuries that could have ended any footballer's career, Shearer has bounced back only to be written off by critics who have questioned his pace and sharpness in front of goal.

Despite that criticism, few would argue that Shearer has been one of the best strikers England has ever produced. At the 1996 European Championships, hosted in England, Shearer showed his importance to the England team by scoring six goals en route to the semi-finals, bagging himself the coveted golden boot trophy. He was a worthy England captain at the 1998 World Cup, but in his final hour at Euro 2000, he was disappointed not to take the team through to the quarter-finals. Shearer was one of the few England players to leave the competition with any credibility and will always treasure one memory – he scored the header which gave England their first tournament win over Germany in 34 years.

After his international swansong at Euro 2000, Shearer has decided to concentrate on his club form this season, aiming to bring back the success that Tyneside has been crying out for. With FA Cup heartbreaks over the last three years, Shearer is adamant he will add some more silverware to his trophy cabinet. MATCH takes a look back at the star striker's long and successful career for both club and country.

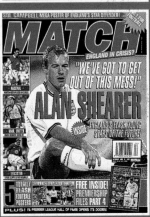

APRIL 1988
DREAM DEBUT

Shearer blasted onto the football scene when he was just 17 years old, scoring a hat-trick on his league debut for Southampton. After that, everyone knew the young striker would become a major force to be reckoned with.

ALAN SAYS: *"I've scored on three of my debuts – Southampton, Blackburn and England – but my league debut is one I won't forget in a hurry. I think I became the youngest player to score three goals on a debut, beating the previous record which was set by Jimmy Greaves. But it wasn't until 1.30pm that the manager told me I was going to be playing in that game. I scored the hat-trick with two headers and a left-foot shot, and I left the field clutching the ball with a smile that lasted for weeks. I have great memories of the first goal I scored for the club."*

FEBRUARY 1992
INTERNATIONAL DEBUT

Four years later, Shearer had established himself at Southampton and with a formidable club scoring record, not even England boss Graham Taylor could ignore Shearer's talents. His first cap was against France at Wembley.

ALAN SAYS: *"It was a great honour. When I was a youngster I had always hoped and dreamed of playing for my country and the time had come. I played up front with David Hirst in the first half, and then Gary Lineker came on at half-time so I partnered him. I managed to get a goal as well in our 2-0 win at Wembley which was great. I found that it was difficult going into the England side at that time because I was so young, but the other more experienced professionals helped me along and it all went very well."*

JULY 1992
JOINING BLACKBURN

After finishing the 1991-92 season as the top scorer at Southampton, Shearer decided it was time to move to pastures new. He left for Ewood Park and big-spending Blackburn for a British transfer record of £3.6million.

ALAN SAYS: *"When I went to Blackburn as the British record signing, I was really relishing playing my first game for the club because it gave me something that I had to live up to. But to be the most expensive player wasn't always easy to live with. I saw it as a privilege to be rated so highly in football and it gave me the extra incentive to go out and show that I could give real value for money. There was a lot of pressure that came with the money that Blackburn had paid for me, but I went out there to show I was worth it."*

BOXING DAY 1992
FIRST MAJOR INJURY

Shearer thrilled the crowd as soon as he pulled on the Blackburn shirt and he even scored on his debut. But after a few months of enjoying life at Ewood Park, he suffered a setback when he picked up a serious injury.

ALAN SAYS: *"I was the league's leading scorer and Blackburn were flying. We played Leeds at Ewood Park and I went to shoot with my left foot, but as I hit the ball, a defender took my right leg away. In the second half I felt my knee go twice so I had to come off. I was very shocked. I thought something had happened, but nothing too serious. Injuries aren't nice and they've made me appreciate the game more when I am playing. I've had two serious injuries in my career and I hope that I can stay injury-free now for the rest of my career."*

MAY 1995
PREMIER LEAGUE WINNER

Shearer formed a formidable partnership with Chris Sutton and with both players in great form, the title race went to the wire. Rovers lost to Liverpool on the last day, but still took the title as Man. United lost at Upton Park.

ALAN SAYS: *"Liverpool's first goal hurt us the most because we'd gone there knowing that we had to win to keep the championship in our hands. After that, despite my equaliser, we were really up against it. For about ten seconds after Jamie Redknapp scored their winner I thought it was all over because I had no idea what the score was between West Ham and Man. United. Then the crowd started cheering and the Blackburn bench erupted, so I knew we'd done it. I wouldn't want to go through those ten seconds again, though."*

DECEMBER 1995
100TH PREMIERSHIP GOAL

Shearer's rise to the very top and his ability to find the net regularly meant he became the first player to blast home a century of goals, the 100th strike coming against Tottenham just three years after the Premiership began.

ALAN SAYS: *"It's nice, but at the end of the day I'm employed to score goals and hopefully I'm doing the job well enough to keep people happy. But I have always maintained that as a goalscorer you are always going to get the headlines and that is harsh on the other players in the team. I thrive on good service and without that I wouldn't score goals. I think it's nice to reach a landmark, but by the same token, others are equally responsible for my achievements because without my team-mates I wouldn't have got this far."*

1995-96
ENGLAND GOAL DROUGHT

Despite his scoring record with Blackburn, Shearer's goals were in short supply during Terry Venables' reign as the England manager. But he answered his critics with the opening goal against Switzerland at Euro '96.

ALAN SAYS: *"I'll always remember either Gary Lineker or Ian Rush saying that when you are on a hot run you should keep practising, but to stop practising when you are struggling. Now that may sound daft but it's quite a good theory. The most important thing as a striker is to play your way out of trouble. If you keep getting into the right position eventually a goal will go in and your confidence will return. I once went 17 games without scoring when I was playing at Southampton, but I eventually started scoring again in the England team."*

JUNE 1996
PENALTY SORROW

After superb wins against Scotland, Holland and then Spain (after penalties), England were on the brink of the Euro '96 Final. But a miss by Gareth Southgate in the penalty shoot-out against Germany meant England were out.

ALAN SAYS: *"It was obviously a disappointing night for us. When we needed a little bit of luck to go our way, we didn't get it. I think that whatever you do in life, you need a bit of luck. But Germany beat us in the semi-finals after a tough 1-1 draw, and to lose on penalties was very tough for the players to take. If we'd got through that semi-final I think we'd have gone on to win the tournament. I would have swapped my goal in that game for an England win, but I think we gave the whole country something to smile about."*

JULY 1996
HOMECOMING

After winning the Golden Boot at Euro '96, clubs were fighting for Shearer's signature. The rumours were of Man. United, but it was Newcastle, his childhood team, who finally got their man for a British record £15 million.

ALAN SAYS: *"I had a trial at Newcastle when I was a youngster and I remember being disappointed at the way things turned out at the time. I always wanted to play for Newcastle United, as I'm sure most boys in Newcastle want to today. Fortunately, the dream to play for the team I supported as a boy came true for me and it's been brilliant. It would have been a dream come true if I had made it with the club from the start, but I can't complain, can I? Destiny brought me back home and I couldn't have been any happier."*

MAY 1997
PLAYER OF THE YEAR

Shearer continued to beat even the toughest of Premiership defences as Newcastle were challenging Man. United for the league title, and it wasn't long before his fellow players acknowledged his outstanding ability.

ALAN SAYS: *"The fact that your fellow players are voting for you is what makes the PFA Player Of The Year award so special. They are the ones who are trying to stop you week in, week out, so it's a great honour to have them vote for you as the best player. I was pleased with my performances and the goals I'd scored that season. It's the greatest feeling in the world to score goals and you work all week to score a goal on a Saturday afternoon. If that feeling ever changes, then I think that will be the time for me to pack in playing football."*

Shearer fought back from another serious cruciate ligament injury to play a part in the Toon Army's march to Wembley in 1998. But a tactically superior Arsenal side beat them 2-0, with Shearer agonisingly hitting the post.

ALAN SAYS: *"It was very disappointing. You never like to lose, let alone at a place like Wembley – but it just wasn't meant to be our day, it's as simple as that. I feel sorry for the fans. The team came back to Newcastle after the final and the fans lined the streets – and we had lost the final. The fans deserve more, they deserve to have the success and I want to stay at Newcastle until I have won them a trophy. I would gladly swap all my honours for winning one winner's medal at Newcastle. You are judged on what you win and we haven't won anything."*

October 1999
ON THE BENCH

There was a long conflict between Shearer and his third boss at Newcastle, Ruud Gullit. It all came to a head when Shearer was left on the bench for the vital derby clash against arch-rivals Sunderland.

ALAN SAYS: *"I have never been dropped before in my career, so to find myself on the subs' bench for such an important game against Sunderland was a big shock. When I spoke to Ruud Gullit before the match he said he didn't think that I was worthy of a starting place in the side. I didn't agree with that and I certainly didn't think I deserved what he said, but I took my place on the bench and I didn't moan. It was the manager's job to select the team that he thought had the best chance of winning the match. But on the night the team didn't win."*

JUNE 2000
ENGLAND RETIREMENT

Euro 2000 was Shearer's last international outing after quitting to spend more time with his family and concentrate on his club career. His hopes of winning a trophy were dashed when England bowed out at the first stage.

ALAN SAYS: *"What was disappointing more than anything is that even with the players we had, we didn't perform. But I've made a decision and I'll stick by it. I've played for my country for the best part of eight years non-stop and you don't let the honour of captaining your country go lightly – being England captain has been the greatest part of my career. It was a tough, tough decision for me, but I'm sure it's going to benefit Newcastle United and myself. It's a relief for me because I want to remain one of the best club strikers around."*

"YOU DON'T LET THE HONOUR OF CAPTAINING YOUR COUNTRY GO LIGHTLY."

THE LITTLE MATCH FOOTBALL PHRASE BOOK

MATCH reveals the true meaning of popular footy sayings.

"It's a game of two halves" =
Anything can happen in a game.
eg: "City are losing 5-0, but it's a game of two halves."

"Football's a funny old game" =
It's not funny at all, just depressing.
eg: "They're losing 4-0 and have lost their strikers, but football's a funny old game."

"He can't catch a bus" =
He's a dodgy goalkeeper.
eg: "Did you see that? The 'keeper can't catch a bus."

"The ball is in our court" =
We've taken control.
eg: "They've made an offer for our striker, and now the ball is in our court."

"As a defender, he's second to none" =
But on the ball he's pants.
eg: "What a brilliant tackle. As a defender, he's second to none."

"At the end of the day, it's up to the gaffer" =
It's the manager's decision.
eg: "I might get a game, but at the end of the day, it's up to the gaffer."

"The lad's got a big heart" =
He's rubbish.
eg: "Whatever you say about Carlton Palmer, the lad's got a big heart."

"He can count himself lucky to get away with that" =
He's a dirty little so-and-so.
eg: "He can count himself lucky to get away with that tackle from behind on my star player."

"I'll have to watch the replays later" =
There's no way that was a penalty and I'll report the ref to the FA.
eg: "I didn't have the best view of the incident. I'll have to watch the replays later."

"We can take something from the game" =
I'm giving my players a good hiding in training on Monday.
eg: "We may have lost here, but we can take something from the game."

"What they lack in skill, they make up for in effort." =
That team is crap.
eg: "It's certainly going to be a tough game for them today, but what they lack in skill, they make up for in effort."

"We will wrap him up in cotton wool" =
We'll keep an eye on him
eg: "When he returns from that bad injury, we will wrap him up in cotton wool to make sure he stays fit."

INJURY TIME

David Batty Leeds United

Feet, Achilles, tendons, broken ribs and even his heart... Poor old David's injury problems just go on and on!

BREATHING DIFFICULTIES

When? It occurred after Batty had an operation for fluid around the heart.

How? The heart problem re-occurred, causing breathing difficulties.

What is it? It becomes a strain to breathe, especially when exercising.

How long out? He responded quickly to the treatment and soon recovered.

Does it hurt? It's not really a pain, it's more of a discomfort.

THE MATCH AGONY RATING 2

FLUID AROUND THE HEART

When? January 1999

Where? He felt problems in training.

How long out? The heart problems came as a result of the rib injury he got in his first game back for Leeds.

What is it? Swelling around the rib injury pressed the lining of his heart and caused discomfort.

How long out? It takes a few months to recuperate after the operation.

Does it hurt? The main pain persists a while after surgery.

THE MATCH AGONY RATING 4

TENDON INJURY

When? November 1999.

Where? Leeds v Bradford

How? Batty realised he had suffered damage to his tendon after the match.

What is it? As Leeds weren't quite sure exactly what the problem was, Batty had to see a specialist in France about the problem tendon between his Achilles and calf.

How long out? After months out recuperating, nothing was happening until it was realised the medication he was taking for his heart condition had weakened his powers of recovery. A set-back meant that Batty needed an operation in June 2000, but he is expected to return at the start of 2001.

Does it hurt? Yes, the injury can be sore, especially after the operation.

THE MATCH AGONY RATING 6

BROKEN RIB

When? December 1998

Where? Leeds v Coventry

How? Received a bang on the chest by a Coventry player during the game.

What is it? A broken rib is where the bone receives such a blow that it breaks, in this case inwards.

How long out? It takes up to three months to recover.

Does it hurt? A broken rib is painful to start with, but the pain turns to discomfort over the following weeks.

THE MATCH AGONY RATING 4

ACHILLES PROBLEM

When? After World Cup '98.

Where? In pre-season training, Batts realised there was something wrong with the Achilles on his left ankle.

How? Batty was playing too much football and, like many players, it put a strain on his body.

How long out? After having an operation to repair the injury, Batty was out for two months. But it wasn't so bad for Newcastle because during that time he was supposed to serve a six-match ban after being sent-off three times the previous season.

Does it hurt? Yes, even more so for David as one of his children rode into the wound while riding his bike and caused a recurrence of the problem.

THE MATCH AGONY RATING 5

SPLIT BONE

When? At the end of 1993-94 season.

Where? In his foot.

What is it? Excessive impact on the foot meant the bone became weak.

How long out? Initial surgery was unsuccessful, so he only played five games as Blackburn won the '95 title.

Does it hurt? Sore, rather than pain.

THE MATCH AGONY RATING 6

ALL SIT DOWN

Most fans have loads of things to moan about. Bad results, bad facilities at their home ground, some well dodgy players and a lack of money to splash out in the transfer market. But it's not often that you hear Man. United fans whinging, they usually just boast about how many trophies they win and what Becks can do with a ball. But now those United fans who actually go to matches are complaining in their thousands. The club is trying to stop fans standing up during matches because it's unsafe, although they don't mind them standing up for the odd goal. Ah well, let them be miserable about something. If only every club just had that to worry about!

DYER THE BAKER

What's this? Kieron Dyer the baker? Surely he's good enough at playing football to make a career out of it? No, don't worry, Dyer didn't take his exclusion from the Euro 2000 squad to heart and he won't be quitting football. Far from it, Kieron loves his life on Tyneside and helped a local supermarket to deliver groceries to show how much he cares! **"The fans at Newcastle are second to none,"** the plucky midfielder said. **"It's a massive club and there's the ambition in the transfer market. I'm enjoying myself here."** After recent stories we don't doubt it for a minute, but can the youngster still keep delivering the goods?

STEVEN GERRARD
Liverpool

WEMBLEY'S FINEST

WEMBLEY TIME LINE...

1923
WHITE HORSE FA CUP FINAL
The first match held at the stadium is the 1923 FA Cup Final, where an estimated 200,000 see Bolton beat West Ham 2-0.

1948
OLYMPICS HOSTS
Wembley hosts Olympics, and Olympic Way is built.

1953
ENGLAND HUMILIATION
Hungary become the first Continental side to win at Wembley when they beat England 6-3.

| 1920 | 1925 | 1930 | 1935 | 1940 | 1945 | 1950 | 1955 |

WEMBLEY STADIUM WILL BE REMEMBERED for being the home of football around the world. Since Wembley was built way back in 1923, millions of fans from across the world have flocked to see top-class matches, as well as other events – such as huge music concerts – in the famous stadium. It was an arena where many dreams came true and where many others were shattered. Any fan who has walked down Wembley Way towards the Twin Towers knows that they may never find another stadium which generates such strong emotions in a collection of people.

Wembley may look great from the outside, but England now needs a more practical and modern stadium. At a grand 77 years old, Wembley can no longer compete with the splendour of Europe's top grounds so a new national stadium is being built. To celebrate the home of football, MATCH recalls Wembley Stadium's finest moments and looks at the ten best matches ever played there.

DID YOU KNOW...

1. The area was developed in 1901 to rival the Eiffel Tower. Sir Edwin Watkins, chairman of the Metropolitan railway, began building work on the Wembley Tower, but the work was left unfinished through a lack of funding.

2. Wembley was originally called The Empire Stadium. It was built to be the centrepiece of a British Empire exhibition after World War I. In its first year, 4.5 million people visited the stadium to see the historic exhibition.

3. The stadium was built in only 300 days at a cost of £750,000. The building work, on the site of a former golf course, was completed just four days before the 1923 FA Cup Final between Bolton Wanderers and West Ham.

4. At the first FA Cup Final there were 24,500 seats under cover, but the capacity was reported to be 125,000. The caterers brought in 10,000 bottles of beer, 500 gallons of tea and 200,000 sandwiches for the massive crowd!

5. Wembley Stadium hosted famous tournaments, such as the 1934 Empire Games, the 1948 Olympics and the 1966 World Cup. It also staged annual sporting events, including the FA and Rugby League Challenge Cup Finals.

6. The star of the 1948 Olympics was a housewife from Holland called Fanny Blankers-Koen, who won four gold medals. Wembley was originally meant to host the Olympics in 1944, but it was postponed due to World War II.

7. England always used the south dressing-room, which carried an England crest, because the north one was regarded as unlucky. At FA Cup Finals, the team whose name came first alphabetically was given the north room.

8. In the 1950s, players in FA Cup Finals had to be wary of the 'Wembley hoodoo'. Between 1952 and 1961, serious injuries were suffered in all but two of the Cup finals – 1954 and 1958.

9. Wembley has staged two major boxing bouts. Henry Cooper fought Cassius Clay (aka Muhammad Ali) and Frank Bruno (aka Emile Heskey!) took on Oliver McCall.

10. Many believe the Wembley pitch is tougher to play on because it's bigger, but it has the same dimensions as Old Trafford.

1966
WORLD CUP FINAL
Sir Alf Ramsey's England beat Germany 4-2 in Final.

1967
LEAGUE CUP FINAL
QPR beat West Brom 3-2 in first League Cup Final at Wembley.

1968
UNITED TRIUMPH
Man. United beat Benfica 4-1 in European Cup Final.

1985
BAND AID
Multi-band charity concert held for starving Africans.

1993
EUROPEAN FINAL
Parma beat Royal Antwerp 2-1 in the Cup Winners' Cup Final.

1999
AUG NEW STADIUM PLANS
The new stadium may feature four 'knitting needles' poles.
NOV BATTLE OF BRITAIN
Scotland win 1-0, but England make Euro 2000 on aggregate.
NOV PLANS CHANGED
New plans are submitted for approval, featuring a giant arch.

1960 1965 1970 1975 1980 1985 1990 1995 2000 2005

10

Over 100,000 unexpected fans turned up for the FA Cup Final in 1923.

Bolton 2 West Ham 0

WHEN? April 28, 1923

WHO SCORED? Bolton Jack 2, Smith 53

WHY IMPORTANT? First FA Cup Final at Wembley

WHAT HAPPENED? West Ham, newly-promoted from Division Two, were the favourites to win the Final, but Bolton had their own ideas. They were ahead after only two minutes courtesy of a brilliant David Jack goal. The Hammers were stunned – their only first-half chance was saved at the second attempt by Pym, after Richards had cleverly steered the ball past two defenders. The second half began immediately due to crowd congestion, and Bolton striker Smith soon made it 2-0. West Ham strongly debated Smith's winning header, after it hit the underside of the crossbar and rebounded out into the field of play, but the referee awarded a goal and Bolton lifted the Cup.

TEAMS BOLTON WANDERERS: Pym, Haworth, Finney, Nuttall, Seddon, Jennings, Butler, Jack, JR Smith, J Smith, Vizard. **WEST HAM UNITED:** Hufton, Henderson, Young, Bishop, Kay, Tresadern, Richards, Brown, Watson, Moore, Ruffell.

WHY WAS IT SPECIAL?

This was the first FA Cup Final played at Wembley. The official attendance was 127,000, but it's thought that 250,000 fans saw the game. At two o'clock, the gates were closed due to the amount of people inside the ground, but some still found their way in. PC George Scorey and his now famous white horse pushed the crowds back to start the game.

9

England were on the wrong end of a right hammering.

England 3 Hungary 6

WHEN? November 25, 1953

WHO SCORED? England Sewell, Mortensen, Ramsey (pen)

Hungary Hidegkuti 3, Puskas 2, Bozsik

WHY IMPORTANT? Hungary became first continental side to win at Wembley

WHAT HAPPENED? Ferenc Puskas and his Hungarian team ran rings around England from the outset. The visitors were 1-0 up inside the first minute when Hidegkuti volleyed past England 'keeper Merrick from 20 yards. The crowd of over 100,000 soon had something to cheer about when Mortensen put Sewell through to equalise. But they had no idea what was coming next. Hidegkuti put Hungary back in front, Puskas made it 3-1 and the impressive winger Bozsik made it 4-1. Mortensen pulled the score back to 4-2, but England were shocked – they hadn't lost at Wembley before. Hungary added two more straight after the break, then sat back on their lead and afforded the home team a consolation penalty. The game finished 6-3 and the England players left the pitch stunned at what had happened.

WHY WAS IT SPECIAL?

England had never lost at home to a continental team when Hungary, unbeaten themselves in three years, visited Wembley. The Hungarians taught the English a footballing lesson with their superior technique and style. Six months later, England were treated to a second lesson in Hungary, losing 7-1.

TEAMS ENGLAND: Merrick, Ramsey, Eckersley, Wright, Johnston, Dickinson, Matthews, Taylor, Mortensen, Sewell, Robb. **HUNGARY:** Goosics (Geller), Buzansskey, Lantos, Bozsik, Lorant, Zakarias, Budai, Kocsis, Hidegkuti, Puskas, Czibor.

8

Keith Houchen scores a stunning equaliser for Coventry.

Coventry 3 Tottenham 2

WHEN? May 16, 1987

WHO SCORED? Coventry Bennett 9, Houchen 63, Mabbutt 96 (og)

Tottenham Allen 2, Kilcline 40 (og)

WHY IMPORTANT? FA Cup Final

WHAT HAPPENED? The odds were stacked against The Sky Blues in this FA Cup Final – Spurs boasted a team of stars, including Hoddle, Waddle, Ardiles and Clive Allen. And while Tottenham had never lost an FA Cup Final, Coventry had never even appeared in one! Tottenham went in front when Waddle crossed to the far post for Allen to score, but Coventry battled back and equalised seven minutes later when Dave Bennett slotted home. Before half-time, Hoddle sent a free-kick over the head of 'keeper Steve Ogrizovic and Brian Kilcline scored an own goal under pressure from Gary Mabbutt to make it 2-1 to Spurs. Coventry improved after the break and Wembley witnessed a memorable goal when Keith Houchen scored a diving header from Bennett's cross to force extra-time. Mabbutt scored an unfortunate own goal to hand hardworking underdogs Coventry the FA Cup.

WHY WAS IT SPECIAL?

Coventry had none of Tottenham's stars but it was a tremendous performance, topped off by Houchen's diving header, which he stretched to reach after a great run into the box. The small club, managed superbly by Sky Blues legend John Sillett, deserved their win with a never-say-die commitment.

TEAMS COVENTRY CITY: Ogrizovic, Phillips, Downs, McGrath, Kilcline (Rodger), Peake, Bennett, Gynn, Regis, Houchen, Pickering. **TOTTENHAM HOTSPUR:** Clemence, Hughton (Claesen), Thomas, Hodge, Gough, Mabbutt, Allen C, Allen P, Waddle, Hoddle, Ardiles (Stevens, G).

7

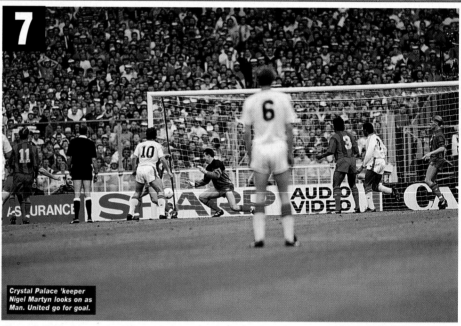

Crystal Palace 'keeper Nigel Martyn looks on as Man. United go for goal.

Crystal Palace 3 Manchester United 3

WHEN? May 12, 1990

WHO SCORED? Crystal Palace O'Reilly 19, Wright 72, 97

Man. United Robson 35, Hughes 62, 113

WHY IMPORTANT? FA Cup Final

WHAT HAPPENED? Neither of these FA Cup finalists were having good seasons. Crystal Palace narrowly escaped relegation and Manchester United finished 13th in the league. But underdogs Palace took a surprise lead through Gary O'Reilly, who headed past Jim Leighton after only 19 minutes. United knew they had their work cut out against Steve Coppell's determined side and captain Bryan Robson led by example to equalise before the break before Mark Hughes put United 2-1 ahead after 62 minutes. Coppell introduced the energetic Ian Wright from the bench and he changed the game, scoring with his first touch to send the game into extra-time. Wrighty added a second to put Palace in the lead for the first time in the match and United were stunned into action. Mark Hughes scored a late goal to send the tie to a replay, which United won, but it failed to live up to this 3-3 Wembley classic.

TEAMS CRYSTAL PALACE: Martyn, Pemberton, Shaw, Gray (sub 118 mins Madden), O'Reilly, Thorn, Barber (sub 69 mins Wright), Thomas, Bright, Salako, Pardew. **MANCHESTER UNITED:** Leighton, Ince, Martin (sub 88 mins Blackmore), Bruce, Phelan, Pallister, (sub 93 mins Robins), Robson, Webb, McClair, Hughes, Wallace.

WHY WAS IT SPECIAL?

Neither side would lie down. It seemed almost cheeky that Palace had taken the lead, so United stamped their authority on the game. But they couldn't contend with the pace of Ian Wright, who had been on the bench because he wasn't match-fit. Mark Hughes' goal made sure the game had turned full circle after Palace were seven minutes away from winning the FA Cup. The ensuing replay was one-way traffic as United won 1-0.

6

Johnston and Matthews are lifted off the ground in the post-match celebrations.

Blackpool 4 Bolton 3

WHEN? 1953

WHO SCORED? **Blackpool** Mortensen 3, Perry

Bolton Lofthouse, Moir, Bell

WHY IMPORTANT? 'Stanley Matthews' Cup final

WHAT HAPPENED? The excitement began after just 90 seconds of this Final when Nat Lofthouse opened the scoring for Bolton with a 20-yard volley. Stan Mortensen equalised for Blackpool, but Bolton were back in the lead again four minutes later with a goal from Moir. After the break it looked like Wanderers' name was surely on the Cup when they scored another goal to make it 3-1. But then disaster struck – one of Bolton's players went down injured, and with 10-man Wanderers struggling, Blackpool started to take full advantage of the situation. Stanley Matthews, who had been a problem for Wanderers all afternoon, began to dominate the game. He set up 'Pool's second, and their fans inside Wembley roared Blackpool on. It looked like the fightback was too late, but with three minutes left another Matthews cross fell to Jackie Mudie, who was fouled, and Mortensen scored from the direct free-kick to level the game at 3-3. In injury-time, Matthews again popped up to lay the ball across for Bill Perry to score the winner for Blackpool from close range.

TEAMS BLACKPOOL: Farm, Shimwell, Garrett, Fenton, Johnston, Robinson, Matthews, Taylor, Mortensen, Mudie, Perry.
BOLTON: Hanson, Ball, Banks, Wheeler, Barrass, Bell, Holden, Moir, Lofthouse, Hassall, Langton.

WHY WAS IT SPECIAL?

Stanley Matthews was a footballing legend and this game was probably his finest hour – or 90 minutes, rather. Matthews dominated the Final, and without him, Blackpool would certainly not have won the game. It was only fitting, for one of the greatest players of his generation, that the game was named after him, the Stanley Matthews Cup Final. He was 38-years old-when he lifted the Cup and the whole country celebrated his triumph with him.

5

Liverpool celebrate as they score past their Merseyside neighbours.

Everton 2 Liverpool 3

WHEN? May 20, 1989

WHO SCORED? **Everton** McCall 90, 102

Liverpool Aldridge 4, Rush 94, 104

WHY IMPORTANT? FA Cup Final

WHAT HAPPENED? This was an emotional game with both sides of Merseyside mourning the deaths of the 95 people who died at Hillsborough. Liverpool wanted a win for their fans and John Aldridge gave them an early lead. It looked like Liverpool's early goal would win the Cup until Everton substitute Stuart McCall scored in the last minute after Bruce Grobbelaar failed to clear the ball. In extra-time, Aldridge made way for Ian Rush, back at Liverpool after a spell with Juventus. Rush made an immediate impact, chesting down a pass in the area and shooting low beyond Southall. Everton wouldn't lie down though, and McCall got a dramatic second when he controlled a clearance and sent it crashing through the crowded penalty box and into the net. Just two minutes later, John Barnes crossed for Rush, who caught enough of the ball with his head to score the winning goal.

WHY WAS IT SPECIAL?

Emotions were running high with Hillsborough on the minds of the Wembley crowd, but both sets of fans stood side by side and experienced a classic Cup final. The advantage swung back and forth, with two substitutes making dramatic impacts, until Liverpool edged it at the end with Rush's glancing header.

TEAMS LIVERPOOL: Grobbelaar, Ablett, Staunton (Venison), Nicol, Whelan, Hansen, Beardsley, Aldridge (Rush), Houghton, Barnes, McMahon. **EVERTON:** Southall, McDonald, Van Den Hauwe, Ratcliffe, Watson, Bracewell (McCall), Nevin, Steven, Sharp, Cottee, Sheedy (Wilson).

Wimbledon 1 Liverpool 0

WHEN? May 14, 1988

WHO SCORED? **Wimbledon** Sanchez 36

WHY IMPORTANT? FA Cup Final

WHAT HAPPENED? This game went down as the biggest giantkilling in FA Cup Final history. Liverpool had run away with the league championship and many thought it was a forgone conclusion that they would secure their second 'double' in three years – especially as the opposition looked to be inferior to a Liverpool side which included Alan Hansen at the back and John Aldridge and Peter Beardsley up front. The match itself was packed with incidents. Aldridge had a shot early on which was well saved by Beasant. Then Beardsley thought he had put The Reds ahead in the 35th minute, but instead of playing the advantage and awarding the goal, the referee called the ball back for a Liverpool free-kick. The Reds were clearly rattled, and while they were arguing with each other about the decision, Dennis Wise took a free-kick at the other end and Lawrie Sanchez rose highest to back-head past Bruce Grobbelaar into the Liverpool goal. Wimbledon had stunned Kenny Dalglish's side, but there was still a chance for Liverpool when Aldridge stepped up to take his 12th penalty of the season, having been successful in his previous eleven spot-kicks. But Wimbledon's Dave Beasant guessed that Aldridge would shoot to his left, and he became the first goalkeeper ever to save a penalty in a Wembley Cup Final. Liverpool threw everything at The Dons, but they couldn't beat Beasant, who collected the FA Cup as captain.

4

Bruce Grobbelaar can do nothing to keep the ball out of the net.

WHY WAS IT SPECIAL?

Wimbledon were never given a chance against mighty Liverpool, but they had fought their way up through the Football League to join the big boys of the top division. They bravely held on to their lead and Dave Beasant had a glorious match in goal for The Dons!

TEAMS WIMBLEDON: Beasant, Goodyear, Phelan, Jones, Young, Thorn, Gibson (Scales), Cork (Cunningham), Fashanu, Sanchez, Wise. **LIVERPOOL:** Grobbelaar, Gillespie, Ablett, Nicol, Spackman (Molby), Hansen, Beardsley, Aldridge (Johnston), Houghton, Barnes, McMahon.

England 4 Holland 1

WHEN? June 16, 1996

WHO SCORED? England Shearer 23 (pen), 57
Sheringham 51, 62

Holland Kluivert 77

WHY IMPORTANT? Group stages of Euro '96

WHAT HAPPENED? A draw would have been enough for England to make it through to the quarter-finals, but the side was on a high after beating Scotland and wanted revenge after Holland had ended England's hopes of qualifying for the 1994 World Cup. Holland had some of the best players in Europe, but their squad was clearly unsettled. Both teams had early chances, but Paul Ince was fouled in the box after a charging run by Steve McManaman and Alan Shearer converted the penalty. Bergkamp almost equalised before half-time, but England managed to keep it tight at the back. Soon after the break, Teddy Sheringham tucked away a neat header from a corner to make it 2-0. England were cruising and they thrilled Wembley with a passing move that ended spectacularly – Sheringham squared the ball to Shearer and the Blackburn striker rifled the ball into the back of the net. Sheringham added a fourth as Van der Sar failed to hold Anderton's shot, and even a late consolation goal from Kluivert couldn't take the shine off England's victory.

WHY WAS IT SPECIAL?

England hadn't beaten Holland for 14 years, but this was a confident team, managed superbly by Terry Venables and boosted by a fabulous Wembley crowd. England played some excellent attacking football but contained Holland when they came forward at speed. This was a thrilling performance – the best England had played for a long time at Wembley.

TEAMS ENGLAND: Seaman, Neville G, Pearce, Ince (sub 67 mins Platt), Adams, Southgate, Gascoigne, Shearer (sub 75 mins Barmby), Sheringham (sub 75 mins Fowler), Anderton, McManaman. **HOLLAND:** Van der Sar, Reiziger, Blind, Seedorf, de Boer (sub 71 mins Cocu), Bergkamp, Hoekstra (sub 71 mins Kluivert), Winter, Witschge (sub 56 mins de Kock), Bogarde, Cruyff.

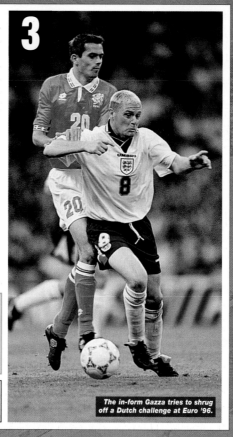

The in-form Gazza tries to shrug off a Dutch challenge at Euro '96.

Man. United go all out in attack to win the European Cup Final.

Manchester United 4 Benfica 1

WHEN? May 29, 1968

WHO SCORED? Man. United Charlton 54, 98, Best 92, Kidd 95

Benfica Jaime Graca

WHY IMPORTANT? European Cup Final

WHAT HAPPENED? In one of only a few European finals ever played at Wembley, Man. United became the first English team to win the European Cup. After a first-half stalemate, Bobby Charlton gave United the lead with a rare headed goal early in the second half, but Benfica equalised with 15 minutes to go. Then, with only seconds remaining on the clock, Portuguese legend Eusebio burst through United's defence with only the 'keeper to beat. But Eusebio chose power over accuracy and Alex Stepney, United's 'keeper, saved his shot to take the match into extra-time. After 90 minutes, Busby told his team to pass the ball around Benfica as both teams were exhausted. After only three minutes of extra-time, George Best received the ball from Brian Kidd and set off on a run. Benfica couldn't touch him – Best beat two players before dribbling around the entire defence and passing the ball calmly beyond the despairing 'keeper. Kidd then scored a minute later, on his 19th birthday, and Bobby Charlton put the game beyond reach with his second and United's fourth. Benfica were too tired to fight back and United took the trophy back home to Manchester.

TEAMS MANCHESTER UNITED: Stepney, Brennan, Dunne, Crerand, Foulkes, Stiles, Best, Kidd, Charlton, Sadler, Aston. **BENFICA:** Henrique, Adolfo, Humberto, Jacinto, Cruz, Jaime Graca, Jose Augusto, Coluna, Eusebio, Torres, Simoes.

WHY WAS IT SPECIAL?

This was the first time an English team had won the European Cup. George Best scored one of the best goals of his career and had a glorious match. The victory came on the tenth anniversary of the tragic Munich air disaster where a young team of Man. United stars lost their lives. Manager Matt Busby and captain Bobby Charlton had survived the crash and openly wept at the final whistle, becoming national heroes for their achievements. Sir Matt Busby retired soon afterwards, having won every trophy possible in club football.

Bobby Moore holds aloft the World Cup trophy, which he had received from the Queen.

Geoff Hurst completes his hat-trick as some people come onto the pitch.

England 4 West Germany 2

WHEN? July 30, 1966

WHO SCORED? England Hurst 19, 100, 119, Peters 78

West Germany Haller 13, Weber 90

WHY IMPORTANT? World Cup Final

WHAT HAPPENED? Both teams started nervously and there were chances at both ends, but West Germany took the lead after 13 minutes through Haller. England weren't behind for long, though. Bobby Moore took a quick free-kick to Geoff Hurst, who powered the ball low into the net. That goal gave England the confidence they needed to press the German team back, with Moore dominant at the back and Hurst a constant threat in attack. The second half was played out at a slower pace, but Wembley sensed victory when Martin Peters made it 2-1 with only 12 minutes left. Then, with the seconds ticking away, Weber scored a dramatic equaliser from close range to force extra-time. Both teams were tired but England coped better, passing the ball around and making the Germans work hard. After ten minutes of extra-time, Hurst crashed the ball off the crossbar and turned to see the Russian linesman signalling a goal. West Germany were stunned by the decision and never fully recovered. With seconds to go, Bobby Moore hit a controlled clearance to Hurst, who ran up the pitch and scored a thundering drive to make it 4-2 to England.

TEAMS ENGLAND: Banks, Cohen, Wilson, Stiles, Charlton J, Moore, Ball, Hurst, Hunt, Charlton B, Peters. **WEST GERMANY:** Tilkowski, Hottges, Schnellinger, Beckenbauer, Schulz, Weber, Held, Haller, Seeler, Overath, Emmerich.

WHY WAS IT SPECIAL?

This was the first time England had won the World Cup and it was a heroic performance from the host team. West Germany wouldn't lie down, but England stepped up a gear in extra-time and Hurst scored a fabulous hat-trick with a bit of help from the Russian linesman. Even the commentary of Kenneth Wolstenholme (below) was legendary: **"There are some people on the pitch, they think it's all over. It is now!"** Over 90,000 saw Bobby Moore lift the World Cup at Wembley – the greatest result in English football history.

Jack Charlton and the team celebrate English football's finest moment.

HOW DID YOU SCORE?
Remember, you get a point for every question you answer, as well as a point for every player's name you can find in the Mega Word Spot. So start searching!

Dennis Wise lifted the 2000 FA Cup for Chelsea.

third XI

The FA Cup is the world's oldest and most loved cup competition, but how much do you know about it?

1 The FA Cup may be the oldest cup competition in the world, but in which year was it first contested?

2 In the history of the FA Cup two teams have won the competition three years running. Can you name any one of the teams?

3 Early FA Cup Finals were played at several different venues, including The Oval, but in which year was the final first played at the now famous Wembley Stadium?

4 Can you work out the highest-scoring FA Cup Final at Wembley, and which two teams contested the thrilling game?

5 Who were the last winners of the FA Cup before the outbreak of the Second World War in 1939?

6 Who scored the winning goal in the 1973 FA Cup Final at Wembley?

7 And can you name the winners of the 100th FA Cup Final?

8 Only one team has ever won the League Cup and FA Cup double in the same year. Who are they and in which year did they do it?

9 Which club has won more FA Cup trophies than any other side in the long history of the competition?

10 And do you know which Premiership team has appeared in the most FA Cup Finals to date?

11 Aston Villa played Chelsea in the last FA Cup Final at Wembley before it was knocked down in 2000 for redevelopment. Can you name the only goalscorer in that historic game?

THE MEGA WORD SPOT

Can you spot these European footballers who have graced the English game in recent years?

```
S T R U P A R O U C S E R T E P G V R
L Q P A H A R S D Z B R N C R K N U I
N I E L S E N M W B Z X O H K R U M E
D Z F L O F H Y Y P I A S F Y E F E D
Z R U S I L V E S T R E S J O N K E L
O A S M N I C E H R W P R Z A K B B E
H W X D E S A I L L Y H A A A I N E J
C H I W T X I X W C I B D B L D E R G
N C L D I C A N I O Z R I D G L S G V
E S J A W G K A N O U T E R I E N K T
H A V I E I R A V C N A R E N V H A O
N I L I S S X I O K K N H I O R O M I
I R E R R E F V M C I J X V L E J P H
W V X K V D D A Y A Y N E A A T D Y C
B O A T E N G C V R B N D Z X F S U H L
Z I E G E O S G N S B D P K O E G Q E
J D P V H A S S E L B A I N K W E O M
H A M A N N M B H U F R E U N D H G N
K I D R P P I V E R S E N S T A M J Q
```

- BAKKE
- BERGKAMP
- BOATENG
- DE BILDE
- DESAILLY
- DI CANIO
- FERRER

- FLO
- FREUND
- GINOLA
- GRIMANDI
- GUDJOHNSEN
- HAMANN
- HASSELBAINK

- HENCHOZ
- HENRY
- HREIDARSSON
- HYYPIA
- IVERSEN
- JONK
- KANOUTE

- MELCHIOT
- NIELSEN
- NILIS
- PAHARS
- PETRESCU
- RIEDLE
- SCHWARZ

- SILVESTRE
- STAM
- STRUPAR
- VIEIRA
- WESTERVELD
- XAVIER
- ZIEGE

2-1

All these games finished 2-1, but who scored the winner?

1 October 1999
Newcastle v Middlesbrough

2 November 1999
Tottenham v Arsenal

3 February 2000
Bradford v Arsenal

4 March 2000
Sunderland v Everton

WHO AM I?

Can you guess the name of the player from these statements?

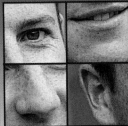

1 I'm a striker.

2 I was born in 1978 in the North-East of England.

3 I'm at my second club.

4 I help people to cross water.

MATCHfacts
CODE BREAKER

CRACK THE CODE!

16	4	5	1	14	14	21

4	1	10	14	21

THE GAFFERS!
What do you know about the men in charge?

1 Name the manager of Third Division Hartlepool.

2 Who won the 1999-2000 LMA Manager Of The Year award?

3 Which manager led his side to last year's Division Two title?

4 Name the Wimbledon manager who quit before they were relegated.

5 Who was in charge when Real Madrid won the Champions League?

2 POINTS PER CORRECT ANSWER

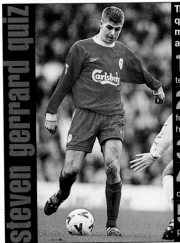

steven gerrard quiz

Try these tough-tacklin' questions on the young midfield star of Liverpool and England.

1 Against which side did Steven make his first team debut for Liverpool?

2 True or false? Gerrard had to stop playing football as a child because he was growing too quickly.

3 What is Steven's preferred position?

4 Against which country did he make his senior debut for England?

5 Name the manufacturer of the boots that Steven prefers to wear.

BARRY FERGUSON

Rangers

BOYS &TH

FIR TOYS!

MANCHESTER UNITED winger **RYAN GIGGS**, who's famed for his love of flashy motors, tells **MATCH** about his latest set of wheels!

RYAN GIGGS IS FAMOUS FOR BEING A FRIGHTENINGLY-TALENTED WINGER WHO HAS AN INCREDIBLE collection of trophies so far with Manchester United. But the other thing he's famous for is his love of flashy cars. Ryan was mad about motors as a child and since becoming a pro he's had as many posh motors as United have had home strips! Last season he was given a top-of-the-range Toyota for being Man Of The Match in the World Club Cup against Palmeiras, which he kindly gave to his brother, Rhodri. But Giggs isn't the only star player to have a flash set of wheels. Parked outside the Premiership's training grounds are some of the most desirable cars around, including Porsches, Jaguars, BMWs and Ferraris. Here, Giggsy talks exclusively to MATCH about his love of cars, and over the page we take a sneaky look at the motors of the stars – just how flashy are they?

WHAT IS IT ABOUT UNITED AND CARS?

"There are many young lads in the team and a lot of them are interested in cars. Then someone like Dwight Yorke, who's not that interested in cars, thinks, 'I've got to have a decent motor or I'm going to get some stick'. I don't know. I've just always been interested in cars."

WERE YOU THE ONE WHO STARTED IT?

"I don't know if I was the one to start it, but I've always enjoyed driving nice cars. I've just sold my Ferrari, but I've got an M5 now, that's a BMW, and I love it. It's the best car I've ever had. It's as quick as any other and the comfort is great – you can drive it every day, whereas the Ferrari you can only drive some days. I've also got a Jeep, which I used to drive all the time. When I went to Australia before the start of last season, people were saying, 'We understand you've got 13 cars'. That was absolute nonsense! I've got two. I sold my DB7."

HAS JAAP STAM GOT THE SAME CAR?

"Yeah, he's got the same car as me. It has a screen in the dashboard, but obviously it doesn't come on when you're driving. You can watch it when you're waiting for someone, but really it's more a navigation system. If you ever want to go somewhere, but you don't know where it is, you just type in the name of the road and it directs you there. You can pick up normal TV, but not Sky!"

DID GARY NEVILLE REALLY TURN UP TO TRAINING ON A BIKE?

"No, he didn't turn up on it! I don't know where all the newspapers got that from. He had an injury so he was just doing a bit of exercise on the bike, which some of the lads do to get back to full fitness when they've been injured. It was nothing to do with the cars."

WHO HAS THE WORST CAR THEN?

"Wes Brown doesn't drive. He's not passed his test yet, but I don't think anyone's got a bad car, they're all nice. Who has the best extras? Probably Dwight Yorke. I think he has got every imaginable extra on his Range Rover. He's got a fridge, the best stereo you can get, it's really nice. The fridge was empty when I looked, though!"

HAVE YOU TRIED A RALLY CAR BEFORE?

"I did get one – a Subaru like Colin McRae's. That was really nice, it was quick. That's in my mum's garage. I'm keeping it so that it hopefully becomes a collector's item as they only ever made 400 of them and only 13 came to Britain so I'm not driving that one, but I've still got it."

WERE YOU INTO CARS AS A KID?

"Yeah, I never had any of the little toy cars, but I always wanted a black BMW 325 when I was growing up. Then I thought they were the bee's knees and I managed to get one when I was 21. It's just gone from there really."

RYAN GIGGS
★ MANCHESTER UNITED ★

JEEP **GRAND CHEROKEE**

COST: £26,525

ENGINE: 4 litres

SPEED: 0-60mph in 9.9s

TOP SPEED: 112mph

FEATURES: Twin airbags, roof bars and a cruise control system. Oh, and you can go off-road if you want to test this beast!

HOW FLASH IS IT? It's very practical and the tinted windows mean Giggsy doesn't get spotted when he's driving about. Loads of Giggsy's team-mates have similar cars, like Land Rovers – including Gary Neville and David Beckham – because it means they can drive without getting any hassle. Not as flash as the M5, but not bad at all.

VERDICT: *PRACTICAL!*

ALAN SHEARER
★ NEWCASTLE UNITED ★

JAGUAR XJ SPORT

COST: £54,405
ENGINE: 4.0 litres
SPEED: 0-60mph in 7.35s
TOP SPEED: 150mph

FEATURES: There are millions of them! As well as having superb handling ability and being a very quiet car to drive, the Jaguar XJ Sport has remote-controlled central locking and automatic climate control, so Alan will feel cool in the summer and warm in the winter. But that's not all! The car also has automatic headlights, which means Shearer doesn't even have to turn on the lights when it starts to get dark! How's that for laziness?

HOW FLASH IS IT? All Jaguars are stylish, but this is a particularly elegant model. The seats are all made of leather, so let's hope Al doesn't get too hot in the summer! Shearer reckons Jaguar cars are 'the best of British' and they are the only cars he drives. The first Jag he had was an XK8 Coupe but he soon swapped his first love for this current model.

VERDICT: *VERY FLASH!*

MICHAEL OWEN
★ LIVERPOOL ★

JAGUAR XKR COUPE

COST: £60,105
ENGINE: 4.0 litre
SPEED: 0-60mph in 5.25s
TOP SPEED: 155mph

FEATURES: A cruise control system for easy motorway driving and good grip on the road.

HOW FLASH IS IT? Well, Owen originally tested a Jaguar XK8, but he wanted a faster model so he went for the XKR Coupe. It's called the 'World's ultimate luxury sports car' so it's very flash! For the days when he's being practical, he also owns a Jaguar S-type sports saloon!

VERDICT: *WAY FLASH!*

MICHAEL BALL
★ EVERTON ★

PORSCHE ★ BOXSTER

COST: £42,161
ENGINE: 2.7 litres
SPEED: 0-60mph in 5.95s
TOP SPEED: 150mph

FEATURES: It doesn't consume as much fuel as the other models here, but it's still expensive to run. The flashy hood opens and closes in 12 seconds, but the car's also practical, with all of the instruments within easy reach.

HOW FLASH IS IT? It's a very stylish car, based on the original Porsche models, and has cutting-edge technology. In other words, it's very flash!

VERDICT: *TASTY MOTOR!*

LEE HENDRIE
★ ASTON VILLA ★

BMW ★ M3

COST: £43,990
ENGINE: 3.2 litres
SPEED: 0-60mph in 5.6s
TOP SPEED: 155mph

FEATURES: It has an extra-strengthened windscreen frame so it's very safe to drive and would be reliable in an accident, despite being a convertible.

HOW FLASH IS IT? The M3 is a very fast car and it's easy to drive, which makes it an ideal car for footballers. It's also elegantly designed, so it looks classy as well – and you're bound to see one in every top club's car park.

VERDICT: *BABE MAGNET!*

LES FERDINAND
★ TOTTENHAM HOTSPUR ★

ASTON MARTIN ★ DB7

COST: £86,000
ENGINE: 3.2 litres
SPEED: 0-60mph in 5.65s
TOP SPEED: 165mph

FEATURES: The stylish Aston Martin has a leather interior and cruise control system. The front seats are electronically-controlled for real comfort. Nice!

HOW FLASH IS IT? Well, it's always been a favourite with top footballers. Dwight Yorke used to have one in racing green when he was at Aston Villa, and James Bond used to have one in his films – now that's flash, Mr Bond.

VERDICT: *UNDISPUTEDLY CLASSY!*

ANDY COLE
★ MANCHESTER UNITED ★

MERCEDES ★ CLK CABRIOLET

COST: £36,090
ENGINE: 4.0 litre
SPEED: 0-60mph in 9.1s
TOP SPEED: 143mph

FEATURES: As well as ABS breaks and passenger sidebags, this Mercedes has a wind detector which controls the wind coming into the car when the hood's down, so Andy's hair isn't ruffled out of place. Not that he has any!

HOW FLASH IS IT? It has an attractive two-tone upholstery design, with a maplewood finish on the dashboard. Could Coley get a flashier motor?

VERDICT: *VERY STYLISH!*

IAN HARTE
★ LEEDS UNITED ★

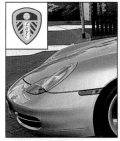

PORSCHE ★ CARRERA

COST: £70,000
ENGINE: 4.0 litre
SPEED: 0-100mph in 11.6s
TOP SPEED: 167mph

FEATURES: The Porsche Carrera uses a permanent four-wheel drive, which makes it easier to grip in all weather conditions. It has six gears on manual drive and the brake system re-aligns the wheels if the driver over-steers.

HOW FLASH IS IT? It's a practical, flashy car and Ian opted for the Carrera with a roof, which is not quite as flashy as the convertible-style Porsche.

VERDICT: *VERY FLASH!*

FRANK SINCLAIR
★ LEICESTER CITY ★

BMW ★ Z8

COST: £86,650
ENGINE: 5.0 litres
SPEED: 0-60mph in 5s
TOP SPEED: 155mph

FEATURES: The Z8 has evolved from BMW's original 507 sports car and its engine has the power of 400 horses! The car is electronically controlled so it can't reach speeds in excess of 155mph, so Frankie can't go out of control!

HOW FLASH IS IT? This two-seater is definitely for someone who loves sports cars and its unbelievable speed and power will impress any driver.

VERDICT: *FAST, VERY FAST!*

FOOTY MAD!

There is always room for a laugh at someone else's expense – as this selection of last season's **MATCH** pics shows.

THEY SAID WHAT!

MATCH looks back at some of the gems we overheard last season…

"English clubs ignore the family too much. I would always encourage the family to be involved in football. I really don't mind players' wives coming down to the training ground." Ex-Wimbledon manager Egil Olsen shows more signs of going completely mad before leaving The Dons.

"I think he treated it like a holiday. When he comes to training with sunglasses on top of his head when it's foggy, you think, 'hang on a minute'." Aston Villa's John Gregory on Gustavo Bartlet, who cost £200,000 and didn't even play a game for the club.

"The Beckhams are mixing their worlds. David must say, 'I'm a footballer and I'm going to concentrate on this'. His wife should then do the same for her world, singing or whatever it is." Johan Cruyff turns father figure to Becks.

"Middlesbrough are a mad team. We play well, then play badly, play well, then play badly. I would prefer it if we were boring and won games. We have to change from playing like a mad team." Bonkers Italian defender Gianluca Festa attempts to explain why Middlesbrough are so inconsistent.

"He can't kick a ball with his left foot, he doesn't score many goals, he can't head the ball and he can't tackle. Apart from that he's alright." George Best on David Beckham, after the Man. United midfielder was named the second best player in the world.

"The reason why the crowd was so low was because we've been playing badly and they don't pay to watch crap." John Gregory makes a technical assessment on why Aston Villa were getting low gates early in the season.

"I can't speak Turkish, but my room-mate for Turkey, Umit Davala, is teaching me. So far I've learnt 20 words!" Leicester midfielder Muzzy Izzet on having to learn the language of the country he plays for.

Ed de Goey uses the 'close my eyes and hope' trick.

Gary Megson couldn't believe the steward's hair.

"He's behind you!" The ref was having none of that panto nonsense.

Shearer auditions for 'Thunderbirds'.

Mark Kinsella loses the 'pull the ugliest face' contest. Just!

Neil Sullivan prays before the kick-off. Hang on, the game's started – Neil!

The Chelsea boys loved to play 'ring-a-roses'.

This Lisbon Lion reckons Martin O'Neill is the mane man.

Marcel's making a meal out of it!

There's nothing like pushing a man when he's down.

Twister proved a popular game with footballers. Even when they didn't have the mat to play on.

Davor Suker couldn't bear to see Highbury before he left.

Yes, it was a great goal, but...

Ever wondered who John Gregory talks to on his mobile?

The new scarf and flag sellers at Ibrox looked very familiar.

Taylor rubbed his eyes. Yes, staying up was just a dream.

The referee tries to escape di Canio's bad breath.

Thierry Henry ponders where all his hair went.

Your mum always said look where you're going.

So you think this scarf makes me look cool, Nic?

That's it, wave the Premiership goodbye.

"This short-range heading is getting us nowhere Boothy."

It's the first time Stevie Mac's washed in years!

CARL CORT
England

MATCH
YOUNG GUNS

A DAY IN THE LIFE

MATCH takes you behind the scenes to show how we covered the FA Cup Final.

HAVE YOU EVER THOUGHT WHAT IT WOULD BE like to be a journalist covering top-flight football games? Not only would you get to watch and write about some of the top players, you'd also get the chance to interview them! The MATCH writers live out these dreams every week, but a bigger team is needed to produce the mag.

There's a team of designers, who make the magazine look great, and sub-editors who check the spelling and make the words fit on the page. The editor decides which stories go in each week and he also makes sure that MATCH is the best football mag on the market. So are you ready to see exactly how the process works?

We decided to make a diary of how we produce the FA Cup Final issue, so you can look behind the scenes at MATCH. The magazine is usually written and produced in the week and sent to the printers on Friday, but Cup Final day is always played on a Saturday. This means the magazine has to go to press a day late and the team works overtime to bring you the best coverage of the game and the reaction of the players after the final whistle has blown. Read on to find out exactly what happens in a day in the life of MATCH.

17.00 FRIDAY PLANNING THE MAGAZINE

In order for the issue to run smoothly, editor Chris Hunt (right) and deputy editor Hugh Sleight (left) have an editorial meeting on the day before the FA Cup Final to discuss just how much coverage the magazine will give to the event. They're looking at the MATCH 'flatplan', a schedule of the entire magazine with page numbers assigned to all of the articles.

It's decided that as well as a five-page feature on the final, there will also be a double-page poster of the winners. The front cover will be the captain of the winning team lifting the famous trophy. Chris and Hugh also read the quotes that the journalists have got from players in the build-up to the final.

MATCH has been allocated a press pass for a reporter to cover the game – which is given to senior writer Kev Hughes, who's over the moon because he's a faithful Aston Villa fan! The photographer's pass is taken by Phil Bagnall, the staff photographer, who has been with MATCH for 20 years and covered 18 FA Cup Finals, so he should know how to get the perfect celebration picture of the winners by now!

As the action starts, Kev takes his place in the press box, which is behind the Royal Box and the steps where Villa or Chelsea will collect the trophy.

13.00 ARRIVING AT WEMBLEY

Photographer Phil arrives at Wembley early to receive his official bib, which all the cameramen have to wear when they're at pitchside. He reserves his place behind the goal ready for the big kick-off. Phil is soon joined by Chris, who has driven to Wembley to be Phil's messenger for the day. He will leave the game at half-time to take the unprocessed photos of the first-half back to the MATCH offices, in Peterborough, to be developed.

18.00 FIGHT TO GET THE PERFECT PICTURE

As the final whistle blows at Wembley, Phil changes the film in his camera. Now comes his most important job of the day. He needs to get a celebration photo for the front cover of the magazine. Chelsea have won the cup 1-0, so Phil gets onto the pitch because he needs a perfect shot of captain Dennis Wise with the trophy. **"Getting the team photo and a shot with the players holding the trophy is the hardest part of the day,"** says Phil. **"I've only missed covering one Cup Final since 1982 but it's still quite hard to get the perfect photograph. You may only get one chance to get it right."**

SATURDAY

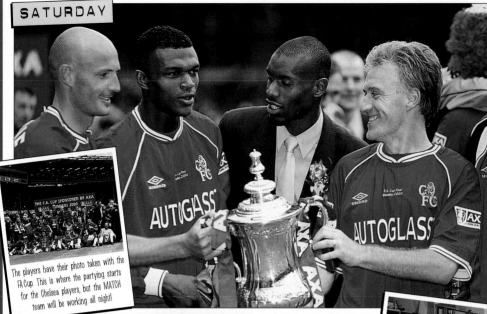

The players have their photo taken with the FA Cup. This is where the partying starts for the Chelsea players, but the MATCH team will be working all night!

17.30 PHONING IN COPY

Kev phones over his match report. When he's finished, he will use his Press pass to go behind the scenes. The tunnel is just outside the dressing rooms and the players walk past the media before meeting their family in the players lounge. Kev will take this opportunity to interview both the Chelsea and Aston Villa players.

Chris is back in the office after driving from London with the first-half photos from Wembley. While waiting for them to be developed, he reads through the report.

19.30 PRODUCTION IS STARTED

Kev rings Chris to tell him who he's been speaking to in the tunnel after the game. Although he hasn't written up the quotes from these players yet, the design team need to know which pictures to research for the FA Cup Final feature. Villa 'keeper David James admits to Kev that he took his eye off the ball for a second, allowing a grateful Chelsea side to score the only goal of the game. He also gets to speak to the jubilant Mario Melchiot, Roberto Di Matteo and Frank Leboeuf. Kev will write out his interviews and ring them through.

20.00 QUOTES ARE FILED

Production editor Phil Smith rings Kev on his mobile phone to take down the player quotes now that he's finished writing them up from his shorthand. Meanwhile, staff writer Bev Ward starts creating the feature, using the quotes that Kev has phoned through to tell the story of Chelsea's delight and Aston Villa's disappointment.

20.30 FEATURE IS IN

The MATCH designers have been working on the design since the final finished, but at 8.30pm they receive the text from the writers and start flowing the words into the laid-out pages. Senior designer Ben Bates must make sure that every word in the feature is in the right typeface and correctly sized!

While the designers work on the feature, MATCH's group art director, Darryl, starts working on the cover because the photo of Dennis Wise with the trophy is finally in.

21.30 CHOOSING THE RIGHT PHOTOS

Ben and fellow designer Becky Booth look through the second set of photos, back from the developers, along with Chris. There are some good celebration shots and a few of these will be included on the poster celebrating Chelsea's win. They take a close look at each picture to make sure they're suitable for publication.

21.45 SCANNING THE PHOTOGRAPHS

Designer Martin Barry is busy at work scanning the transparency photos which have been picked to go in the magazine. Each scan will be saved into a file on the computer, while the 'trannies' are taken to the reproduction company so they can produce high-quality scans. Martin picks out the pictures he will be using for the FA Cup poster, because he needs to get it designed quickly and off to the printers.

23.30 TIME TO CHECK THROUGH IT ALL

Phil looks over Bev's shoulders to make sure she's finished writing because it's close to midnight and approaching the deadline! Phil's checked the feature for mistakes and written all the photo captions, but Chris has a final check for errors before it's sent to the reproduction company. In the meantime, Bev starts writing the words on the front cover now that Darryl has finished the design. The coverline has to explain the main feature in just a few words, which can be a difficult task, while the other sell lines have to tell readers about the rest of the exciting issue.

It's nearly midnight and Becky is checking the final print-outs of the feature and the cover to make sure the design is perfect. Then everything is sent and we go home!

SUNDAY

04.00 PAPER READY

After the reproduction company has finished scanning the photos and pages, the courier sets off with the final pages to the printers, which is based in Kidderminster. The first job for the guys in the factory is to put two huge reels of paper on to the reel stand of the printing presses.

04.15 REELING THEM IN

It's 4.15 in the morning and the paper is loaded, ready to start. It takes 20 tonnes of paper to print MATCH every week – that's 25 of those huge reels of paper to load! The machine swaps the reel automatically, so there must always be two reels loaded at once. This is crucial to keep the printing going and maintain MATCH's schedule!

04.30 SETTING UP THE PAGES

The printers are given colour proofs of the pages to be printed and these are put on to the printer so that the images can be copied on to the paper – this is the printing process. It is important to make sure the proofs are set down properly because otherwise the text won't match up. The colours of the ink in the presses are then matched up to the colours on the proofs.

The guys at the printers really can't help but have a read of the magazine as it's coming off the presses. They get to see it two days before it hits the newsagents!

05.00 A WATCHFUL EYE

The guys at the printers need to keep an eye on the pages which are being printed to make sure there aren't any problems – like the ink changing colour during the printing. Magazines are constantly coming off the presses. Here you can see MATCHfacts being trimmed by a rotor, so the pull-out section will be smaller than the mag itself, making all your fave players' ratings easy to find!

The MATCHfacts section of the magazine is designed to be a pull-out, so statistic lovers can keep the sections. This is one of the first parts of the magazine to be printed.

08.00 SETTING UP

As the printing presses spurt out page after page of the MATCHfacts section and the features covering the FA Cup Final, the printers set up each section ready for the next stage in the printing process. This worker is setting up the last machine in the process. Checks are still being made to ensure everything is working well.

09.00 TYING IT ALL UP

Once most of the magazine has been printed, the pages are carefully put together, because you don't want to read it upside down! The pages are cut and bound together on these machines. Every printed section that goes in MATCH is threaded on to the machine, which puts all the sections together to make the final magazine!

10.00 PACKING THE MAGAZINE

The final pages come off the printing presses and are sent to be cut on the scary-looking rotor machine. Meanwhile all the magazines that the printers have finished are bound together and packed on wooden pallets ready for the fork-lift trucks to carry them all on to the lorry when it arrives to distribute the mags. The workers are nearing the end of their shift, but they have to tidy up before they leave because they will be printing different magazines later in the day!

11.00 MONDAY, READY FOR SHOPS

There are 30 pallets left at the printing house, which the lorries will distribute to newsagents across the country before the next morning! Each pallet holds 5,000 magazines, so it's a big load to take!

MONDAY

11.30 THE MAGAZINE ARRIVES BACK

The magazine arrives in the office on Monday! Everyone is thrilled with the finished product, making all the effort worthwhile. When you see next year's FA Cup Final issue you'll know how it's done! The MATCH team, from left to right, is: *Katherine Hannah, James Bandy, Darryl Tooth, Richard Adams, Kevin Pettman, Kev Hughes, Chris Hunt, Ian Foster, Hugh Sleight, Phil Bagnall, Martin Barry, Bev Ward, Leyton Edwards, Dawn Brown, Calum Booth, Becky Booth and Giles Milton (missing!).*

ISN'T IT ABOUT TIME...

Man. United lost the title again? We want to put some fun back into the Premier League and a real race for the title would be great!

WHAT'S THE BEST, INTERNATIONAL OR LEAGUE FOOTY?

5 reasons why the league's got to be a winner

1 Unless it's the boring close season, the action comes thick and fast all year long. Whatever you're doing, you know that you're never more than a week away from watching your favourite team play.

2 Nothing beats the feeling of streaming towards your team's ground with all the other fans. It's what Saturday afternoons were made for!

3 The league lasts much longer than international competitions. Let's face it, no matter how bad your team is playing, you don't get knocked out before May so you get to see them loads and loads of times!

4 It's a great way to see the country. Following your team around for all their away games takes you to places you'd never have visited otherwise, like Hartlepool and Torquay!

5 You get to know loads of other mad supporters, so you can just talk footy all day long. And some even support the same team as you!

5 reasons why your country always gets you going!

1 You know the whole country is on the same side as you, so if your team wins, you're guaranteed to get some non-stop partying wherever you go! And none of your friends will take the mickey out of you when your country loses either.

2 For once, you get the likes of David Beckham, Steven Gerrard and Michael Owen playing for your side. How cool is that? No more dodgy passes, bad mistakes in defence and long-ball football. Or is there?

3 If your team pulls off a cracking victory against a world-class team, you can spend the next five or so years reminding them about it. If it's the World Cup, you can brag for 34 years. It's a great way to grab some glory!

4 When it comes to a major international competition, the build-up lasts for months and by the time it comes to kick-off you just can't help being madly excited about it!

5 The big tournaments always happen in the summer, so it gives us a break from the lack of footy that we usually have to suffer. Getting more footy can never be a bad thing!

CONCLUSION

LEAGUE FOOTY WINS, BUT IT'S A CLOSE-RUN THING!

WHY WEAH LEFT CHELSEA...

Do you want to know the real reason why George Weah and Chris Sutton left Chelsea? There may have been talk that Gianluca Vialli couldn't afford to buy George Weah or that Sutton moved to Celtic to make way for Jimmy Floyd Hasselbaink, but Route 1 has got to the bottom of the problem. We sent a team of detectives to Chelsea's training ground and they unearthed this rather revealing set of photographs. Now you can find out what really happened!

Jody Morris fools George Weah into thinking he's a friendly guy...

...before he pulls a karate pose to attack the striker!

Morris then approaches George to 'finish him'.

But Chris Sutton thwarts him as George fumes.

George, a fan of 'The Karate Kid', moves to defend himself.

"I laugh at your moves. Ha, ha! You are no match for me!"

Sutton misses his pop-shot as Morris goes for the killer kick!

"What are you looking at Sutton? You can get out of here as well!"

---

my favourite... OTHER SPORT

ALAN SHEARER
NEWCASTLE

SO AL, WHAT SPORT DO YOU LIKE – OTHER THAN FOOTY, OF COURSE?
"I play some golf when I get the time, but I also like watersports."

DO YOU DO A LOT OF WATERSPORTS?
"No, only when I go away on holiday. I can't really do much of that up here in Newcastle, can I?"

NOT UNLESS YOU WANT A SWIM IN THE TYNE. WHAT ELSE DO YOU LIKE?
"I haven't got much time for anything else!"

BUT YOU'RE RETIRED FROM ENGLAND NOW!

F.R.I.E.N.D.S

match asks the stars who's their best mate in footy?

"I have a lot of friends in football, but I have two good friends who I grew up with – Scott McGleish who is at Barnet and Jonathan Hunt who plays for Birmingham. We all grew up in the same area and we still talk regularly."

• **Gary Breen** • **Coventry City** •

TIME ON HIS HANDS

You know when you're playing footy and you do something so brilliant that you get a funny feeling it happened in slow motion? Well, that very thing happened to ex-Hereford goalkeeper David Icke when he played at Barnet and made a top save. **"It was just like a slow-mo replay and everything was like some quiet mystical dream,"** barked bonkers Ickey. **"That was until my right hand made contact with the ball. Then everything zipped back into conscious time and the noise erupted."** Blimey. And he didn't have a clue what had just gone on. **"I was utterly bewildered. 'How the hell did I stop that?' I thought. Now I know – time does not exist."** Ah, that explains it then, 'Oh Great One'. Yeah, we understand what you mean now Dave – NOT!

GARETH LOVES GREGORY

It hasn't been an easy ride for John Gregory since he took over as Aston Villa manager, but one player who's got nothing but praise for him is Gareth Barry. **"He's been a big influence for me,"** Gareth confided to Route 1. **"Obviously he's had faith in me since I was 17 and he's given me a run in the team. He has rested me at the times he felt was right, and he's played me at the times he felt was right. He's been very good to me over the last few years."** Now who's a little teacher's pet, eh Gareth?

KEANE

" I've had a fantastic ten years in England, three at Nottingham Forest and seven years at Manchester United, and long may it continue."

OVER THE YEARS, IRELAND HAS PRODUCED MANY STARS but few can come close to Manchester United's fiery captain Roy Keane. Voted by his peers as the PFA and Football Writers' Player Of The Year last season, Keane is one of the most complete players in the Premiership and the most influential member of Alex Ferguson's victorious side.

His leadership abilities inspire his team-mates, whether it's in a dogged Premiership battle or a crucial match against Europe's finest in the Champions League. There was a good reason why United ended 1997-98 with no trophies – Keane was ruled out for most of the season with a serious knee injury. When he returned to the side, United brushed everyone aside and won their historic treble.

The inspirational midfielder brings an extra dimension to The Red Devils. He excels in all aspects of his demanding position. Watching him play, it's hard to know whether he's a blood and guts scrapping midfielder or an attacking playmaker that creates and scores vital goals. The truth is Keane can produce both of these qualities at will, and he can use them against the very best teams in the world.

His meteoric rise to Old Trafford's millionaire XI wasn't an easy ride though. It could have been a very different story for the man they affectionately call 'Keano'.

He was a boxer in his teenage years in Ireland and loved the cut and thrust of Gaelic football, a sport which helped him to develop the aggressive and committed sides of his game. But football was his real ambition and it wasn't long before he was putting all his energy into the game he loved.

His career began with Cobh Ramblers, a non-league Irish team. Keane was so determined to be a success that he wrote to Nottingham Forest asking for a trial. The letter was unsuccessful, but the midfielder didn't have long to wait before tough-talking Brian Clough snapped him up for the bargain price of £10,000.

From there, his natural ability did the rest, and after three impressive seasons at the City Ground, Keane was signed by Alex Ferguson for a British record fee of £3.75 million. He's won every trophy on offer since joining Manchester United, and there doesn't seem to be any sign of him slowing up.

Roy Keane is already an Old Trafford legend and although his demands of more than £50,000 a week seemed over the top to some, he has consistently proved his worth to United. His goals in the Champions League took Alex Ferguson's side to the 1999 final in the Nou Camp, even though Keane was suspended after being booked in the semi-final against Juventus. The treble wouldn't have been possible without him and the trophy cabinet at Old Trafford wouldn't be full of Premiership crowns if it wasn't for their captain.

MATCH charts Roy Keane's amazing career, from an Irish non-league side to the giddy heights of the Premiership.

June 1990
SIGNING FOR FOREST

After choosing to follow a career in football it wasn't long before Keane's potential as a top player was noticed, but he had to work hard for it. The tough-tackling midfielder was soon on his way to Nottingham Forest for £10,000.

ROY SAYS: *"I wrote to Forest in a desperate bid to get a trial in England but unfortunately they turned me down. I was then called up to play an important game for the league of Ireland and, although we got beaten 4-0, I was told I'd left a good impression on one of the Forest scouts. I really liked the club and a few weeks later I returned to the City Ground and played in front of Brian Clough. After the game he said he wanted to sign me and it wasn't a difficult decision to make."*

August 1990
PROFESSIONAL DEBUT

At the time the Forest boss was none other than ol' big head, Brian Clough. Despite the manager's legendary status, Keane had an excellent relationship with him and it wasn't long before he made his first start for Forest.

ROY SAYS: *"I came in one day just to do some extra training and not expecting to play at all, but one of the coaches took me to one side and told me to get my boots because I'd been selected to play in the squad of 16 against Liverpool. I really enjoyed it when I walked out of the tunnel and took to the field at Anfield and I was just trying to savour the atmosphere of the place, surrounded by the rest of the team who were all asking me who I was! It was a great experience."*

May 1991
INTERNATIONAL DEBUT

While still playing for Nottingham Forest, the young Keane was drafted into Jack Charlton's Republic Of Ireland squad. He went on to be instrumental to their success and went to the 1994 World Cup.

ROY SAYS: *"My Irish debut was against Chile, but it seems like absolutely ages ago now. The game was a dull 1-1 draw and I was a bit nervous during that match. I was okay at international level after that, but I don't normally get nervous before games. It wasn't much of a shock when I was first called into the Republic Of Ireland squad because I was a regular in the Forest team at the time and a lot of people had been putting pressure on Jack Charlton to include me in his squads."*

May 1993
RELEGATION WITH FOREST

By now Keane was an established member of the Forest midfield. But despair was just around the corner as the team suffered a disappointing season and were relegated to the First Division.

ROY SAYS: *"On the field, the lowest moment of my career was probably going through relegation with Forest. Nobody likes to get relegated and it was a very frustrating season because we were dominating all of our games, but we were still getting beaten. That was happening to us nearly every game. It's frustrating because people don't believe you, they think you can't be playing that well, but we were – we just weren't getting the results at the end of games and it cost us dearly."*

July 1993
JOINING MAN. UNITED

After suffering relegation with Forest, Keane was faced with the prospect of First Division football. Despite the club's efforts to keep the midfield star, Forest were forced to sell him to Manchester United for £3.75 million.

ROY SAYS: *"The move to Manchester United was a dream come true for me. Obviously I don't mean any disrespect to Forest because I had three good seasons playing with them and I really like the club, but when we got relegated I felt that with the World Cup coming up I couldn't really be playing in the First Division. When I heard that United had come in for me it was like a dream – I think it's every player's dream, so I had absolutely no hesitation in moving to Old Trafford."*

August 1993
MAN. UNITED DEBUT

At Old Trafford, Keane found himself playing in a squad of stars, including Steve Bruce, Bryan Robson and Eric Cantona. But that wasn't going to unnerve him as he set about creating a big name for himself.

ROY SAYS: *"My debut was away to Norwich City and we won the game 2-0 with Bryan Robson and Ryan Giggs scoring the goals. My next match was my Old Trafford debut on the following Wednesday against Sheffield United – we won 3-0 and I scored two of the goals. That really helped me and it got me off to the perfect start at the club, because obviously I was the record signing at the time and the pressure was on me not just to play well but to score as well."*

May 1996
HIGHEST POINT OF CAREER

The Red Devils were unstoppable, claiming their third Premier League title in four years and then beating Liverpool in the FA Cup Final to win an unprecedented double Double, after winning the same trophies in 1994.

ROY SAYS: *"Obviously I really wanted to win the Premiership as many times as I possibly could, and I still do, but in the end I really wanted to move up to another level and take my career to a real peak, and I think that's what we did that year. At the time, it was the highest point in my career when we won the double Double with Man. United. It's nice for me to know that there are only seven players who have ever achieved that, and I'm one of them. That's a nice feeling."*

August 1997
BECOMING CAPTAIN

With his ability to control the midfield and direct those around him, it was impossible for Alex Ferguson to overlook Keane's leadership qualities. With Robson and Cantona gone, it was time for Keane to get another honour.

ROY SAYS: *"For me to be awarded the captaincy of Manchester United was a really great honour and hopefully I haven't let anybody down during my time as captain. I've always been one to encourage the lads out on the pitch and every so often I give them a rollicking, but I used to be like that anyway so in that sense being captain doesn't make too much difference. I just hope that I've done as well as Eric Cantona and Bryan Robson did when they were the captain of Manchester United."*

September 1997
OUT OF ACTION

Keane was out for most of the season with a self-inflicted injury which he sustained while going in for a late tackle on Alf-Inge Haaland in the match against Leeds at Elland Road. He'd become a victim of his own style.

ROY SAYS: *"I knew there were a lot of people out there thinking that it was a silly thing for me to do, but I definitely paid the price for it and I was out of action for the entire season. You know, nobody needs to remind me of that, the whole thing was an absolute nightmare from beginning to end. I just hope I've learned from the tackle which got me the injury – the ball was even going out of play, so it was a silly and really unnecessary thing for me to do. I won't be doing that again!"*

May 1999
CUP FINAL INJURY

With the '90s drawing to a close, Man. United were determined to go out with a bang, and that's exactly what they did. But Keane was injured early into the FA Cup Final and it was left to his team-mates to win the game 2-0.

ROY SAYS: *"Obviously I was very disappointed to get injured because it was the FA Cup Final and everyone wants to take part in that, but if I'd been told that I was going to get a winner's medal before the game had kicked-off, I would have settled for that. I was confident going into the match because I knew that if we just went out there and played anywhere near as well as we'd played in other matches throughout the season we were going to win the cup comfortably."*

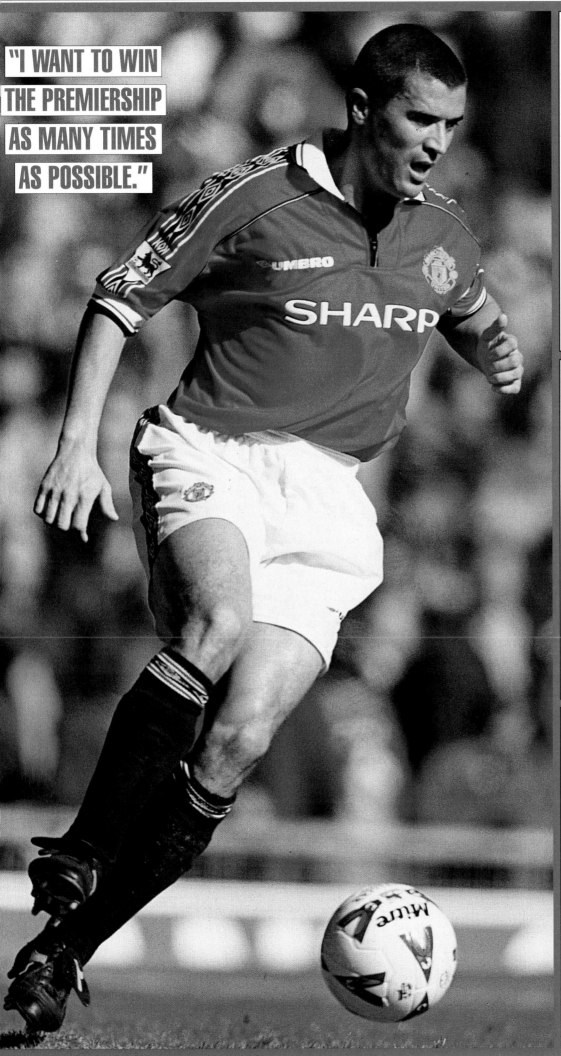

"I WANT TO WIN THE PREMIERSHIP AS MANY TIMES AS POSSIBLE."

After picking up a booking in the semi-final clash with Juventus, where he had been an inspirational force, Keane was suspended for the crucial Champions League Final against German rivals Bayern Munich.

ROY SAYS: *"I knew I would miss the final, but if I had focused on that, I would have been useless to the team in the semi-final. My only aim was to see the club into the final. That was all that mattered. Of course I was disappointed to miss the final in Barcelona, but I know the rules of the game and we all have to live by them. I've been very fortunate in football. You have your ups and downs and that was just a down for me personally. But for the club, the players and the staff, it was fantastic."*

April 2000
PFA PLAYER OF THE YEAR

Having already won the Football Writers' Player Of The Year Award, Keane did the double once more and landed the PFA Player Of The Year accolade. It capped yet another successful season for the United skipper.

ROY SAYS: *"All the nominees had a good chance of winning the award, so I'm fortunate that it was me and I thanked all the professionals who voted for me, even the ones that didn't! I've had a fantastic ten years in England, three at Nottingham Forest and seven years at Manchester United, and long may it continue. I have been extremely fortunate to work under two fantastic managers. I owe a lot to Brian Clough for bringing me over from Ireland and Alex Ferguson has helped my career both on and off the pitch."*

May 2000
PREMIERSHIP WINNERS

United clinched the title with a 3-1 win over Southampton at The Dell and Keane added another medal to his collection. Due to his hamstring injury, he played no part in the final three games of what was an eventful season.

ROY SAYS: *"To win the league is always nice and now hopefully next year we can push ourselves even more to do a lot better. I think it was far from a perfect season and there were many disappointments for all of us at the club. The Real Madrid game at home was one of the worst games and not being able to defend the FA Cup was a shame for us as well. But the next three or four years should see me in the prime of my football career and I'm really delighted that it will be with Manchester United."*

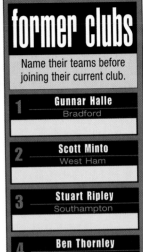

Arsenal and Galatasaray battle it out in the final.

fourth XI

The UEFA Cup features the cream of Europe's clubs not in the Champions League. What do you know about it?

1 Can you remember the name of the competition before it was changed to the UEFA Cup?

2 In what year did the first UEFA Cup take place under its current name?

3 Before 1998, the UEFA Cup Final was always held over two legs – home and away. True or false?

4 Do you know which team won the first UEFA Cup under its current name?

5 Who was the manager of Ipswich Town when they won the competition in 1981, beating Dutch opponents AZ 67 Alkmaar in the final?

6 Who were the last side to win the competition two years running?

7 Which Italian side did exceptionally well in the competition and won the UEFA Cup an impressive three times in the '90s?

8 Can you name the last English side to lift the UEFA Cup trophy way back in 1984 by beating Anderlecht?

9 Who were the winners of the last UEFA Cup Final to be played over two legs, which was in 1997?

10 The final of the 1998-99 UEFA Cup was held in Eastern Europe. Parma beat Olympique Marseille 3-0 to lift the trophy, but in which city was the final held?

11 After changing the competition's structure for the 1999-2000 season, the UEFA Cup incorporated the European-Cup Winners' Cup, which is no longer contested. Can you name the team that dramatically won the first UEFA Cup of the new millennium on penalties?

CROSSWORD

Use your footy knowledge to solve the crossword below!

ACROSS
1. Came bottom of Northern Ireland's Euro 2000 qualifying group (5)
3. Brazilian full-back at Highbury (8)
7. Forest's former Villa central defender, Riccardo (7)
9. Homeland of Arsenal's Alex Manninger (7)
11. ...... Marsh, opinionated Sky TV pundit (6)
12. Newcastle's former Wimbledon and England full-back, Warren (6)
14. Country that Freddie Ljungberg plays for (6)
15. Piece of woodwork supported by the posts (8)
18. Sunderland superstriker – Premiership golden boot winner (8)
20. Stuart, now assistant manager of The Bantams (6)
24. Nickname associated with Hamilton Academicals (6)
26. Leyton ......, Third Division club (6)
28. 2000 FA Cup winners (7)
29. Nickname of Second Division Bury (7)
30. Gianluca Vialli's French centre-back, Marcel (8)
31. Veteran full-back, Lee, with The Gunners (5)

DOWN
1. Lucky club figures – like Cyril the Swan (7)
2. Andre, South African 'keeper for Fulham and Oxford (7)
3. Ex-Dons and Liverpool defender, John, now at Ipswich (6)
4. Transfer move conducted on a temporary basis (4)
5. Sir Geoff, Englishman who scored a World Cup Final hat-trick (5)
6. Millwall's former Anfield 'keeper, Tony (6)
8. Nationality of West Ham and Celtic man Eyal Berkovic (7)
10. Mansfield Town's club nickname (5)
13. Well-travelled ex-Barnet and Birmingham manager, Barry (3)
16. Southampton's one-time Blackburn forward, James (7)
17. Injury-dogged, veteran West Ham and England full-back (6)
19. Third-placed Premiership club managed by David O'Leary (5)
21. Alec, ex-Rangers full-back reunited with Walter Smith at Everton (7)
22. Celtic's Scandinavian forward, Henrik, who broke a leg last year (7)
23. ...... Road, home ground of 25 Down (6)
25. The Railwaymen from Division One (5)
27. Liverpool-born England Under-21 left-back, Michael (4)

former clubs
Name their teams before joining their current club.

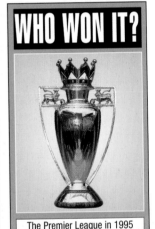

1 Gunnar Halle
Bradford

2 Scott Minto
West Ham

3 Stuart Ripley
Southampton

4 Ben Thornley
Huddersfield

WHO WON IT?

The Premier League in 1995

1 POINT FOR CORRECT ANSWER

MATCHfacts
CODE BREAKER
Can you decode this to find a Premiership star?

CRACK THE CODE!

5	20	26	9

2	18	13	6	9	16	2

CIVVY STREET

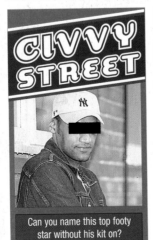

Can you name this top footy star without his kit on?

who plays where?
Can you match these Second Division clubs with their grounds?

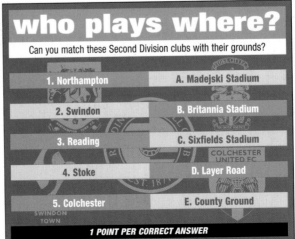

1. Northampton	A. Madejski Stadium
2. Swindon	B. Britannia Stadium
3. Reading	C. Sixfields Stadium
4. Stoke	D. Layer Road
5. Colchester	E. County Ground

1 POINT PER CORRECT ANSWER

connections...
Which Division One club links Sunderland's Danny Dichio and West Ham's Trevor Sinclair?

NICKY WEAVER
Manchester City

MATCH
YOUNG GUNS

EURO SUPER

MATCH gets out its crystal ball to see just what a European Super League might look like.

FOOTBALL IS NOW CLOSER THAN EVER TO A LEAGUE INVOLVING THE TOP clubs from Europe. UEFA's Champions League is already made up of mini leagues of teams battling it out for a place in the quarter-finals of the competition. But what would happen if UEFA selected the most successful clubs on the continent to form a European Super League? MATCH took on the task, looking at which teams would qualify for the league.

First, teams have to be successful at home, winning loads of league titles and cup competitions. Second, they need plenty of European honours in the trophy cabinet so UEFA would know they could compete with the very best. Money often talks loudest these days in football, so the clubs would have to compete financially to build huge stadiums and buy the best players. And you can guarantee the European Super League would showcase the finest players in the world, from Zidane of Juventus to Rivaldo of Barcelona and from Beckham of Manchester United to Owen of Liverpool. If these clubs had a top manager and proven goalscorers, they'd have a winning combination for a place in the best club competition in the world. So who would win if UEFA launched the European Super League for 2001-2002?

HERE'S WHAT COULD HAPPEN...

EUROPEAN SUPER LEAGUE 2001-2002

		P	W	D	L	F	A	Pts
1.	Real Madrid	34	21	8	5	85	51	71
2.	Manchester United	34	20	9	5	89	46	69
3.	Lazio	34	19	8	7	79	48	65
4.	Juventus	34	18	8	8	80	48	62
5.	Barcelona	34	17	11	6	80	50	62
6.	Arsenal	34	15	10	9	69	47	55
7.	AC Milan	34	15	9	10	71	55	54
8.	Inter Milan	34	13	10	11	69	54	49
9.	Bayern Munich	34	12	11	11	62	52	47
10.	Rangers	34	9	12	13	52	58	39
11.	Liverpool	34	9	11	14	59	60	38
12.	PSV Eindhoven	34	8	12	14	55	63	36
13.	Benfica	34	9	9	16	48	69	36
14.	FC Porto	34	7	9	18	46	71	30
15.	Ajax	34	7	8	19	41	74	29
16.	Celtic	34	6	10	18	39	75	28
17.	Borussia Dortmund	34	5	7	22	33	81	22
18.	Marseille	34	4	7	23	31	86	19

EUROPEAN SUPER LEAGUE'S TOP TEN GOALSCORERS

		CLUB	GOALS
1.	Andriy Shevchenko	AC Milan	28
2.	Raul	Real Madrid	25
3.	Patrick Kluivert	Barcelona	25
4.	Ruud Van Nistelrooy	PSV Eindhoven	23
5.	Jardel	Porto	23
6.	Dwight Yorke	Manchester United	22
7.	Thierry Henry	Arsenal	21
8.	Christian Vieri	Inter Milan	20
9.	Filippo Inzaghi	Juventus	19
10.	Michael Owen	Liverpool	19

1

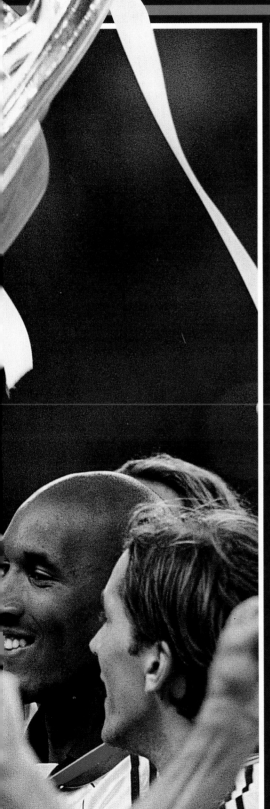

REAL MADRID
Spain

Manager: Vincente Del Bosque

World's richest club status: 3rd

In the trophy cabinet: 27 Spanish League titles, 17 Spanish Cups, 8 European Cups, 2 UEFA Cups, 2 World Club Cups

Top scorer: Raul, 17

Star Players: Roberto Carlos, Fernando Morientes, Redondo

Why they're there: Qualified as 2000 Champions League winners. One of Europe's most successful sides with a team packed full of superstars.

2

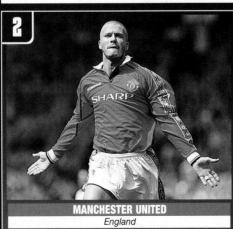

MANCHESTER UNITED
England

Manager: Alex Ferguson

World's richest club status: 1st

In the trophy cabinet: 13 English League titles, 10 English FA Cups, 1 English League Cup, 2 European Cups, 1 Cup-Winners' Cup, 1 European Super Cup

Top scorer: Dwight Yorke, 20

Star players: Jaap Stam, David Beckham, Roy Keane

Why they're there: Dominated English football in the '90s and won the 1999 Champions League. Also the world's richest club.

3

LAZIO
Italy

Manager: Sven Goran Eriksson

World's richest club status: 19th

In the trophy cabinet: 2 Italian League titles, 3 Italian Cups, 1 Cup Winners' Cup

Top scorer: Marcelo Salas, 12

Star players: Juan Sebastien Veron, Marcelo Salas, Sinisa Mihajlovic

Why they're there: Winners of the 1999-2000 Serie A title, just edging out Juventus in a thrilling championship race. Lazio have shown excellent form domestically over the last few seasons in Italy and can boast a team packed with a number of established foreign stars. The club are renowned for making big moves in the world transfer market and Lazio now pose a serious threat to the very finest club sides in Europe.

4

JUVENTUS
Italy

Manager: Carlo Ancelotti

World's richest club status: 4th

In the trophy cabinet: 25 Italian League titles, 9 Italian Cups, 2 European Cups, 1 Cup-Winners' Cup, 3 UEFA Cups, 2 European Super Cups, 2 World Club Cups

Top scorer: Filippo Inzaghi, 15

Star players: Zinedine Zidane, Edgar Davids, Alessandro Del Piero

Why they're there: Juventus boast an impressive history of European titles and are the fourth richest club in the world. They have a superbly talented team, including the world's best player, Zinedine Zidane.

5

BARCELONA
Spain

Manager: To be announced

World's richest club status: 2nd

In the trophy cabinet: 16 Spanish League titles, 24 Spanish Cups, 1 European Cup, 4 Cup-Winners' Cups, 2 European Super Cups, 3 Fairs Cups

Top scorer: Patrick Kluivert, 15

Star players: Luis Figo, Rivaldo, Kluivert

Why they're there: A bulging trophy cabinet and a team consisting of some of the finest players in the world.

6

7

AC MILAN
Italy

Manager: Alberto Zaccheroni

World's richest club status: 6th

In the trophy cabinet: 16 Italian titles, 4 Italian Cups, 5 European Cups, 2 Cup-Winners' Cups, 3 European Super Cups, 3 World Club Cups

Top scorer: Andriy Shevchenko, 24

Star players: Paolo Maldini, Oliver Bierhoff, Andriy Shevchenko

Why they're there: The huge trophy cabinet speaks for itself. A real force.

8

INTER MILAN
Italy

Manager: Marcello Lippi

World's richest club status: 10th

In the trophy cabinet: 13 Italian League titles, 3 Italian Cups, 2 European Cups, 3 UEFA Cups, 2 World Club Cups

Top scorer: Christian Vieri, 13

Star players: Christian Vieri, Ronaldo, Luigi Di Biagio

Why they're there: In the shadow of AC Milan in the past, but in Ronaldo and Vieri, Inter have two of the best strikers in the world.

ARSENAL
England

Manager: Arsene Wenger

World richest club status: 20th

In the trophy cabinet: 11 English League titles, 7 FA Cups, 2 League Cups, 1 European Cup-Winners' Cup, 1 Fairs' Cup

Top scorer: Thierry Henry, 17

Star players: Dennis Bergkamp, Marc Overmars, Patrick Vieira

Why they're there: Only serious challengers to Man. United in England. They reached the final of the UEFA Cup in 1999-2000 and are very difficult to beat at their home ground, Highbury.

9

BAYERN MUNICH
Germany

Manager: Uli Hoeness

World's richest club status: 5th

In the trophy cabinet: 16 German League titles, 10 German Cups, 3 European Cups, 1 Cup-Winners' Cup, 1 UEFA Cup, 1 World Club Cup.

Top scorer: Giovanni Elber, 14

Star players: Oliver Kahn, Steffen Effenberg, Carsten Jancker

Why they're there: Lost the 1999 Champions League Final, but dominant in Germany and successful in Europe.

10

RANGERS
Scotland

Manager: Dick Advocaat

World's richest club status: 14th

In the trophy cabinet: 48 Scottish League titles, 28 Scottish FA Cups, 21 League Cups, 1 Cup-Winners' Cup

Top scorer: Jorg Albertz, 17

Star players: Michael Mols, Giovanni van Bronckhorst, Barry Ferguson

Why they're there: Rangers find it difficult to transfer their dominance in Scotland to the European stage. But they are still a very wealthy club and boast several big-name stars. The Glasgow outfit were unlucky not to qualify for the second stage of the UEFA Champions League last season.

11 LIVERPOOL
England

Manager: Gerard Houllier

World's richest club status: 10th

In the trophy cabinet: 18 League titles, 5 FA Cups, 5 English League Cups, 4 European Cups, 2 UEFA Cups, 1 European Super Cup.

Top scorer: Michael Owen, 12

Star players: Michael Owen, Sami Hyypia, Robbie Fowler

Why they're there: Liverpool have fallen behind the other top teams in England in recent years after dominating the domestic and European stage for nearly 20 years in the '70s and '80s. But The Reds remain a huge club and are enjoying something of a resurgence under the guidance of inspirational manager Gerard Houllier. The Frenchman has created an exciting young side at Anfield, made up of emerging England stars and experienced foreign international players.

12 PSV EINDHOVEN
Holland

Manager: Frank Arnesen

World's richest club status: N/A

In the trophy cabinet: 15 Dutch League titles, 7 Dutch Cups, 1 European Cup, 1 UEFA Cup

Top scorer: Ruud van Nistelrooy, 29

Star players: Jan Heintze, Ivica Kralj, Ruud van Nistelrooy

Overcame Ajax to be crowned Dutch champions in 1999-2000 but have yet to enjoy the same success in Europe.

13

BENFICA
Portugal

Manager: Jupp Heynckes

World's richest club status: N/A

In the trophy cabinet: 30 League titles, 26 Portuguese Cups, 2 European Cups.

Top scorer: Nuno Gomes, 18

Star players: Jorge Cadete, Karel Poborsky, Nuno Gomes

Why they're there: European Cups in 1961 and 1962. Portugal's team of the '70s and '80s. Lost ground to Porto but could be a force in Europe.

14 FC PORTO
Portugal

Manager: Fernando Santos

World's richest club status: N/A

In the trophy cabinet: 18 Portuguese League titles, 14 Portuguese Cups, 1 European Cup, 1 European Super Cup, 1 World Club Cup

Top scorer: Mario Jardel, 38

Star players: Mario Jardel, Ljubinko Drulovic, Fernando Mendes

Why they're there: Portugal's top club had European success in 1980s.

15 AJAX
Holland

Manager: Morten Olsen

World's richest club status: 17th

In the trophy cabinet: 27 League titles, 14 Dutch Cups, 4 European Cups, 1 Cup Winners' Cup, 1 UEFA Cup, 3 European Super Cups, 2 World Club Cups

Top scorer: Richard Knopper, 15

Star players: Aron Winter, Jesper Gronkjaer, Brogdan Lobont

Why they're there: Have a fine tradition as one of Europe's most successful club sides.

16 CELTIC
Scotland

Manager: Martin O'Neill

World's richest club status: N/A

In the trophy cabinet: 36 League titles, 30 Scottish FA Cups, 10 Scottish League Cups, 1 European Cup

Top scorer: Mark Viduka, 25

Star players: Mark Viduka, Mark Burchill, Henrik Larsson

Why they're there: First British team to win the European Cup, Celtic will be looking to Martin O'Neill to bring back the glory days.

17

BORUSSIA DORTMUND
Germany

Manager: Michael Meier

World's richest club status: 7th

In the trophy cabinet: 5 German League titles, 2 German Cups, 1 European Cup, 1 Cup Winners' Cup, 1 World Club Cup

Top scorer: Fredi Bobic, 8

Star players: Jens Lehmann, Christian Worns, Lars Ricken

European Cup and World Club Cup winners in 1997, Dortmund had a bad season in 1999-2000 but are sure to bounce back sooner rather than later.

18 MARSEILLE
France

Manager: Rolland Courbis

World's richest club status: N/A

In the trophy cabinet: 8 French League titles, 10 French Cups, 1 European Cup.

Top scorer: Florian Maurice 8, Ibrahim Bakayoko 8

Star players: Ivan de la Pena, Ibrahim Bakayoko, Sebastien Perez

Fought their way back to prominence in Europe after the disgrace of being found guilty of match-fixing and banned from European competition. European Cup winners in 1993, it looks like Marseille could be ready to rise to the top again soon.

ISN'T IT ABOUT TIME...

We saw some new goal celebrations? More time should be put aside in training for rehearsing those post-goal fun and frolics!

MARTYN ON KEEGAN

The size of goals should be changed to 'this big'. That'll make my job easier!

Nigel Martyn is a lucky bloke.
Not only is he part of a highly-promising Leeds side, he also gets to play under one of the best managers in the Premiership – David O'Leary. But he's also keen to learn from the experience of Kevin Keegan when he's with the England squad and he still gets very excited by this.

"One of the first things you notice about Kevin Keegan is how positive he is, and how he can make the opposition seem inferior to you," Nigel revealed to Route 1.

"His teamtalks are inspirational. They're also technical – you can't have a teamtalk saying, 'Come on boys, let's go and get them!'. He gets the technical stuff out of the way, then emphasises the pride in what you're doing. He's very good at giving players confidence. He really builds you up, it's great to be around his teamtalks and he lifts everyone."

But Keegan couldn't lift the players enough at Euro 2000, so let's hope the rest of the team feel as inspired as Martyn when the 2002 World Cup comes around!

The next step is the England No. 1 jersey.

So Kev says: "Nige, you're playing!".

Martyn is lapping it up with both Leeds and England.

Playing like girls

No, don't start moaning girls, that isn't an insult. Football's ever-increasing popularity means more and more women want to turn professional. What's surprising is the idea that we could soon see female players alongside their male counterparts in competitive matches. Huh? No, this isn't a script for some TV series. Professor Ellis Cashmore from Staffordshire University believes women would be successful in the same team as men and that many would do well in the Scottish Premier League today. Ah, now he's got a good argument. **"If you look at the progress women have made in sport over the past 30 years, you'll find that they actually outpace men,"** says the (very nutty) professor. Mind you, they probably could hold their own – have you seen those strapping Scottish lasses? They'd scare the life out of poor old Henrik Larsson, with his dodgy flowing locks!

GROWING OLD DISGRACEFULLY

David Seaman has absolutely no intention of doing a 'Shearer' and bowing out of international stardom, despite mounting pressure from Nigel Martyn and Richard Wright. The England 'keeper wants to hang on to the No.1 jersey and aims to keep going until his back gives way and he succumbs to the perils of old age. **"I don't want Euro 2000 to be my last championship,"** stuttered Dave, while pushing his false teeth back in. **"I want to go on and hopefully I can get another World Cup under my belt."** Aye, you'll probably still be at Arsenal, but will you be the first-choice in goal at Highbury, Seamo? The penalty king is planning to go on until he's at least 38 – that'll be nearly ten years older than Shearer was when he called it a day with England. It seems like senility has set in already!

MICHAEL BRIDGES
Leeds United

MICHAEL OWEN

THE STORY SO FAR!

MATCH charts the meteoric rise and rise of Liverpool and England scoring sensation Michael Owen, from Liverpool debutant to World Cup hero.

FROM THE VERY FIRST MOMENT THAT LIVERPOOL LAID EYES ON Michael Owen, they knew they had unearthed a special talent. It's well known now that Owen broke all of Ian Rush's youth goalscoring records on Deeside, but did you know teams as far away as Chelsea knew about him even then? It was Liverpool who nurtured Owen's raw talent and unleashed him on the footballing world in May 1997, when he more than justified his inclusion with a goal on his debut. It would be the first of many.

Football has always had its heroes and Michael Owen was a phenomenon waiting to happen. Not only had he developed into an outstanding prospect on the pitch, he was about to become a superstar off the pitch, too. Following in the footsteps of Ryan Giggs, Jamie Redknapp and David Beckham before him,

Owen became a commercial dream – wearing Umbro boots, driving a Jaguar and coaching football on BBC television. But he has always strived to keep his personal life totally private from his profession and concentrates fully on his game.

Last season Owen was dogged by injury, but he came back to play in all of England's Euro 2000 games in the summer and started the new season with Liverpool in August. He only turns 22 this Christmas, so there's still plenty of time for the striker to win some silverware with a rejuvenated Liverpool side and to make an even bigger impact on the international stage.

MATCH traces back every competitive game Owen has played and relives every goal he's scored for Liverpool. And check out the definitive guide to his already impressive England career.

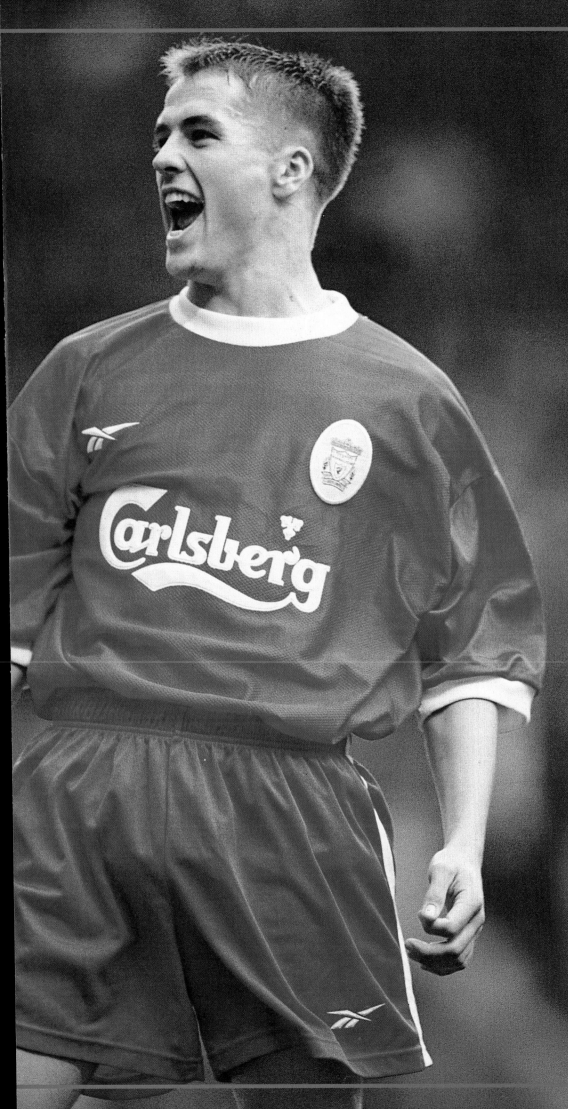

MICHAEL OWEN STORY

TAKEN FROM THE PAGES OF MATCH facts

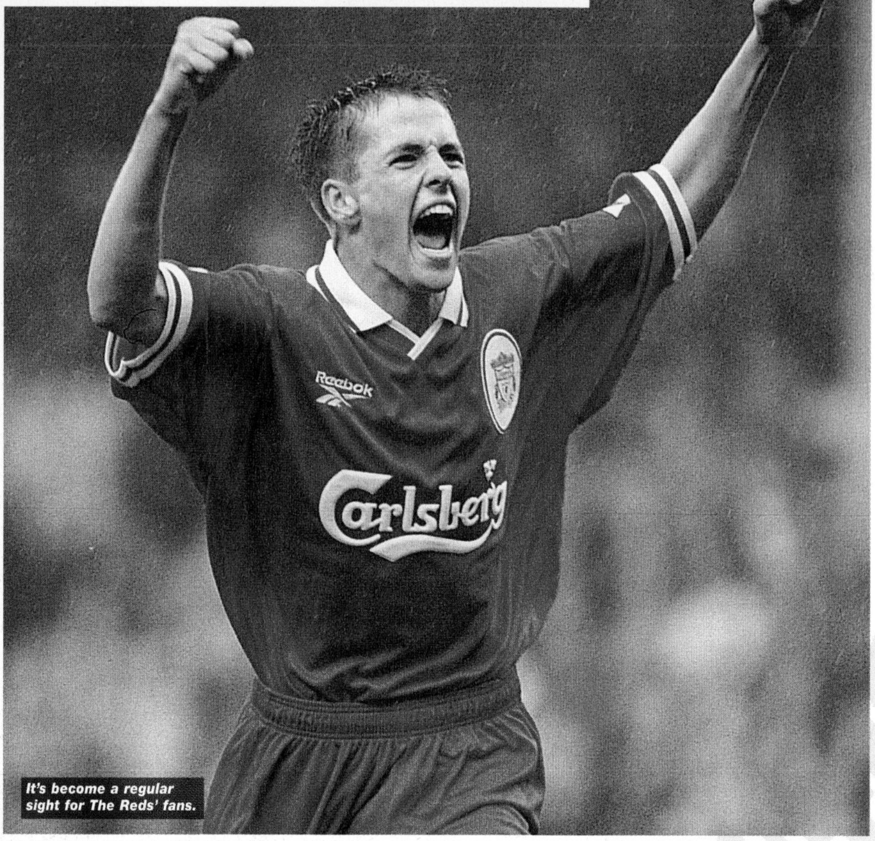

It's become a regular sight for The Reds' fans.

1 FA CARLING PREMIERSHIP — TUESDAY MAY 6, 1997

WIMBLEDON	2
LIVERPOOL	1

Attendance: 20,016

Scorers: Owen 74

The Game: Liverpool missed top scorer Fowler as their slim title hopes vanished. The one comfort of a poor team performance was the much anticipated debut of Michael Owen. The youth team graduate scored just 16 minutes into his professional career and he showed enough promise in his first game to have the visiting fans cheering his name at the end.

Team: James 7, Kvarme 7, McAteer 6, Wright 7, McManaman 7, Collymore 5, Redknapp 6, Ruddock 6, Berger 5 (sub 58 mins Owen 7), Thomas 8, Bjornebye 7.

***OWEN GOAL! 74 mins:** Owen showed incredible pace to run onto a Bjornebye throughball and slot home his first goal as a pro from inside the area.*

2 FA CARLING PREMIERSHIP — SUNDAY MAY 11, 1997

SHEFFIELD WEDNESDAY	1
LIVERPOOL	1

Attendance: 38,943

Scorers: Redknapp 83

The Game: Liverpool missed out on a Champions League place in this extraordinary game in which three Wednesday players shared the goalkeeping duties. Owen made his first start for Liverpool and the 17-year-old did not look out of his depth as he partnered first Collymore and then Barnes up front.

Team: James 6, Kvarme 7 (sub 46 mins Matteo 7), McAteer 8, McManaman 6, Wright 7, Collymore 6 (sub 46 mins Barnes 6), Redknapp 9, Ruddock 6 (sub 16 mins Harkness), Thomas 6, Owen 7, Bjornebye 7.

3 FA CARLING PREMIERSHIP — SATURDAY AUGUST 9, 1997

WIMBLEDON	1
LIVERPOOL	1

Attendance: 26,106

Scorers: Owen 72

The Game: Owen earned Liverpool a vital point on the opening day of the season with a sweetly struck second-half penalty. Things were looking grim for Liverpool when Gayle put Wimbledon ahead with a memorable 30-yard free-kick, but Jones handed the Reds a lifeline. He up-ended Riedle in the box before Owen kept his cool and converted the resulting spot-kick to earn The Reds a hard-fought draw away from home.

Team: James 7, Jones 7 (sub 82 mins McAteer), Wright 6, Babb 6, Riedle 6, McManaman 8, Ruddock 6 (sub 22 mins Harkness 6), Thomas 7, Ince 7, Owen 7, Bjornebye 7 (sub 67 mins Murphy 6).

***OWEN GOAL! 72 mins:** Owen blasted his shot past Sullivan after Karl-Heinz Riedle had been bundled over by Jones in the penalty area.*

4 FA CARLING PREMIERSHIP — WEDNESDAY AUGUST 13, 1997

LIVERPOOL	1
LEICESTER CITY	2

Attendance: 35,007

Scorers: Ince 84

The Game: Liverpool could not find a way past Leicester's three giant centre-backs, while Foxes 'keeper Keller had to wait until the 84th minute for a Liverpool shot on goal and when it came he was beaten by Ince's low strike. For Leicester, Heskey proved too much for Wright, setting up both goals.

Team: James 6, Jones 6, Wright 5, Babb 6 (sub 73 mins Matteo), Harkness 7, McManaman 5, Riedle 5, Thomas 5 (sub 77 mins Carragher), Ince 7, Owen 6, Bjornebye 5.

5 FA CARLING PREMIERSHIP — SATURDAY AUGUST 23, 1997

BLACKBURN ROVERS	1
LIVERPOOL	1

Attendance: 30,187

Scorers: Owen 53

The Game: Rovers came back to equalise after Owen's spectacular effort had put Liverpool ahead. Dahlin was a substitute for the third successive game and claimed his first Premiership goal for Blackburn. It was a fair result in a thrilling game.

Team: James 7, Jones 7, Kvarme 7, Wright 7, Harkness 6, Bjornebye 6, McManaman 6, Ince 7, Thomas 6, Owen 8, Riedle 7 (sub 80 mins Berger).

***OWEN GOAL! 53 mins:** Owen robbed Wilcox inside the Liverpool half and raced 50 yards to finish with a low shot from near the penalty spot.*

6 FA CARLING PREMIERSHIP — TUESDAY AUGUST 26, 1997

LEEDS UNITED	0
LIVERPOOL	2

Attendance: 39,775

Scorers: McManaman 23, Riedle 75

The Game: Liverpool put their stuttering start to the season behind them as McManaman struck only his third Premiership goal since December. With the Leeds defence caught asleep, Reidle grabbed his first goal for Liverpool 15 minutes from the end.

Team: James 9, Jones 7, Kvarme 8, Wright 8, McManaman 7, Harkness 8, Riedle 8 (sub 82 mins Berger) Thomas 7, Ince 8, Owen 8, Bjornebye 8.

7 FA CARLING PREMIERSHIP — SATURDAY SEPTEMBER 13, 1997

LIVERPOOL	2
SHEFFIELD WEDNESDAY	1

Attendance: 34,705

Scorers: Ince 55, Thomas 68

The Game: The victory would have been easier for Liverpool if Wednesday 'keeper Pressman hadn't been in inspired form. Ince, Bjornebye, Thomas and Owen were all left holding their heads as goalbound shots were spectacularly saved. There was a tense last ten minutes, as substitute Berger missed two golden chances, firing wide when finding the net seemed to be the only possible outcome.

Team: James 7, Jones 7 (sub 89 mins McAteer), Kvarme 7, McManaman 8, Wright 8, Harkness 7 (sub 28 mins Matteo 7), Riedle 7 (sub 74 mins Berger), Thomas 7, Ince 9, Owen 8, Bjornebye 8.

8 UEFA CUP R1 L1 — TUESDAY SEPTEMBER 16, 1997

CELTIC	2
LIVERPOOL	2

Attendance: 50,000

Scorers: Owen 6, McManaman 89

The Game: Both teams came away feeling that they should have won, with chances at either end in a game of immense excitement, which climaxed with McManaman's spectacular solo effort.

Team: James 7, Jones 7, Bjornebye 7, Kvarme 6, Wright 6, McManaman 8, Matteo 6, Ince 8, Riedle 7, Owen 8, Thomas 8.

***OWEN GOAL! 6 mins:** Owen broke clear of the Celtic defence to calmly slot the ball past 'keeper Gould from 12 yards out for his first European goal.*

9 FA CARLING PREMIERSHIP — SATURDAY SEPTEMBER 20, 1997

SOUTHAMPTON	1
LIVERPOOL	1

Attendance: 15,252

Scorers: Riedle 37

The Game: Riedle scored with Liverpool's first effort on target, but Southampton equalised through Davies and both sides then had opportunities for a winner. James made a superb save from Davies and Fowler forced an excellent save from Jones.

Team: James 7, McAteer 6, Bjornebye 7, Kvarme 6, Wright 6, McManaman 7, Matteo 6, Ince 8, Riedle 6, (sub 69 mins Berger 7), Owen 6 (sub 60 mins Fowler 7), Thomas 6.

10 FA CARLING PREMIERSHIP — MONDAY SEPTEMBER 22, 1997

LIVERPOOL	3
ASTON VILLA	0

Attendance: 34,843

Scorers: Fowler 56, McManaman 79, Riedle 90

The Game: The Liverpool machine coughed and spluttered in the first-half before moving into top gear after the break when Owen went down in the area under Southgate's challenge. Fowler, who was making his first start of the season, scored from the spot and two further goals clinched victory.

Team: James 8, Kvarme, 7, Babb 7, McManaman 9, Fowler 8, (sub 75 mins Riedle), Berger 6, Thomas 6, Owen 9, Bjornebye 6, Carragher, 7, Murphy 6 (sub 73 mins Thompson).

11 FA CARLING PREMIERSHIP — SATURDAY SEPTEMBER 27, 1997

WEST HAM UNITED	2
LIVERPOOL	1

Attendance: 25,908

Scorer: Fowler 52

The Game: Eyal Berkovic cancelled out Fowler's fantastic equaliser to end West Ham's three-match losing streak. "This smacks of last season," said Liverpool boss Roy Evans. "We got back into the game but we just didn't take it on from there."

Team: James 7, Kvarme 6 (sub 70 mins Murphy 6), Babb 6, McManaman 7, Fowler 7, Berger 6 (sub 75 mins Riedle), Thomas 6 (sub 70 mins McAteer 7), Ince 8, Owen 7, Bjornebye 7, Carragher 6.

12 UEFA CUP R1 L2 — TUESDAY SEPTEMBER 30, 1997

LIVERPOOL	0
CELTIC	0

Attendance: 38, 205

The Game: Liverpool squeezed past Celtic due to McManaman's wondergoal in Glasgow in the first leg of the tie. The Reds were well below par for the first hour and it seemed Celtic could steal the win. However, strong performances from McManaman and Babb sealed qualification on away goals.

Team: James 5, Jones 7, Kvarme 7, Babb 8, Ince 7, McManaman 8, Fowler 6 (sub 84 mins Riedle), Berger 6, Owen 7, Bjornebye 7, Carragher 7.

13 FA CARLING PREMIERSHIP — SATURDAY OCTOBER 18, 1997

EVERTON	2
LIVERPOOL	0

Attendance: 40,112

The Game: Everton turned the form book on its head with a good win over their rivals. From the start they looked sharp, while Liverpool seemed disinterested. Everton's opening goal came thanks to a defensive mix-up, and Cadamarteri's strike that finally sealed the game was also due to a lapse of concentration at the heart of the Liverpool defence.

Team: James 6, Kvarme 6, McAteer 6, Ruddock 6, McManaman 7, Fowler 6, Riedle 6, (sub 50 mins Owen 6), Berger 6 (sub 56 mins Leonhardsen 6), Thomas 6, Ince 7, Bjornebye 6.

14 UEFA CUP R2 L1 — TUESDAY OCTOBER 21, 1997

STRASBOURG	3
LIVERPOOL	0

Attendance: 18,183

The Game: It was another poor showing from a disappointing Liverpool team that seemed to be lacking in any imagination or conviction. Strasbourg looked a very dangerous side, stretching Liverpool's three central defenders time and time again until they powered into a three-goal lead. The French team were then content to sit back and allow The Reds to take a grip on the game, but to no avail.

Team: James 6, McAteer 4, Bjornebye 6, Harkness 5, Kvarme 6, Ruddock 5 (sub 75 mins Owen), Ince 6, Redknapp 7, Leonhardsen 5, McManaman 5, Fowler 6.

15 FA CARLING PREMIERSHIP — SATURDAY OCTOBER 25, 1997

LIVERPOOL	4
DERBY COUNTY	0

Attendance: 38,017

Scorers: Fowler 27, 84, Leonhardsen 65, McManaman 88

The Game: Roy Evans could smile again as his side ripped apart in-form Derby. The Reds, with McManaman having an absolutely brilliant game, overcame early nerves to first wear down and then overwhelm Derby. The Rams had chances with their unpredictable striker Wanchope the main culprit.

Team: James 5, Jones 5, Kvarme 7, McManaman 9, Leonhardsen 7, Fowler 7, Redknapp 7, Ince 8, Owen 7, Matteo 7, Bjornebye 7.

16 FA CARLING PREMIERSHIP — SATURDAY NOVEMBER 1, 1997

BOLTON WANDERERS	1
LIVERPOOL	1

Attendance: 25,000

Scorers: Fowler 1

The Game: Liverpool should have been home and dry with the amount of possession and goalscoring chances they had. However, a moment of madness by Fowler and some astute substitutions by Bolton boss Colin Todd turned the game in Bolton's favour. In the end it was the visiting Liverpool fans who found themselves calling for the final whistle.

Team: James 7, Jones 6, Kvarme 7, McManaman 6, Leonhardsen 6, Fowler 6, Redknapp 5, Ince 6, Owen 7 (sub 74 mins Riedle), Bjornebye 6, Matteo 8.

17 UEFA CUP R2 L2 — TUESDAY NOVEMBER 4, 1997

LIVERPOOL	2
STRASBOURG	0

Attendance: 32,426

Scorers: Fowler 63, Riedle 84

The Game: Liverpool claimed their 100th victory in Europe but were left to rue their costly blunders from the disastrous first leg in France. Second-half goals from Robbie Fowler and Karl-Heinz Riedle brought them within a whisker of forcing the game into extra-time and the opportunity to progress further in Europe but lost 3-2 on aggregate.

Team: James 6, Jones 7 (sub 55 mins Riedle 8), Kvarme 8, McManaman 8, Leonhardsen 7, Fowler 8, Redknapp 9, Ince 8, Owen 7, Bjornebye 6 (sub 51 mins Berger), Matteo 8.

18 FA CARLING PREMIERSHIP — SATURDAY NOVEMBER 8, 1997

LIVERPOOL	4
TOTTENHAM HOTSPUR	0

Attendance: 38,006

Scorers: McManaman 48, Leonhardsen 50, Redknapp 65, Owen 86

The Game: Two early second-half strikes from Liverpool killed off the brave challenge of Spurs to leave them still searching for their first league victory of the season away from White Hart Lane. The Reds consolidated their lead with goals from Redknapp and Owen to complete the rout.

Team: James 6, Jones 8, (sub 87 mins McAteer), Kvarme 7, McManaman 8 (sub 87 mins Berger), Leonhardsen 8, Fowler 6, Redknapp 9, Riedle 7 (sub 75 mins Owen), Ince 7, Bjornebye 6, Matteo 6.

***OWEN GOAL! 86 mins:** Owen sprinted forward to meet Ince's pass, beating 'keeper Walker to the ball and rolling his shot into an empty net.*

19 COCA-COLA CUP R4 — TUESDAY NOVEMBER 18, 1997

LIVERPOOL	3
GRIMSBY TOWN	0

Attendance: 28,515

Scorers: Owen 28, 44, 57

The Game: Owen completed his first hat-trick for Liverpool in a virtual one-man display to demolish Grimsby Town's Coca-Cola Cup campaign and put Liverpool into the quarter-finals of the competition.

Team: James 6, Jones 6, Kvarme 7, McManaman 8, Leonhardsen 8, Redknapp 7 (sub 66 mins Berger 6), Riedle 7, Ince 6, Owen 9, Bjornebye 7, Matteo 7.

***OWEN GOAL! 28 mins:** Redknapp's shot from just outside the box was blocked by the Grimsby 'keeper and Owen poked home from the rebound.*

***OWEN GOAL! 44 mins (pen):** Owen was fouled by Handyside in the Grimsby penalty area, but he converted the spot-kick with the minimum of fuss.*

***OWEN GOAL! 57 mins:** Owen fired in a superb shot from outside the area which sailed past the stranded 'keeper and straight into the top corner.*

20 FA CARLING PREMIERSHIP — SATURDAY NOVEMBER 22, 1997

LIVERPOOL	0
BARNSLEY	1

Attendance: 41,011

The Game: Liverpool seemed to be in control with no great pressure on them as Barnsley set out to sit

MICHAEL OWEN'S STRIKE RATE RATIOS

PREMIERSHIP	95 games/48 goals	51%
FA CUP	3 games/2 goals	67%
LEAGUE CUP	6 games/5 goals	75%
EUROPE	10 games/3 goals	30%
OVERALL	58 goals in 114 games	51%

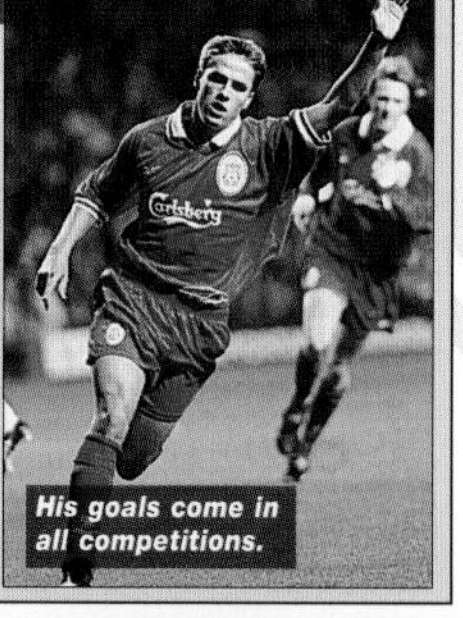

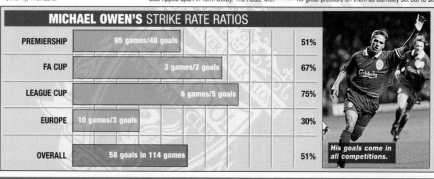

His goals come in all competitions.

back and attack on the break. The Reds had two strikes on goal in the first half an hour, but seemed stunned by Barnsley's goal. Liverpool dominated the second-half but missed four excellent chances.
Team: James 6, Kvarme 7, McAteer 7, Riedle 6, Redknapp 8, Berger 5, Bjornebye 6 (sub 67 mins Murphy 8), Owen 7, Matteo 5, McManaman 8, Leonhardsen 7.

21 FA CARLING PREMIERSHIP
SUNDAY NOVEMBER 30, 1997

ARSENAL	**0**
LIVERPOOL	**1**

Attendance: 38,094
Scorers: McManaman 56
The Game: Liverpool worked hard, closing down spaces well and hitting Arsenal on the break with speed and accuracy. If it wasn't for the valiance of skipper Tony Adams and a couple of magnificent saves from David Seaman, the scoreline would have reflected Liverpool's dominance more favourably.
Team: James 7, Kvarme 7, McAteer 6, Matteo 7, McManaman 8, Leonhardsen 7, Redknapp 7, Riedle 7, Owen 7 (sub 88 mins Murphy), Bjornebye 7, Carragher 7.

22 FA CARLING PREMIERSHIP
SATURDAY DECEMBER 6, 1997

LIVERPOOL	**1**
MANCHESTER UNITED	**3**

Attendance: 41,027
Scorers: Fowler 60
The Game: The blood and guts first-half gave no indication of the goal rush that followed. Liverpool showed glimpses of what they were capable of early on, but once United took the lead there was no stopping them – despite Fowler's disputed penalty. The Reds left the field to a chorus of boos.
Team: James 5, Kvarme 5 (sub 60 mins Berger 6), McAteer 5, McManaman 7, Leonhardsen 6, Fowler 7, Redknapp 6, Owen 6, Bjornebye 6 (sub 71 mins Riedle), Matteo 6, Carragher 6.

23 FA CARLING PREMIERSHIP
SATURDAY DECEMBER 13, 1997

CRYSTAL PALACE	**0**
LIVERPOOL	**3**

Attendance: 25,790
Scorers: McManaman 39, Owen 55, Leonhardsen 61
The Game: Liverpool cruised to a comfortable win, their superiority never in doubt. Despite losing Lombardo and Padavano, Palace didn't give up, but Liverpool never took their foot off the pedal and ended up winning this game in convincing style.
Team: James 7, Kvarme 7, McAteer 7, McManaman 8, Leonhardsen 7 (sub 89 mins Bjornebye), Fowler 7, Redknapp 8, Harkness 7 (sub 89 mins Berger), Owen 9, Matteo 7, Carragher 7.
***OWEN GOAL! 55 mins:** Redknapp's pass split the defence and Owen lobbed over the 'keeper.*

24 FA CARLING PREMIERSHIP
SATURDAY DECEMBER 20, 1997

LIVERPOOL	**1**
COVENTRY CITY	**0**

Attendance: 39,707
Scorers: Owen 14
The Game: Owen's ninth goal of the season put an end to Liverpool's poor run of form at home and ensured Coventry were beaten at Anfield for the first time in four seasons. Liverpool should have won the game with ease, but the longer it went on the more frustrating it became for The Reds in front of goal.
Team: James 5, Kvarme 4, McAteer 5, McManaman 7, Leonhardsen 6, Fowler 5, Redknapp 6, Harkness 5, Owen 8, Matteo 6, Carragher 6.
***OWEN GOAL! 14 mins:** Jamie Redknapp's super pass found skipper McManaman in space on the right touchline and his cross found Owen at the far post. The young striker didn't need an extra touch and finished convincingly with a left-footed shot.*

25 FA CARLING PREMIERSHIP
FRIDAY DECEMBER 26, 1997

LIVERPOOL	**3**
LEEDS UNITED	**1**

Attendance: 43,854
Scorers: Owen 46, Fowler 79, 83
The Game: A battling performance by Liverpool wore down Leeds. The visiting team were intent on disrupting The Reds, their game based purely on graft and effort. Haaland was detailed to man-mark McManaman, but it was Owen who Leeds couldn't pin down. The 18-year-old broke the deadlock 50 seconds into the second-half. His enthusiasm was infectious and the youngster took further plaudits as he presented strike partner Fowler with his second goal seven minutes from time.
Team: James 7, Kvarme 6, McAteer 6,Harkness 8, Matteo 8, McManaman 8, Leonhardsen 7, Fowler 8 (sub 85 mins Riedle), Redknapp 7 (sub 85 mins Berger), Ince 8 (sub 85 mins Carragher), Owen 9 .
***OWEN GOAL! 46 mins:** Oyvind Leonhardsen rolled the ball back for Owen, who lashed home right-footed past 'keeper Martyn from 15 yards.*

26 FA CARLING PREMIERSHIP
SUNDAY DECEMBER 28, 1997

NEWCASTLE UNITED	**1**
LIVERPOOL	**2**

Attendance: 36,718
Scorers: McManaman 31, 43
The Game: Steve McManaman's two well-taken half-volleys kept Liverpool's title hopes on course.
Team: James 7, Kvarme 6, Matteo 6, Harkness 7, McAteer 7, Ince 7, McManaman 9, Leonhardsen 6, Redknapp 7, Fowler 7 (sub 80 mins Carragher), Owen 7.

27 COCA-COLA CUP QF
WEDNESDAY JANUARY 7, 1998

NEWCASTLE UNITED	**0**
LIVERPOOL	**2**

Attendance: 33,207
Scorers: Owen 95, Fowler 105
The Game: Newcastle United crashed out of the Coca-Cola Cup to leave their season in tatters, whereas Liverpool appeared to rescue theirs. The Reds were indebted to their dynamic duo, Michael Owen and Robbie Fowler, for seeing them through to the semi-final with a goal each in extra-time.
Team: James 7, McAteer 7, Harkness 7, Babb 8, Matteo 8, McManaman 7, Leonhardsen 7, Ince 6, Redknapp 6, Fowler 7, Owen 9 (sub 115 mins Riedle).
***OWEN GOAL! 95 mins:** Owen used his pace to get onto a throughball from Fowler and kept his cool to lift the ball into the net, right-footed from ten yards over the advancing Hislop*

28 FA CARLING PREMIERSHIP
SATURDAY JANUARY 10, 1998

LIVERPOOL	**2**
WIMBLEDON	**0**

Attendance: 38,011
Scorers: Redknapp 72, 84
The Game: A brace from Jamie Redknapp gave Liverpool only their second victory in 14 attempts against Wimbledon's Crazy Gang.
Team: James 6, McAteer 6, Babb 7, McManaman 7, Leonhardsen 5 (sub 71 mins Berger), Fowler 5, Redknapp 8, Harkness 5, Ince 6, Owen 6, Matteo 6.

29 FA CARLING PREMIERSHIP
SATURDAY JANUARY 17, 1998

LEICESTER CITY	**0**
LIVERPOOL	**0**

Attendance: 21,633
The Game: Liverpool's march up the table was halted by a gritty Leicester City performance, as the partnership of Owen and Fowler failed to get going against a towering defensive display by Leicester's Scotland centre-back Matt Elliott.
Team: James 6, McAteer 7, Babb 7, McManaman 6, Leonhardsen 6, Fowler 6, Redknapp 7, Harkness 6, Ince 6, Owen 5 (sub 79 mins Berger), Matteo 8.

30 FA CARLING PREMIERSHIP
TUESDAY JANUARY 20, 1998

LIVERPOOL	**1**
NEWCASTLE UNITED	**0**

Attendance: 42,791
Scorers: Owen 17
The Game: This 1-0 win made it three in a row for Liverpool against the Geordies, but the match was no repeat of the 4-3 classics of previous seasons. Neither side could be faulted for effort, but it was Owen who shined the brightest on the night.
Team: James 5, McAteer 6, Babb 7, McManaman 6, Leonhardsen 6, Fowler 5, Redknapp 7, Harkness 7, Ince 7, Owen 8, Matteo 7.
***OWEN GOAL! 17 mins:** Ince won a vital tackle against the dithering Tomasson, allowing McAteer to find Owen, who chested the ball down and then side-footed a powerful, dipping volley with his right foot over Hislop from 12 yards.*

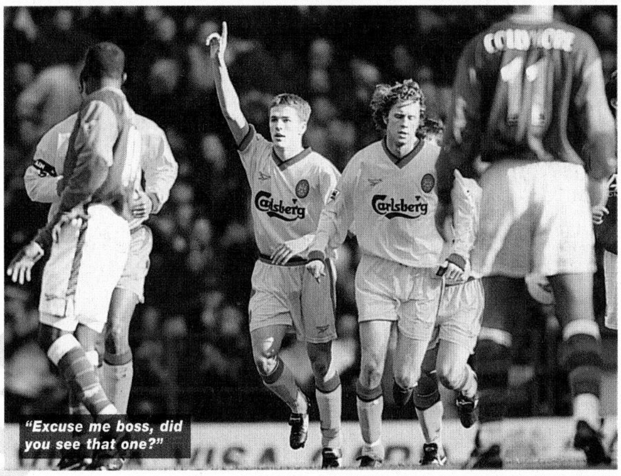
"Excuse me boss, did you see that one?"

31 COCA-COLA CUP SF L1
TUESDAY JANUARY 27, 1998

LIVERPOOL	**2**
MIDDLESBROUGH	**1**

Attendance: 33,438
Scorers: Redknapp 31, Fowler 82
The Game: The Reds recovered well after going 1-0 behind to Merson's superb strike and laid siege to the visitors' goal for the entire second period. Owen, Leonhardsen and Fowler went close before the out-of-sorts Fowler finally finished one of many gilt-edged chances to set up a tense second leg.
Team: James 7, McAteer 7, Babb 7, McManaman 7, Leonhardsen 7, Fowler 6, Redknapp 8, Harkness 7 (sub 76 mins Riedle), Ince 7, Owen 7, Matteo 7.

32 FA CARLING PREMIERSHIP
SATURDAY JANUARY 31, 1998

LIVERPOOL	**0**
BLACKBURN ROVERS	**0**

Attendance: 43,890
The Game: This was a bruising game with three players leaving the field injured and several more needing treatment. Rovers defended resolutely and The Reds could not find a way past Tim Flowers.
Team: James 6, McAteer 6 (sub 65 mins Jones 6), Babb 8, McManaman 6 (sub 46 mins Berger 8), Leonhardsen 6, Fowler 6, Harkness 7, Ince 8, Owen 7, Matteo 9, Carragher 7.

33 FA CARLING PREMIERSHIP
SATURDAY FEBRUARY 7, 1998

LIVERPOOL	**2**
SOUTHAMPTON	**3**

Attendance: 43,550
Scorers: Owen 24, 90
Slack defending allowed The Saints to win the game. Liverpool had piled on the pressure, but produced very little and were punished. Owen's late reply was nothing more than a consolation.
Team: James 6, Jones 6, Matteo 6, Babb 6, Harkness 6, McManaman 6, Ince 6, Carragher 5 (sub 58 mins Murphy 7), Leonhardsen 5 (sub 58 mins Berger 6), Fowler 5, Owen 7.
***OWEN GOAL! 24 mins:** Rob Jones crossed from the right, Leonhardsen's shot was blocked and Owen smashed the ball into the roof of the net.*
***OWEN GOAL! 90 mins:** Jones palmed away Owen's first effort, then saved again from Fowler, only for Owen to head home from close range.*

34 FA CARLING PREMIERSHIP
SATURDAY FEBRUARY 14, 1998

SHEFFIELD WEDNESDAY	**3**
LIVERPOOL	**3**

Attendance: 35,405
Scorers: Owen 27, 73, 78
The Game: Three goals from Owen did his hopes of making the World Cup squad absolutely no harm. The trio of strikes helped to clinch Owen's place for France following his fine debut for the England side.
Team: James 7, Jones 6 (sub 71 mins Riedle 6), Kvarme 6 (sub 71 mins Berger 6), McManaman 8, Leonhardsen 7, Fowler 6, Harkness 6, Ince 7, Owen 10, Matteo 7, Carragher 7.
***OWEN GOAL! 27 mins:** Owen's pace had left Newsome trailing as he collected McManaman's throughball and slid a shot past Pressman.*
***OWEN GOAL! 73 mins:** Fowler's shot hit the post and Owen rifled home an angled shot.*
***OWEN GOAL! 78 mins:** McManaman and Ince were involved in the build-up and ice cool Owen produced another shot of the highest quality.*

35 COCA-COLA CUP SF L2
WEDNESDAY FEBRUARY 18, 1998

MIDDLESBROUGH	**2**
LIVERPOOL	**0**

Attendance: 29,828
The Game: Liverpool lost their chance to return to Wembley after going behind in an astonishing burst at the start of the game. Boro deserved their place in the final against a disappointing Liverpool side that under-performed on the night.
Team: James 6, Jones 5, McManaman 7, Fowler 6, Harkness 5, Berger 5 (sub 65 mins Riedle 5), Ince 6, Owen 6, Matteo 5 (sub 46 mins Leonhardsen 6), Bjornebye 5, Carragher 5.

36 FA CARLING PREMIERSHIP
MONDAY FEBRUARY 23, 1998

LIVERPOOL	**1**
EVERTON	**1**

Attendance: 44,501
Scorers: Ince 66
The Game: Duncan Ferguson's winner helped Everton to extend their unbeaten run in Merseyside derbies to eight games. Liverpool lost even more ground in their quest for the Champions League.
Team: James 5, Jones 6, Kvarme 5, McManaman 7, Leonhardsen 6, Fowler 7 (sub 90 mins Murphy), Redknapp 7, Ince 8, Harkness 6, Owen 7, Carragher 7.

37 FA CARLING PREMIERSHIP
SATURDAY FEBRUARY 28, 1998

ASTON VILLA	**2**
LIVERPOOL	**1**

Attendance: 39,377
Scorers: Owen 5
The Game: Aston Villa celebrated the arrival of new boss John Gregory with a welcome home win. Villa produced some excellent form in preparation for their UEFA tie against Atletico Madrid. Liverpool old boy Collymore was a revelation in the Aston Villa attack and the team deserved this belated success.
Team: Friedel 6, Jones 6 (sub 77 mins Murphy), McManaman 7, Leonhardsen 7 (sub 80 mins Berger), Harkness 6, Riedle 6, Ince 8, Owen 6, Bjornebye 6, Carragher 6, Thompson 6.
***OWEN GOAL! 5 mins (pen):** Leonhardsen was brought down by Bosnich and Owen coolly scored.*

38 FA CARLING PREMIERSHIP
SATURDAY MARCH 7, 1998

LIVERPOOL	**2**
BOLTON WANDERERS	**1**

Attendance: 44,532
Scorers: Ince 58, Owen 65
The Game: In this Jekyll and Hyde game, the first period belonged to the visitors, but The Reds came out with all guns blazing after the break. Liverpool, led by a fired-up Paul Ince, completely dominated the last 40 minutes and should have punished the opposition by scoring several more goals.
Team: Friedel 6, Jones 7, McManaman 7, Matteo 7, Leonhardsen 7, Redknapp 8, Harkness 8, Riedle 6 (sub 34 mins Kennedy 80, Ince 9, Bjornebye 7, Owen 8,
***OWEN GOAL! 65 mins:** Owen latched on to a wonderful throughball and took one touch to control the pass before firing across Branagan.*

39 FA CARLING PREMIERSHIP
SATURDAY MARCH 14, 1998

TOTTENHAM HOTSPUR	**3**
LIVERPOOL	**3**

Attendance: 30,245
Scorers: McManaman 20, 88, Ince 63
The Game: David Ginola was simply outstanding, scoring one and setting up the other two Tottenham goals. For Liverpool Ince was superb, running the show in defence, midfield and sometimes in attack! Owen's pace caused problems for Tottenham and he could have claimed a hat-trick, thwarted only by Baardsen, on two occasions, and the post.
Team: Friedel 7, Jones 7, McManaman 8, Leonhardsen 6 (sub 67 mins Babb 6), Redknapp 8, Harkness 6, Ince 9, Owen 7, Bjornebye 7, Matteo 7, Carragher 7 (sub 60 mins Thompson 7).

40 FA CARLING PREMIERSHIP
SATURDAY MARCH 28, 1998

BARNSLEY	**2**
LIVERPOOL	**3**

Attendance: 18,684
Scorers: Riedle 44, 59, McManaman 90
The Game: It looked like Neil Redfearn's penalty had given his Barnsley side a share of the spoils in this pulsating Premiership clash at Oakwell. But in a bad-tempered game in which three of the home side were dismissed, McManaman's last-gasp goal kept Liverpool pressing for the runners-up spot.
Team: Friedel 6, Jones 6, Babb 6, McManaman 7, Leonhardsen 6 (sub 88 mins Murphy), Redknapp 7, Harkness 7, Riedle 8, Ince 7, Owen 6, Matteo 7.

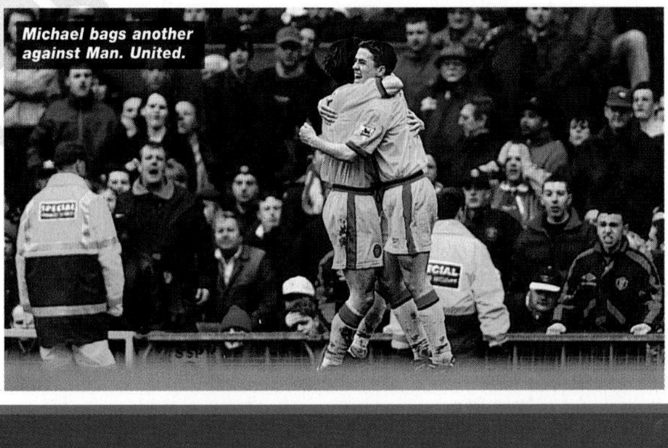
Michael bags another against Man. United.

THE LIVERPOOL STRIKE FORCE

With so many top strikers now at Anfield, Owen must be at his best just to get a game! **MATCH** looks at the partners that he's linked up with over the past year for Liverpool.

OWEN & FOWLER

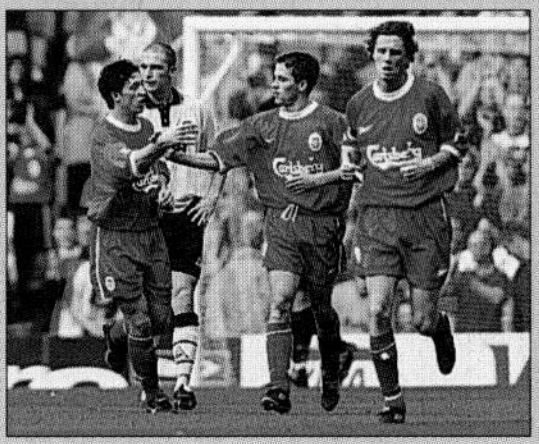

Liverpool's top strikers were both dogged by injury last season, so Gerard Houllier's first-choice pairing of Owen and Fowler hardly even played together. A dynamic duo when firing on all cylinders, both strikers have bursts of pace and are blessed with deadly accuracy. Fowler holds the ball up more and feeds Owen's darting runs, and both are happy to take on defenders and attempt the spectacular with confidence.

OWEN & HESKEY

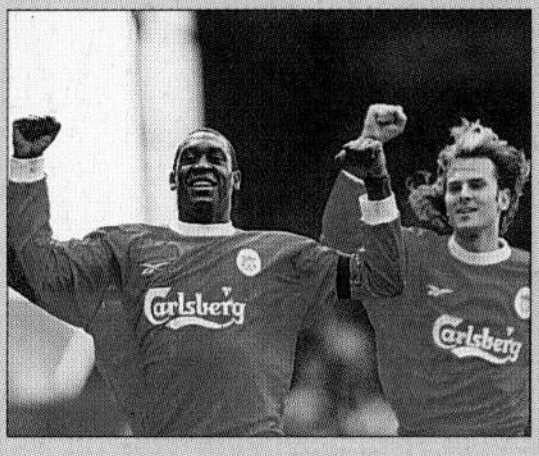

The £11 million striker working with Owen could be one of the most awe-inspiring partnerships of the Premiership. The pace and sharpness of Owen combines well with Heskey's power, strength and pace to inflict maximum damage on opposing defences. The new partnership came to the fore at the end of last season against Coventry in a 3-0 demolition of the Sky Blues. Heskey scored his first goal for Liverpool in that game, while Owen collected a fine brace.

OWEN & CAMARA

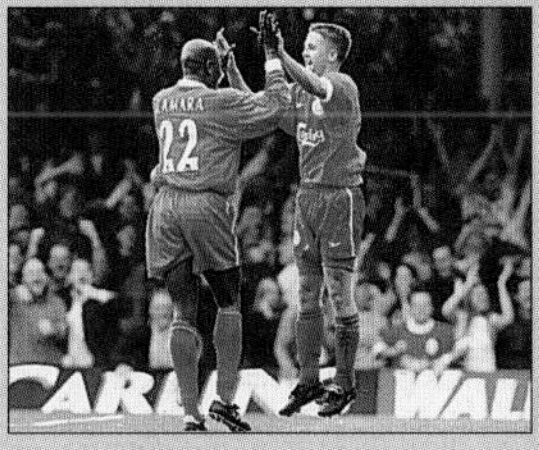

Yet another striker bursting with power and pace, the unpredictable Camara certainly causes problems when he plays up front for Liverpool. The maverick striker hasn't really clicked with Owen yet, though, and Heskey seems a better option. However, Camara and Owen successfully linked up to score against Derby County and Coventry last season, providing Gerard Houllier with yet another attacking option if required, with Camara effective from the bench.

OWEN & BERGER

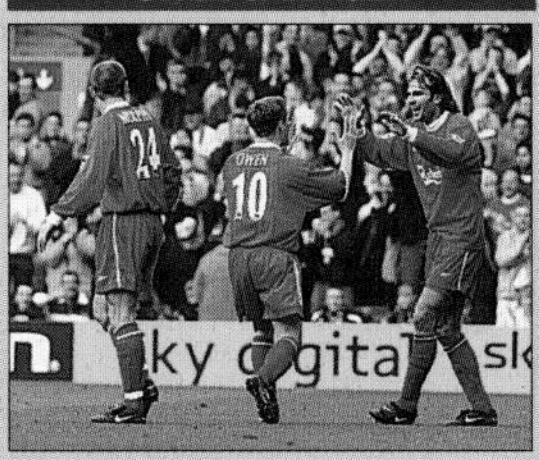

Berger, the Czech Republic international, is certainly capable of scoring spectacular goals, as demonstrated with two superb strikes against Leeds last season. Both Berger and Owen are lightening quick, but it's not necessarily a dream combination. Their styles of play may be too similar to work as an effective partnership, rather than complementing each other and offering a combined range of skills.

MICHAEL OWEN STORY

TAKEN FROM THE PAGES OF MATCH facts

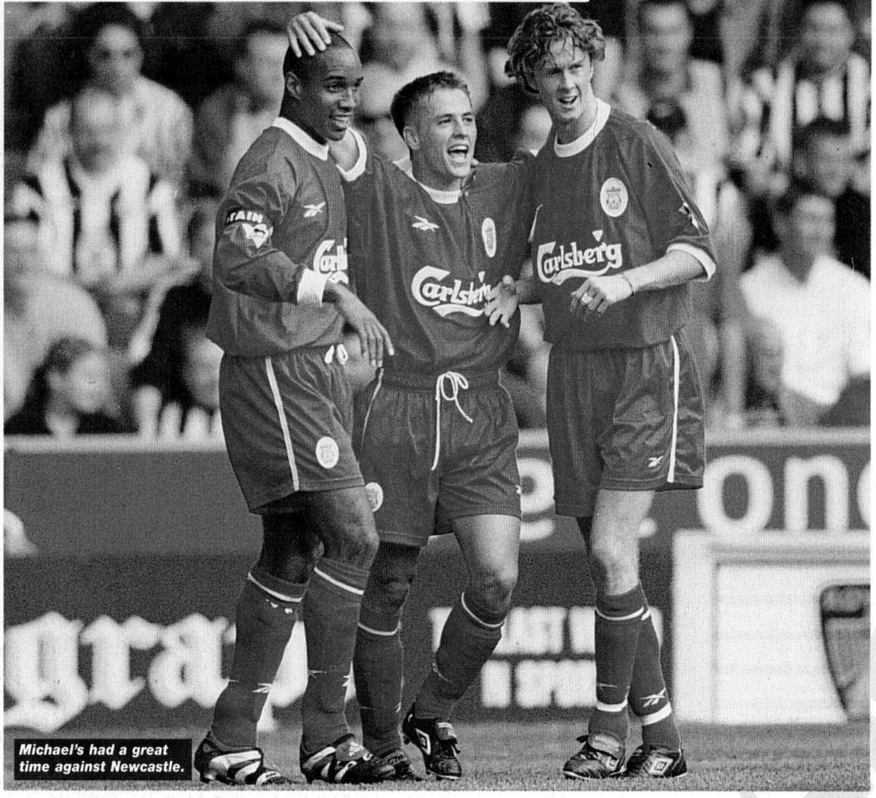
Michael's had a great time against Newcastle.

41 FA CARLING PREMIERSHIP
FRIDAY APRIL 10, 1998

MANCHESTER UNITED	**1**
LIVERPOOL	**1**

Attendance: 55,171

Scorers: Owen 36

The Game: Manchester United failed to break down a ten-man Liverpool after Owen had been dismissed for his second bookable offence, which occurred as early as the 40th minute. United lacked the guile and quality of finishing they're usually associated with and should have taken advantage against ten men – but Liverpool defended brilliantly.
Team: Friedel 7, Jones 7, Matteo 7, Babb 7, Ince 7, Harkness 7, McManaman 7, Redknapp 8, Murphy 7 (sub 74 mins Berger), Leonhardsen 7, Owen 7, .

***OWEN GOAL! 36 mins:** Owen sprinted on to Redknapp's well-struck throughball and indecision between Pallister and Schmeichel allowed him the opportunity to clip home a delicate finish from the edge of the Manchester United penalty area.*

42 FA CARLING PREMIERSHIP
MONDAY APRIL 13, 1998

LIVERPOOL	**2**
CRYSTAL PALACE	**1**

Attendance: 43,007

Scorers: Leonhardsen 29, Thompson 85

The Game: This lacklustre affair was reminiscent of a veteran's testimonial as neither side sparkled, but Owen had a steady game up front for The Reds.
Team: Friedel 6, Jones 7, Babb 7, McManaman 6, Leonhardsen 9, Redknapp 7, Harkness 7 (sub 63 mins Kvarme 6), Ince 7, Owen 7, Matteo 7, Murphy 7 (sub 70 mins Thompson 8).

43 FA CARLING PREMIERSHIP
SUNDAY APRIL 19, 1998

COVENTRY CITY	**1**
LIVERPOOL	**1**

Attendance: 22,721

Scorers: Owen 33

The Game: Dion Dublin's 21st goal of the season denied Liverpool success at Coventry. Liverpool were on top after a fine individual goal from Owen in the first-half as the youngster proved a constant threat, but The Sky Blues held out for a point.
Team: Friedel 6, Jones 7, Babb 5, McManaman 7, Leonhardsen 6, Ince 7, Redknapp 7 (sub 74 mins Riedle), Owen 8, Bjornebye 6, Matteo 5, Murphy 7.

***OWEN GOAL! 33 mins:** Owen controlled a pass from Bjornebye to turn and rifle home a right-footed shot past Ogrizovic from ten yards.*

44 FA CARLING PREMIERSHIP
SATURDAY MAY 2, 1998

LIVERPOOL	**5**
WEST HAM	**0**

Attendance: 44,414

Scorers: Owen 14, McAteer 21, 25, Leonhardsen 45, Ince 61

The Game: The Hammers were thrashed as five goals ensured Liverpool a place in the following season's UEFA Cup. Owen was electric throughout, his pace absolutely destroying the opposition.
Team: Friedel 7, Kvarme 6, McAteer 8, Babb 7, Leonhardsen 7, Harkness 7, Riedle 7, Ince 8, Owen 9, Bjornebye 7, Carragher 7.

***OWEN GOAL! 4 mins:** Sloppy defending gave McAteer the ball, and he fed the ultra-fast Owen, who sprinted clear and coolly slotted home to the goalkeeper's left.*

45 FA CARLING PREMIERSHIP
WEDNESDAY MAY 6, 1998

LIVERPOOL	**4**
ARSENAL	**0**

Attendance: 44,417

Scorers: Ince 28, 30, Owen 40, Leonhardsen 86

The Game: Liverpool clinched third place in the Premiership and became the only team of the season to do the double over eventual Double Winners Arsenal, who were missing seven first team regulars. Owen netted his 18th league goal of the season, but missed a 43rd-minute penalty.
Team: Friedel 6, McAteer 6 (sub 55 mins Thomas 6), Babb 7, McManaman 8, Leonhardsen 7, Harkness 7, Riedle 7 (sub 89 mins Murphy), Ince 9, Owen 8, Bjornebye 7, Carragher 7.

***OWEN GOAL! 40 mins:** Owen's waist-high right-footed volley on the turn followed a knock down by Ince from McManaman's right-wing corner which beat Manninger at his near post.*

46 FA CARLING PREMIERSHIP
SUNDAY MAY 10, 1998

DERBY COUNTY	**1**
LIVERPOOL	**0**

Attendance: 30,492

The Game: The scoreline flattered a Liverpool side who seemed unable to string more than two passes together. It could have been a lot more.
Team: Friedel 6, Kvarme 6, Babb 5, Harkness 5, Riedle 6, Berger 6, Thomas 5, Owen 6, Bjornebye 6, Carragher 6, Murphy 7.

47 FA CARLING PREMIERSHIP
SUNDAY AUGUST 16, 1998

SOUTHAMPTON	**1**
LIVERPOOL	**2**

Attendance: 15,202

Scorers: Riedle 39, Owen 71

The Game: Everyone expected fireworks from Owen and he didn't disappoint, setting up the first goal and scoring the second. The Reds were stunned in the 36th minute when Ostenstad gave Southampton the lead, but that was short-lived as Owen turned provider for Riedle to head home. Owen's inevitable winner came in the 72nd minute.
Team: Friedel, 6, Heggem, 6, Staunton 7, Owen 7, Carragher 7, McAteer, 6, Babb 6, Ince 6, Berger 7, (sub 75 mins Harkness), McManaman 6, Riedle 8 .

***OWEN GOAL! 72 mins:** Owen showed his poaching instincts when Steve Staunton's throw was flicked on by Ince and 'keeper Jones was unable to gather, allowing the loose ball to drop nicely for the young Liverpool striker to volley home, right-footed from eight yards out.*

48 FA CARLING PREMIERSHIP
SATURDAY AUGUST 22, 1998

LIVERPOOL	**0**
ARSENAL	**0**

Attendance: 44,429

The Game: The Gunners should have won and Liverpool always looked second best, although Owen was Liverpool's best player and could have won the game late on for The Reds.
Team: Friedel 8, McAteer 7, Staunton 7, Babb 6, McManaman 7, Owen 8, Riedle 7, Heggem 8, Ince 7, Berger 7 (sub 67 mins Redknapp 6), Carragher 7.

49 FA CARLING PREMIERSHIP
SUNDAY AUGUST 30, 1998

NEWCASTLE UNITED	**1**
LIVERPOOL	**4**

Attendance: 36,740

Scorers: Owen 15, 18, 32, Berger 45

The Game: Owen ran the home side ragged all game, hitting a hat-trick in 15 minutes in the first half with a display of scintillating finishing. He even managed to miss a couple of sitters as well!
Team: Friedel 7, Staunton 7, Babb 6, McManaman 8 (sub 89 mins Thompson), Owen 10, Redknapp 7 (sub 85 mins McAteer), Riedle 7, Heggem 7, Berger 8, Ince 8, Carragher 7.

***OWEN GOAL! 15 mins:** Given did superbly to dive to his left to parry Ince's right-footed drive, but the ball rebounded to Owen 12 yards out and his magnificently hammered right-foot shot squeezed inside the 'keeper's left-hand upright.*
***OWEN GOAL! 18 mins:** Another flowing move by The Reds resulted in McManaman slipping an inch-perfect throughball into the path of Owen, who drew Given before slotting home through the 'keeper's legs from ten yards.*
***OWEN GOAL! 32 mins:** Owen robbed Charvet and raced forward down the left channel to shrug off Albert's tentative challenge, before surprising Given with an early shot, flicked with the outside of his right foot and high into the net from 15 yards out.*

50 FA CARLING PREMIERSHIP
WEDNESDAY SEPTEMBER 9, 1998

LIVERPOOL	**2**
COVENTRY CITY	**0**

Attendance: 41,771

Scorers: Berger 25, Redknapp 48

The Game: Liverpool cruised back to the top of the Premiership with a dazzling 2-0 win at Anfield. Jamie Redknapp capped a brilliant display in midfield, tapping in from ten yards after brilliant dribbling skills from the irresistable Owen.
Team: Friedel 7, Staunton 7, Babb 7, McManaman 8, Owen 8, Redknapp 8, Riedle 7, Heggem 8, Berger 9, Ince 6, Carragher 7.

51 FA CARLING PREMIERSHIP
SATURDAY SEPTEMBER 12, 1998

WEST HAM	**2**
LIVERPOOL	**1**

Attendance: 26,029

Scorers: Riedle 87

The Game: The Hammers knocked Liverpool off the top of the Premiership in the game at Upton Park as Owen, waiting for strike partner Fowler to return after injury, ploughed a lone furrow up front.
Team: Friedel 6, Staunton 6, (sub 61 mins Matteo 7), Babb 6, Owen 6, McManaman 7, Redknapp 8, Harkness 6 (sub 53 mins Riedle 7), Heggem 6 (sub 70 mins McAteer 7), Berger 7, Ince 7, Carragher 7.

52 UEFA CUP R1 L1
TUESDAY SEPTEMBER 15, 1998

FC KOSICE	**0**
LIVERPOOL	**3**

Attendance: 4,750

Scorers: Berger 19, Riedle 23, Owen 59

The Game: Liverpool kicked off their 27th European campaign with a thoroughly professional performance, the return of Robbie Fowler capping a comfortable 3-0 victory. Fowler's introduction after 58 minutes was a welcome sight to the 200 travelling fans. Just 17 seconds later they saw him put Owen through superbly to score his side's third.
Team: Friedel 7, Babb 7, Staunton 7, Carragher 8, Heggem 8, Harkness 8, McManaman 9 (sub 78 mins McAteer), Redknapp 8, (sub 83 mins Leonhardsen), Riedle 7 (sub 58 mins Fowler 7), Owen 8, Berger 8.

***OWEN GOAL! 59 mins:** Fowler's wonderful chest control and inch-perfect throughball sent Owen racing clear of the Slovakian defence, and the England striker coolly slid home a right-footed shot past Molnar's left-hand post from 16 yards.*

53 FA CARLING PREMIERSHIP
SATURDAY SEPTEMBER 19, 1998

LIVERPOOL	**3**
CHARLTON ATHLETIC	**3**

Attendance: 44,526

Scorers: Fowler 33, 82, Berger 67

The Game: Fowler marked his Premiership return with two goals in a six-goal thriller. Owen looked relieved to have him back in action and was happy to let his team-mate grab the deserved glory.
Team: Friedel 5, Staunton 5 (sub 64 mins Matteo 5), Babb 4, McManaman, 6, Fowler, 7, Owen 6, Redknapp 5, Harkness 5 (sub 61 mins McAteer 6), Heggem 5 (sub 85 mins Thompson), Berger 8, Carragher 6.

54 FA CARLING PREMIERSHIP
THURSDAY SEPTEMBER 24, 1998

MANCHESTER UNITED	**2**
LIVERPOOL	**0**

Attendance: 55,181

The Game: Owen looked lively in patches and benefited from the introduction of Fowler near the end, but at Old Trafford, United clinched the points.
Team: Friedel 5, McAteer 6, Babb 6, McManaman 9, Owen 6, Redknapp 6, Riedle 6 (sub 74 mins Fowler), Berger 7, Ince 7, Bjornebye 6, Carragher 6.

55 UEFA CUP R1 L2
TUESDAY SEPTEMBER 29, 1998

LIVERPOOL	**5**
FC KOSICE	**0**

Attendance: 23,792

Scorers: Redknapp 23, 55, Ince 52, Fowler 53, 90

The Game: Fowler and Redknapp were superb for Liverpool, and although Owen failed to score, he provided the touches for his team-mates. The Reds put on a show, with Ince rounding off a leader's performance, scoring his first goal of the season.
Team: James 7, McAteer 6 (sub 66 mins Heggem 7), Babb 6 (sub 63 mins Matteo 6), Leonhardsen 7, Fowler 8, Owen 7, Redknapp 9, Berger 7, Ince 7 (sub 71 mins Staunton), Bjornebye 6, Carragher 7.

56 FA CARLING PREMIERSHIP
SUNDAY OCTOBER 4, 1998

LIVERPOOL	**1**
CHELSEA	**1**

Attendance: 44,404

Scorers: Redknapp 84

The Game: The Blues came away with a 1-1 draw after outclassing Liverpool in every department. The Liverpool fans and management were outraged at the poor performance and Owen put in his worst performance in a Liverpool shirt, as he was well shackled by Chelsea's ultra-mean defence.
Team: James 6, McAteer 6 (sub 57 mins Heggem 7), Babb 5, (sub 25 mins Matteo 6), Leonhardsen 5, (sub 64 mins Riedle 6), Fowler 6, Owen 5, Redknapp 7, Berger 6, Ince 7, Bjornebye 5, Carragher 6.

57 FA CARLING PREMIERSHIP
SATURDAY OCTOBER 17, 1998

EVERTON	**0**
LIVERPOOL	**0**

Attendance: 40,185

The Game: The 159th Merseyside derby ended in a dour goalless draw with Everton still looking for their first Premiership goal in front of their fans at Goodison Park. Liverpool again failed to record a derby victory, with Owen having a decent chance in the second-half, but scuffing his shot wide.
Team: James 7, Staunton 6, Fowler 6, Heggem 7, McManaman 9, Owen 6, Redknapp 5 (sub 46 mins McAteer 6), Berger 6 (sub 87 mins Riedle), Ince 6, Bjornebye 7, Carragher 6 (sub 50 mins Kvarme 7).

58 UEFA CUP R2 L1
TUESDAY OCTOBER 20, 1998

LIVERPOOL	**0**
VALENCIA	**0**

Attendance: 26,004

The Game: Valencia went home with mission accomplished following a well-earned goalless draw

MICHAEL OWEN'S PREMIERSHIP GOALSCORING RECORD

MATCH shows Owen's record against all the Premiership teams he's faced. Newcastle, Forest and Wednesday don't look forward to facing him, whereas he's found goals hard to come by against the likes of Everton, Derby, Spurs and Leicester.

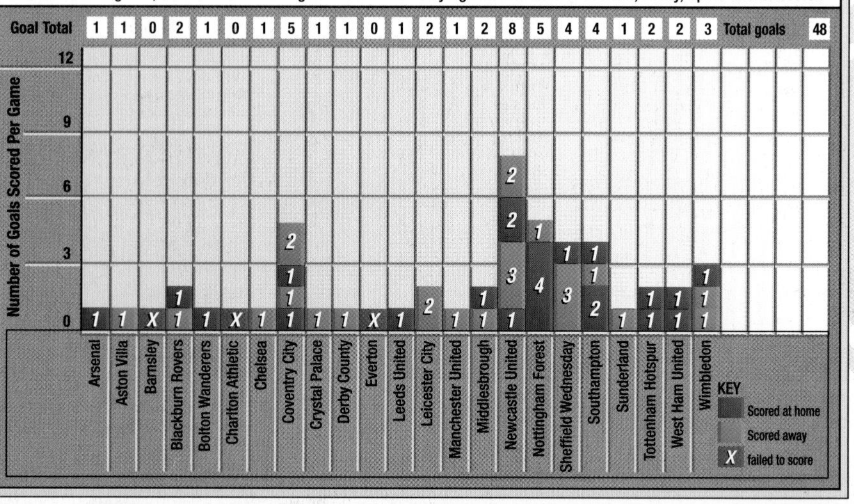

Goal Total 1 1 0 2 1 0 1 5 1 1 0 1 2 1 2 8 5 4 4 1 2 2 3 Total goals 48
Number of Goals Scored Per Game
Arsenal
Aston Villa
Barnsley
Blackburn Rovers
Bolton Wanderers
Charlton Athletic
Chelsea
Coventry City
Crystal Palace
Derby County
Everton
Leeds United
Leicester City
Manchester United
Middlesbrough
Newcastle United
Nottingham Forest
Sheffield Wednesday
Southampton
Sunderland
Tottenham Hotspur
West Ham United
Wimbledon
KEY
Scored at home
Scored away
X failed to score

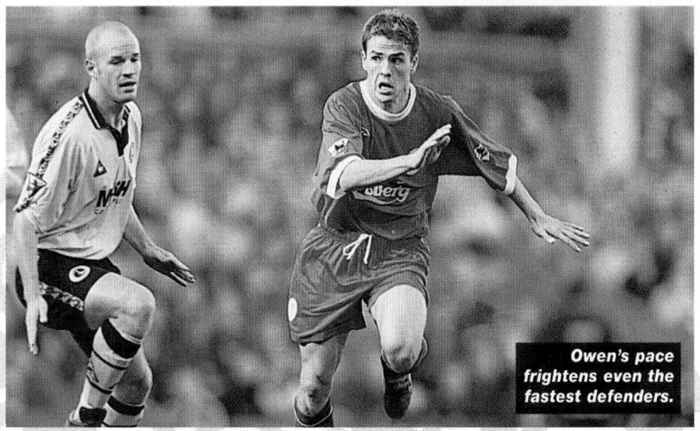

Owen's pace frightens even the fastest defenders.

against clueless Liverpool. Owen started on the bench for the first time in more than a year.
Team: James 7, McAteer 5, Staunton 6, McManaman 6, Fowler 7 (sub 73 mins Owen), Riedle 6, Heggem 6, Berger 7 (sub 75 mins Leonhardsen), Ince 8, Bjornebye 6, Carragher 6.

59 FA CARLING PREMIERSHIP
SATURDAY OCTOBER 24, 1998

LIVERPOOL	**5**
NOTTINGHAM FOREST	**1**

Attendance: 44,595
Scorers: Owen 10, 38, 71, 77, McManaman 23
The Game: Owen silenced talk of early burn-out with his second hat-trick of the season. Four superb goals showed that he has got what it takes to be the best – both mentally and physically!
Team: James 7, McAteer 5, Staunton 7, Carragher 7 McManaman 7 (sub 78 mins Thompson), Owen 10, Riedle 7, Heggem 7, Berger 7, Ince 8, Bjornebye 7.
OWEN GOAL! 10 mins: *Berger played Owen into space down the left and Owen sent a brilliant right-footed curler over the 'keeper from 14 yards.*
OWEN GOAL! 38 mins: *Owen, put through by Berger, beat the covering defender before firing a fierce low shot across into the left-hand corner.*
OWEN GOAL! 71 mins: (pen) *Riedle was hacked down by Alan Rogers to give away a penalty and Owen tucked away a right-footed spot-kick.*
OWEN GOAL! 77 mins: *Owen received a long throw from James and netted at the second try.*

60 WORTHINGTON CUP R3
TUESDAY OCTOBER 27, 1998

LIVERPOOL	**3**
FULHAM	**1**

Attendance: 22,296
Scorers: Morgan og 53, Fowler 66, Ince 76
The Game: Keegan's return to Anfield as manager of Fulham was not a happy one. Class eventually told as the visitors finally folded. Owen ran all night for The Reds before being replaced by Dundee for the last ten minutes of the game at Anfield.
Team: Friedel 7, McAteer 6, Staunton 7, Fowler 7, Owen 8 (sub 82 mins Dundee), Ince 9, Bjornebye 7, Carragher 7, Murphy 6, Thompson 7, Berger 7.

61 FA CARLING PREMIERSHIP
SATURDAY OCTOBER 31, 1998

LEICESTER CITY	**1**
LIVERPOOL	**0**

Attendance: 21,837
The Game: Cottee's strike was no more than The Foxes deserved after dominating their visitors. Liverpool midfielder McAteer completed a miserable day for The Reds as he was sent-off in the dying moments. Owen was again well marked by the Leicester defence, who are beginning to become a bogey team for the England striker.
Team: James 7, McAteer 5, Staunton 7, Ince 5, McManaman 6, Owen 6, Riedle 6, Heggem 7, Berger 6 (sub 80 mins Fowler), Bjornebye 6, Carragher 7.

62 UEFA CUP R2 L2
TUESDAY NOVEMBER 3, 1998

VALENCIA	**2**
LIVERPOOL	**2**

Attendance: 48,500
Scorers: McManaman 80, Berger 86
The Game: In an extraordinary finale Liverpool progressed to the third round of the UEFA Cup after Valencia appeared home and dry. The withdrawal of the dangerous Ilie with 15 minutes remaining coincided with Liverpool's late show, as a rare bullet header from McManaman and a Berger special turned the game on its head. The Spaniards did man-marked Owen, but failed to pick up wide men Berger and McManaman when it really mattered.
Team: James 8, Heggem 7 (sub 79 mins Dundee), Carragher 7, Staunton 6, Bjornebye 6, McManaman 7, Ince 6, Redknapp 7 (sub 90 mins Harkness), Fowler 5 (sub 84 mins McAteer), Owen 8.

63 FA CARLING PREMIERSHIP
SATURDAY NOVEMBER 7, 1998

LIVERPOOL	**1**
DERBY COUNTY	**2**

Attendance: 44,020
Scorers: Redknapp 84
The Game: Derby recorded a famous victory at Anfield, their first since 1970, as Liverpool slipped to their first home league defeat since February. Owen was out of sorts after three games in a week and looked like he could benefit from a good rest.
Team: James 6, Staunton 6, McManaman 6, Fowler 7, Owen 5, Redknapp 6, Heggem 5 (sub 66 mins Thompson 8), Berger 4 (sub 31 mins McAteer 5), Ince 5, Bjornebye 5, Carragher 6.

64 WORTHINGTON CUP R4
TUESDAY NOVEMBER 10, 1998

LIVERPOOL	**1**
TOTTENHAM HOTSPUR	**3**

Attendance: 20,772
Scorers: Owen 81
The Game: Roy Evans jumped out of the frying pan and into the fire after a wretched Liverpool performance at the hands of a slick and hungry looking Spurs. The half-hearted boos from the home fans summed up the Anfield apathy. Owen did all he could, but was replaced with ten minutes to go.
Team: Friedel 5, McAteer 4, Staunton 6, Leonhardsen 5 (sub 46 mins Riedle 6), Fowler 5, Owen 7 (sub 80 mins Murphy), Heggem 6, Ince 6, Bjornebye 6, Carragher 6, Thompson 8.
OWEN GOAL! 81 mins: *England's pint-size striker got a lucky rebound from his first effort to slot home left-footed from ten yards, but he picked up a hamstring injury in the process.*

65 FA CARLING PREMIERSHIP
SATURDAY NOVEMBER 21, 1998

ASTON VILLA	**2**
LIVERPOOL	**4**

Attendance: 39,241
Scorers: Ince 2, Fowler 7, 58, 66
The Game: The Premiership leaders were sent crashing to their first league defeat of the season by the classy Reds, thanks to an impressive hat-trick from Robbie Fowler. While Owen may have allowed Fowler to grab the goals and the headlines, but he still looked very much the part himself.
Team: James 7, Heggem, 7, Harkness (sub 8 mins Bjornebye 7), Babb 7, Staunton 7, Carragher 6, Redknapp 7, Berger 7 (sub 63 mins McAteer 6), Ince 7, Owen 7 (sub 79 mins Riedle), Fowler 9.

66 UEFA CUP R3 L1
TUESDAY NOVEMBER 24, 1998

CELTA VIGO	**3**
LIVERPOOL	**1**

Attendance: 31,800
Scorer: Owen 35
The Game: Celta Vigo gave Liverpool a lesson in attacking football and ran out deserved winners, despite falling behind to Owen's first-half effort. Liverpool were then outclassed by the Spanish side.
Team: James 7, Heggem 5, Kvarme 5, Staunton 7, Bjornebye 6, Berger 6 (sub 85 mins Babb), Redknapp 7, Carragher 6, Thompson 6 (sub 77 mins Riedle), Owen 8, Fowler 7.
OWEN GOAL! 35 mins: *A superb ball over the top of Vigo's defence by Thompson released Owen midway inside the opposition half for the England striker to beat Caceres for pace and coolly slide the ball past the advancing Dutruel from 12 yards out.*

67 FA CARLING PREMIERSHIP
SUNDAY NOVEMBER 29, 1998

LIVERPOOL	**2**
BLACKBURN ROVERS	**0**

Attendance: 41,753
Scorers: Ince 30, Owen 33
The Game: Liverpool brushed aside clueless Rovers to climb up to eighth in the table. The Reds dominated throughout the game, scoring twice in three first-half minutes with an Ince wonder-strike and Owen's fortunate second.
Team: James 7, Staunton 7 (sub 75 mins Kvarme), Babb 7, Fowler 6, Owen 7, Redknapp 8, Heggem 9 (sub 90 mins Gerrard), Berger 8, Ince 8, Bjornebye 7, Carragher 6.
OWEN GOAL! 33 mins: *Owen netted home from a lucky rebound off 'keeper Flowers, after Fowler's initial shot was parried away.*

68 FA CARLING PREMIERSHIP
SATURDAY DECEMBER 5, 1998

TOTTENHAM HOTSPUR	**2**
LIVERPOOL	**1**

Attendance: 36,125
Scorers: Berger 54
The Game: Spurs fully deserved their win despite needing Carragher's own goal to help them on their way. Liverpool rarely looked like taking anything from the game, while Armstrong and Ginola were a constant menace for Spurs. Fowler and Owen barely troubled a solid Tottenham defence.
Team: James 7, Staunton 7, Babb 7, Fowler 6, Owen 7, Heggem 6, Berger 8, Ince 7, Bjornebye 7 (sub 75 mins Murphy), Carragher 6, Gerrard 7 (sub 55 mins Thompson 7).

69 UEFA CUP R3 L2
TUESDAY DECEMBER 8, 1998

LIVERPOOL	**0**
CELTA VIGO	**1**

Attendance: 30,289
The Game: Liverpool crashed out of the UEFA Cup following a wonder goal by Revivo. The tie was almost over when a mistake by Babb let in Sanchez. Owen and Fowler caused problems to Celta Vigo but were unable to capitalise on any of the chances.
Team: James 6 (sub 63 mins Friedel 7), McAteer 6, Staunton 7, Babb 5 (sub 45 mins Murphy 7), Fowler 7, Owen 7, Berger 7, Matteo 6, Gerrard 6, Carragher 7, Thompson 7 (sub 58 mins Riedle 7).

70 FA CARLING PREMIERSHIP
SUNDAY DECEMBER 13, 1998

WIMBLEDON	**1**
LIVERPOOL	**0**

Attendance: 26,080
The Game: The Dons stretched their unbeaten home run to four, but they did it the hard way. For most of the game they were on the defensive and had to be grateful for the generosity of Owen. The England international wasted a delightful pass from Redknapp before missing a 78th-minute penalty.
Team: James 7, Staunton 6, Babb 7, Fowler 7 (sub 60 mins Riedle 7), Owen 6, Redknapp 7, Heggem 7, Berger 8, Ince 8, Bjornebye 7, Carragher 7.

71 FA CARLING PREMIERSHIP
SATURDAY DECEMBER 19, 1998

LIVERPOOL	**2**
SHEFFIELD WEDNESDAY	**0**

Attendance: 40,003
Scorers: Berger 18, Owen 33
The Game: Christmas came early for crisis-hit Liverpool with a well-earned 2-0 win. The Reds were in dire need of a pre-Christmas tonic after suffering their worst league run since 1954. Berger scored on 13 minutes and Owen killed the game off with a lovely move.
Team: James 7, Staunton 6, Babb 7, Fowler 5, Owen 8 (sub 88 mins Riedle), Redknapp 7, Heggem 9 (sub 83 mins Kvarme), Berger 7, Ince 7, Bjornebye 7, Carragher 7.
OWEN GOAL! 33 mins: *Owen jinked past Des Walker to blast home past Srnicek from 15 yards.*

72 FA CARLING PREMIERSHIP
SATURDAY DECEMBER 26, 1998

MIDDLESBROUGH	**1**
LIVERPOOL	**3**

Attendance: 34,626
Scorers: Owen 16, Redknapp 35, Heggem 88
The Game: Liverpool inflicted Boro's first league defeat at the Riverside Stadium for 14 months. The home side could have taken a two-goal lead in the opening exchanges but Liverpool improved their fluency and Heggem rounded off their display with a super individual goal. Owen and Fowler found the Boro defence hard work and were both substituted.
Team: James 6, Staunton 7, Fowler 7 (sub 60 mins Riedle 6), Owen 7 (sub 76 mins McManaman), Redknapp 8 (sub 89 mins Harkness), Heggem 8, Ince 6, Berger 7, Bjornebye 6, Babb 6, Carragher 8.
OWEN GOAL! 33 mins: *Carragher's goal-bound shot from a Staunton corner was turned in by the alert Owen, who pounced from close range.*

73 FA CARLING PREMIERSHIP
MONDAY DECEMBER 28, 1998

LIVERPOOL	**4**
NEWCASTLE	**2**

Attendance: 44,605
Scorers: Owen 66, 79, Riedle 71, 84
The Game: Liverpool ended the year on a high after they powered to a 4-2 victory over Newcastle. Gullit's revitalised troops looked like causing an upset, going 2-0 ahead with ten men. However, Liverpool sprang into life with four goals in 18 minutes with Owen suddenly finding his touch.
Team: James 7, Staunton 7, Babb 6 (sub 59 mins McAteer 6), McManaman 5 (sub 25 mins Gerrard 6 (sub 45 mins Thompson 6), Redknapp 7, Heggem 8, Riedle 9, Berger 7, Bjornebye 7, Carragher 7, Owen 8.
OWEN GOAL! 66 mins: *A 25-yard volley from Carragher was touched in by Owen from five yards.*
OWEN GOAL! 79 mins: *Jamie Redknapp's bobbling long-range effort rebounded off the post for Owen to score from just five yards.*

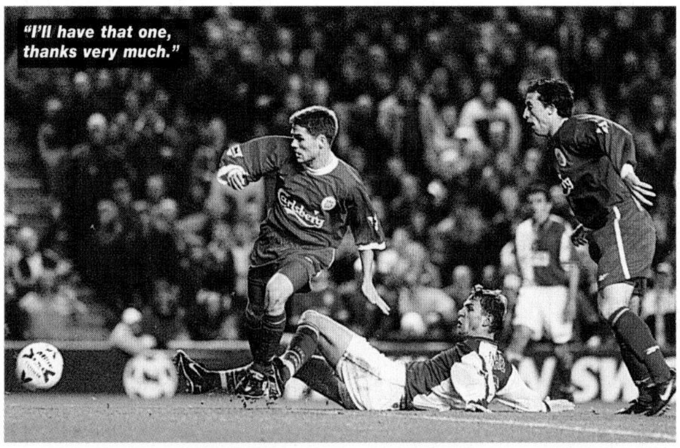

"I'll have that one, thanks very much."

74 FA CUP THIRD ROUND
SUNDAY JANUARY 3, 1999

PORT VALE	**0**
LIVERPOOL	**3**

Attendance: 16,557
Scorers: Owen 34, Ince 38, Fowler 90
The Game: Liverpool enjoyed this comfortable passage through to the fourth round and secured a clash with Man. United after an easy victory at Vale Park. Owen's penalty opened the scoring when the youngster proved too sharp for Dave Barnett.
Team: James 8, McAteer 8, Staunton 7, Babb 8, Owen 8, Redknapp 8, Riedle 8 (sub 61 mins Fowler 7), Berger 8, Ince 8, Bjornebye 7 (sub 70 mins Harkness 7), Carragher 7.
OWEN GOAL! 34 mins: *Owen glided past Beesley but was upended by Barnett. The striker placed his spot-kick low to Pilkington's right.*

75 FA CARLING PREMIERSHIP
SATURDAY JANUARY 9, 1999

ARSENAL	**0**
LIVERPOOL	**0**

Attendance: 38,107
The Game: The game might have ended in a 0-0 draw, but the game was far from unexciting. The Gunners' backline had the beating of Owen though, who was looking strangely out of sorts at Highbury.
Team: James 8, Staunton 6 (sub 62 mins Matteo 6), Babb 7, Fowler 7, Owen 5 (sub 88 mins Riedle), Redknapp 6, Harkness 7, Heggem 8, Berger 6, Ince 6, Carragher 7.

76 FA CARLING PREMIERSHIP
SATURDAY JANUARY 16, 1999

LIVERPOOL	**7**
SOUTHAMPTON	**1**

Attendance: 44,011
Scorers: Fowler 21, 36, 47, Matteo 35, Carragher 54, Owen 63, Thompson 73
The Game: Liverpool put on an exhibition of scintillating football against Southampton. It was an awful day for Saints' 'keeper Paul Jones who could do nothing right and the half-time introduction of Matt Le Tissier did little to halt the flood of goals.
Team: James 7, Babb 7, Fowler 9, Owen 8 (sub 72 mins Riedle), Redknapp 7, Heggem 8, Berger 7, Ince 7 (sub 72 mins Thompson), Bjornebye 7, Matteo 8, Carragher 8 (sub 79 mins Kvarme).
OWEN GOAL! 63 mins: *Owen rounded off a three-man move with a finish from five yards.*

77 FA CUP ROUND 4
SUNDAY JANUARY 24, 1999

MANCHESTER UNITED	**2**
LIVERPOOL	**1**

Attendance: 54,591
Scorers: Owen 3
The Game: United saved themselves from FA Cup elimination as two goals in the last two minutes saw them cancel out Owen's early header and secure their place in the Fifth Round of the competition.
Team: James 6, Fowler 6, Owen 6, Redknapp 6, Harkness 7, Heggem 9, Berger 8, Ince 7, (sub 71 mins McAteer), Bjornebye 6, Matteo 7, Carragher 7.
OWEN GOAL! 3 mins: *Owen scored a free header from close range as he nipped between Neville and Berg on the edge of the six-yard box.*

78 FA CARLING PREMIERSHIP
SATURDAY JANUARY 30, 1999

COVENTRY CITY	**2**
LIVERPOOL	**1**

Attendance: 23,056
Scorers: McManaman 86
The Game: The Sky Blues had the better of this exciting contest, ending Liverpool's five-match unbeaten run. Owen failed to shine up front and looked to be carrying a niggling thigh injury.
Team: James 6, Song 6 (sub 68 mins McManaman 5), Staunton 7 (sub 86 mins Gerrard), Heggem 7, Matteo 7, Ince 6, Redknapp 8, Berger 5 (sub 77 mins Riedle), Bjornebye 6, Fowler 6, Owen 6.

FIVE SCORING DEBUTS

Making that first appearance is likely to put the nerves on edge, but for Michael Owen it's just another game. **MATCH** picks out five of the Liverpool striker's goalscoring debuts.

PREMIERSHIP DEBUT
Liverpool v Wimbledon May 6, 1997

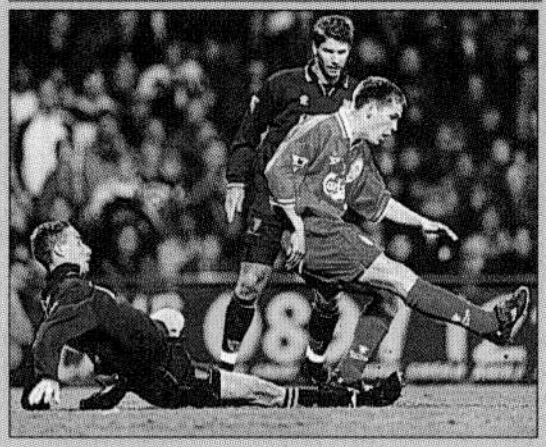

Owen became Liverpool's youngest ever goalscorer in an end of season encounter with bogey side Wimbledon in 1997. It was his first start as a professional footballer.

EUROPEAN DEBUT
Liverpool v Celtic Sep. 16, 1997

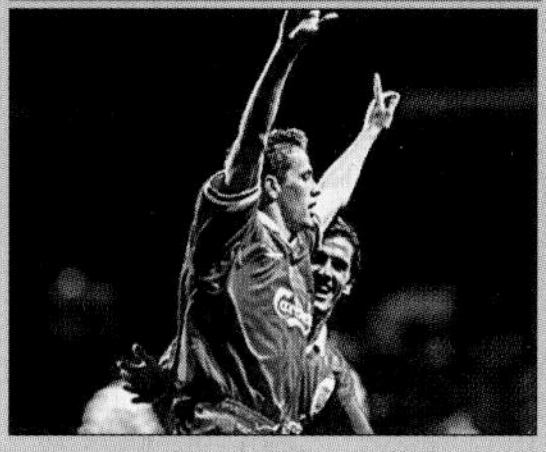

The European arena might be a frightening place to play, but Owen showed no nerves at all by netting after only six minutes of his European debut to set up a thrilling game.

LEAGUE CUP DEBUT
Liverpool v Grimsby Nov. 18, 1997

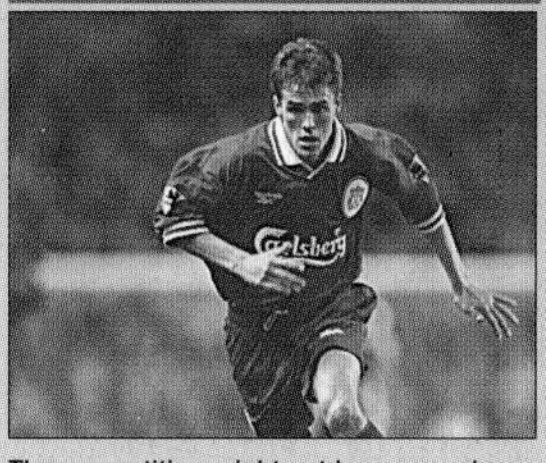

The competition might not be as grand as the FA Cup, but you'll never take away the hat-trick Owen scored against First Division Grimsby on his debut in the League Cup.

ENGLAND UNDER-21 DEBUT
England v Greece Dec. 17, 1997

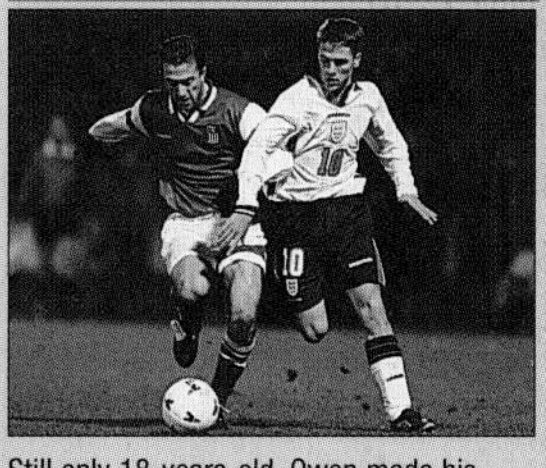

Still only 18-years-old, Owen made his England Under-21 debut against a strong Greek side, but they struggled to contain the rampant partnership of Heskey and Owen, in his only appearance for the U21s.

FA CUP DEBUT
Liverpool v Port Vale Jan. 3, 1997

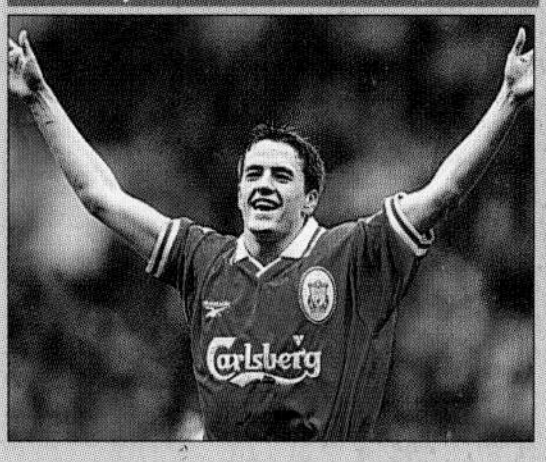

After 18 months, Owen finally got to play in his first FA Cup tie. Naturally he marked the occasion by scoring in the 3-0 victory over lowly Port Vale with a coolly taken penalty after he had been brought down in the box.

MICHAEL OWEN STORY

TAKEN FROM THE PAGES OF MATCHfacts

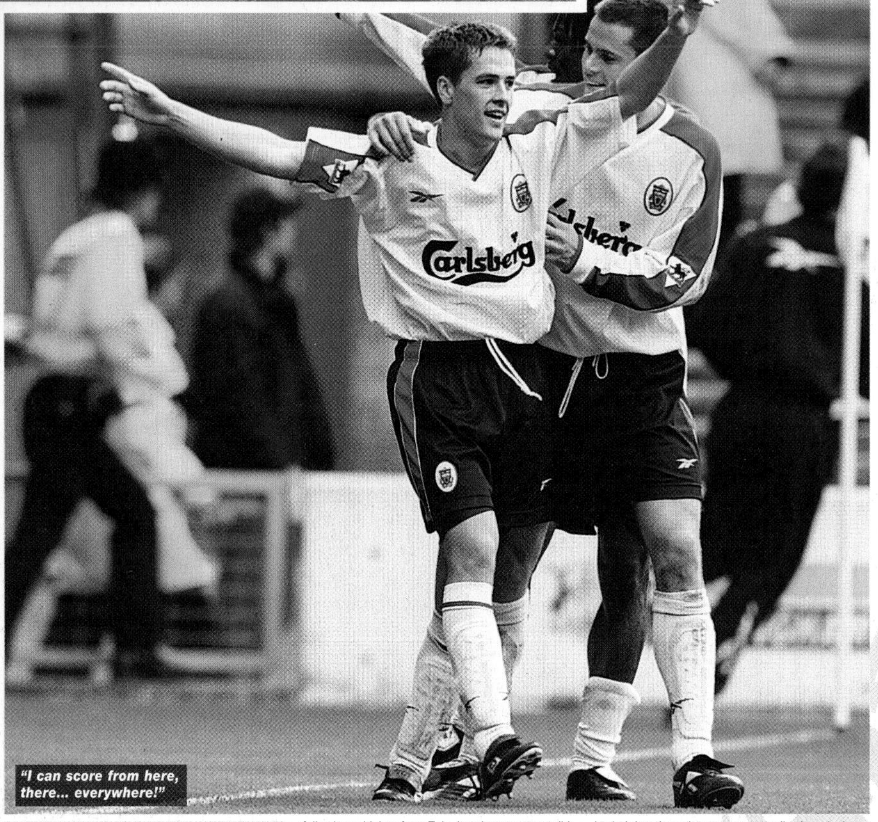

"I can score from here, there... everywhere!"

79 FA CARLING PREMIERSHIP
SATURDAY FEBRUARY 6, 1999

LIVERPOOL	3
MIDDLESBROUGH	1

Attendance: 44,384

Scorers: Owen 9, Heggem 44, Ince 45

The Game: Two goals in a minute before the break from Heggem and Ince added to Owen's 19th of the season and put The Reds in a strong position, despite being down to ten men.

Team: James 5, Staunton 6, Fowler 6, McManaman 7 (sub 81 mins Riedle), Owen 7 (sub 81 mins Gerrard), Ince 6, Redknapp 8, Heggem 7, Bjornebye 5, Matteo 5, Carragher 6.

***OWEN GOAL! 9 mins:** Redknapp's corner from the right-wing was headed away from goal by Ince before Robbie Fowler redirected it across the face of the goal for Owen to tap home.*

80 FA CARLING PREMIERSHIP
SATURDAY FEBRUARY 13, 1999

CHARLTON ATHLETIC	1
LIVERPOOL	0

Attendance: 20,043

The Game: Liverpool were very disappointing with Owen and Fowler failing to register a single shot on target. Carragher was ordered off the field for elbowing Charlton's on-loan striker Pringle.

Team: James 8, Staunton 6, Fowler 6, Carragher 6, McManaman 7, Owen 6 (sub 81 mins Riedle), Redknapp 7, Heggem 6 (sub 81 mins Gerrard), Ince 7, Bjornebye 6 (sub 74 mins Song), Matteo 7.

81 FA CARLING PREMIERSHIP
SATURDAY FEBRUARY 20, 1999

LIVERPOOL	2
WEST HAM UNITED	2

Attendance: 44,511

Scorers: Fowler 22, Owen 45

The Game: West Ham kept their hopes of a UEFA Cup place alive with a deserved draw at Anfield. There were nine first-teamers missing for West Ham, but Ferdinand was outstanding in defence and kept Owen at bay for most of the game.

Team: James 6, Song 8, Staunton 7, Babb 7, McManaman 6 (sub 65 mins Berger 6), Fowler 7, Owen 7, Redknapp 7, Heggem 9, Bjornebye 6 (sub 76 mins Riedle), Carragher 7.

***OWEN GOAL! 45 mins:** Owen ended a superb passing move involving Carragher, McManaman and Redknapp. Owen's long-range effort from 25 yards out left the 'keeper with no chance.*

82 FA CARLING PREMIERSHIP
SATURDAY FEBRUARY 27, 1999

CHELSEA	2
LIVERPOOL	1

Attendance: 34,822

Scorers: Owen 77

The Game: A brand new pitch but the same old result for Liverpool. Chelsea had ripped up the turf following criticism from Zola, but the new grass did nothing for Liverpool's poor record at the Bridge. Owen found it tough going against Leboeuf and Desailly, and did little apart from scoring late on.

Team: James 6, Kvarme 7, Babb 7, Fowler 7, Owen 7, Redknapp 7, Heggem (sub 9 mins McManaman), Berger 6 (sub 80 mins Riedle), Ince 7 (sub 47 mins Ferri 7), Bjornebye 7, Matteo 8.

***GOAL! 77 mins:** Owen beat the offside trap and clipped a right-footed chip over the advancing 'keeper from inside the Chelsea penalty box.*

83 FA CARLING PREMIERSHIP
SATURDAY MARCH 13, 1999

DERBY	3
LIVERPOOL	2

Attendance: 32,913

Scorers: Fowler 36, 57

The Game: Liverpool again paid the price for poor defending as Derby reinforced their challenge for a UEFA Cup place. All three of the home team's strikes resulted from some fundamental errors in defence and Liverpool's bad luck continued when Owen was withdrawn at half-time. The young striker suffered an injury going into a tough challenge with Derby central defender Spencer Prior.

Team: James 6, Song 6, Staunton 6 (sub 24 mins Bjornebye 6), Babb 6, Fowler 6, Owen 6 (sub 46 mins Riedle 6), Redknapp 8, Heggem 6, Berger 7, Matteo 6, Gerrard 6.

84 FA CARLING PREMIERSHIP
SATURDAY APRIL 3, 1999

LIVERPOOL	3
EVERTON	2

Attendance: 44,852

Scorers: Fowler 14, 20, Berger 83

The Game: Liverpool ended their bad run against their arch-rivals thanks to goals from Robbie Fowler and Patrik Berger in the 160th Merseyside derby. In the end it was Fowler took the scoring honours, but his strike partner Owen destroyed Everton's defence with his endless running, phenomenal pace and clever runs to take away defenders.

Team: James 7, Song 9, Staunton 6, McManaman 6, Fowler 8 (sub 85 mins Riedle), Owen 7, Redknapp 7, Heggem 7 (sub 70 mins Gerrard), Berger 8, Ince 8, Matteo 7.

85 FA CARLING PREMIERSHIP
MONDAY APRIL 5, 1999

NOTTINGHAM FOREST	2
LIVERPOOL	2

Attendance: 28,374

Scorers: Redknapp 15, Owen 72

The Game: Liverpool's skill in the first half earned them a thoroughly deserved lead through a cleverly worked free-kick routine. But once they found themselves ahead, The Reds took their foot off the gas. Forest dragged themselves back into the game with Rogers' equaliser, but Owen had other ideas and stepped forward to hammer home a trademark individual strike. The home side appeared dead and buried, but the points were eventually shared when van Hooijdonk struck home a glorious last-gasp free-kick to earn Nottingham Forest a point.

Team: James 6, Song 7, Staunton 6, McManaman 7 (sub 68 mins Riedle 7), Fowler 6 (sub 79 mins Gerrard), Owen 8, Redknapp 8, Berger 7, Ince 6, Matteo 7, Carragher 7.

***OWEN GOAL! 72 mins:** A long ball over the Forest defence found Owen in space. The young ace took one headed touch, superbly cushioning the ball into his path, before volleying right-footed past Crossley's right hand from 12 yards. It was a superb strike and one for the Owen scrapbook.*

86 FA CARLING PREMIERSHIP
MONDAY APRIL 12, 1999

LEEDS	0
LIVERPOOL	0

Attendance: 39,451

The Game: Leeds were on a great run, having won their previous seven games, equalling a club record, but they failed to score for the first time in two months when Liverpool visited Elland Road. Both sides passed the ball well, but United had most of the possession. Owen left the field on 25 minutes after suffering a thigh injury that would rule him out for the rest of the season and England's vital Euro qualifiers with Sweden and Bulgaria.

Team: James 6, Gerrard 7, Babb 7, Carragher 7, Matteo 7, Redknapp 6, Ince 7, Berger 7, Fowler 6, McManaman 6, Owen 6 (sub 25 mins Riedle 8).

87 FA CARLING PREMIERSHIP
SATURDAY AUGUST 28, 1999

LIVERPOOL	2
ARSENAL	0

Attendance: 44,886

Scorers: Fowler 8, Berger 76

The Game: Liverpool ran rings around an Arsenal side which found it hard to put away any chances that came their way. The Reds dominated the game and had gone ahead through a Fowler goal in the eighth minute. Berger made it two after 76 minutes and Houllier thought it would be a good occasion to bring Owen on for his first start of the new season. The striker came on with three minutes left, but didn't have time to impress an expectant Anfield.

Team: Westerveld 7, Song 7, Carragher 7, Redknapp 7, Hyypia 7, Berger 8, Matteo 7, Camara 9 (sub 89 mins Owen), Fowler 9, Thompson 7 (sub 70 mins Heggem 6), Gerrard 7.

88 FA CARLING PREMIERSHIP
SATURDAY SEPTEMBER 11, 1999

LIVERPOOL	2
MANCHESTER UNITED	3

Attendance: 44,929

Scorers: Hyypia (23), Berger (68)

The Game: Liverpool were 3-1 down when Owen came on to the field as a second-half substitute. Carragher was the villain when he put two own goals past Westerveld and left Liverpool with a mountain to climb. Even Andy Cole's sending-off for his second bookable offence didn't help and United held on to beat their North-West rivals.

Team: Westerveld 6, Song 7, Hyypia 7, Matteo 5, Carragher 5, Redknapp 7, Berger 8, Thompson 5 (sub 46 mins Smicer 6), Gerrard 5 (sub 64 mins Heggem 7), Fowler 6, Camara 5 (sub 64 mins Owen 6).

89 WORTHINGTON CUP R3 L1
TUESDAY SEPTEMBER 14, 1999

HULL CITY	1
LIVERPOOL	5

Attendance: 10,034

Scorer: Murphy 4, 31, Meijer 48, 75, Staunton 89

The Game: Liverpool dominated much of the game against their Third Division opposition, but The Reds seemed content to take a comfortable win back to Anfield rather than inflict a heavier defeat. Hull rallied in the final 20 minutes and were rewarded for their efforts with a consolation goal.

Team: Westerveld 6, Heggem 7, Hyypia 6, Traore 7, Staunton 7, Thompson 8, Carragher 6, Murphy 8, Smicer 8 (sub 46 mins Berger 6), Meijer 7, Owen 6 (sub 76 mins Camara).

90 FA CARLING PREMIERSHIP
SATURDAY SEPTEMBER 18, 1999

LEICESTER	2
LIVERPOOL	2

Attendance: 21,623

Scorers: Owen 23, 39

The Game: Owen made his first Premiership start of the season and showed Liverpool just why they had been missing him. His first goal was a penalty which sent Arphexad the wrong way in the Leicester goal after Taggart brought down Berger in the area. Owen's second, to put Liverpool 2-1 ahead, was side-footed into the net from just five yards out after a fine cross from Camara. But Owen's day was spoiled with Muzzy Izzet's 86th minute equaliser, sending The Reds home with just a point.

Team: Westerveld 7, Matteo 7, Hyypia 7, Heggem 6, Carragher 6, Berger 7, Thompson 6, Redknapp 6 (sub 79 mins Murphy), Gerrard 7, Camara 7 (sub 55 mins Meijer 6), Owen 8.

***OWEN GOAL! 23 mins:** Owen slotted home past the Leicester 'keeper after Berger had been fouled by Taggart in the penalty area.*

***OWEN GOAL! 39 mins:** Camara curled a cross from the left-wing which fell to the feet of Owen just five yards out. The England man wasted no time in firing the ball, side-footed into the net.*

91 FA CARLING PREMIERSHIP
MONDAY SEPTEMBER 27, 1999

LIVERPOOL	0
EVERTON	1

Attendance: 44,802

The Game: The game was marred by the fight between Liverpool 'keeper Westerveld and Everton striker Jeffers, for which they were both sent-off. The Reds also had substitute Gerrard sent-off for a high tackle in a pulsating end-to-end derby game which was won by the blue half of Merseyside.

Team: Westerveld 5, Staunton 6, Smicer 5 (sub 70 mins Camara 6), Fowler 6 (sub 64 mins Gerrard 4), Owen 6, Redknapp 6, Hyypia 6, Heggem 5, Berger 7, Hamann 5 (sub 64 mins Meijer 6), Carragher 6.

92 FA CARLING PREMIERSHIP
SATURDAY OCTOBER 2, 1999

ASTON VILLA	0
LIVERPOOL	0

Attendance: 39,217

The Game: This was an easily forgettable match as both sides pounded out a goalless draw to take a share of the spoils. Staunton was harshly sent-off for Liverpool when he encroached on a free-kick to earn his second bookable offence.

Team: Westerveld 7, Song 6, Hyypia 6, Henchoz 6, Staunton 5, Smicer 5 (sub 32 mins Gerrard 8), Hamann 7 (sub 72 mins Carragher), Redknapp 6, Berger 6, Meijer 7, Owen 6 (sub 81 mins Camara).

93 WORTHINGTON CUP R3 L2
WEDNESDAY OCTOBER 13, 1999

SOUTHAMPTON	2
LIVERPOOL	1

Attendance: 13,822

Scorer: Owen 53

The Game: Liverpool were unlucky to go out of the League Cup in the third round after The Saints scored an injury-time winner, but it would have been a different story if Owen had been on song. The star striker missed a string of chances to wrap the game up for Liverpool after he had earlier put The Reds ahead on 53 minutes.

Team: Friedel 6, Henchoz 7, Berger 6, Hyypia 6, Staunton 7, Song 6 (sub 74 mins Heggem), Carragher 6, Owen 7, Meijer 7, Redknapp 6, Thompson 8 (sub 81 mins Camara).

***OWEN GOAL! 53 mins:** Owen deftly took the ball from Southampton defender Claus Lundekvam and struck a low shot into the corner of the net from 12 yards.*

94 FA CARLING PREMIERSHIP
SATURDAY OCTOBER 16, 1999

LIVERPOOL	1
CHELSEA	0

Attendance: 44,826

Scorer: Thompson 47

The Game: Owen was involved in the goal and he could have made it 2-0. The striker was fouled near the touchline by Chelsea defender Leboeuf and Thompson scored for The Reds from the resulting free-kick. Owen could have made it two when he stepped up to take a penalty after Murphy had been fouled in the area by Desailly, but he missed.

Team: Friedel 6, Henchoz 6, Song 7, Staunton 6, Smicer 7, Owen 5 (sub 86 mins Meijer), Redknapp 7, Hyypia 7, Carragher 7, Murphy 8 (sub 80 mins Heggem), Thompson 6.

95 FA CARLING PREMIERSHIP
SATURDAY OCTOBER 23, 1999

SOUTHAMPTON	1
LIVERPOOL	1

Attendance: 15,241

Scorer: Camara 81

The Game: Owen had a miserable afternoon as Liverpool had to cling on for a point, just ten days after they had gone out of the League Cup at The Dell. Owen started the match on the subs' bench after the disappointing game he had against Chelsea the week before. He came on early in the second half and missed a good opportunity to equalise before limping off with a hamstring injury. With ten men left on the field, it was left to Camara, who had a superb game for The Reds to equalise late on.

Team: Friedel 7, Henchoz 6, Song 7, Staunton 6, Smicer 6 (sub 73 mins Heggem), Redknapp 7, Hyypia 7, Meijer 6 (sub 58 mins Owen 6), Camara 8, Carragher 6, Murphy 6 (sub 58 mins Thompson 6).

96 FA CARLING PREMIERSHIP
SATURDAY NOVEMBER 20, 1999

SUNDERLAND	0
LIVERPOOL	2

Attendance: 42,015

Scorer: Owen 62, Berger 85

The Game: Owen helped Liverpool to their fourth win in a row at The Stadium Of Light, but it was perhaps their most important as they inflicted Sunderland's first home defeat in 12 months. The sides looked evenly matched on the day, except for a fine performance by Westerveld in the Reds goal and Owen's finishing up front. He took his goal well and set Liverpool up nicely for their

Team: Westerveld 8, Song 7, Henchoz 7, Hyypia 7, Matteo 7, Gerrard 6 (sub 81 mins Thompson), Hamann 6, Redknapp 6, Murphy 6 (sub 73 mins Meijer), Berger 7, Owen 6 (sub 90 mins Heggem).

***GOAL! 62 mins:** Owen held off Craddock, then stumbled through a Sunderland defender's tackle before toe-poking the ball over Sorensen.*

MICHAEL OWEN'S CLUB STRIKE PARTNERS

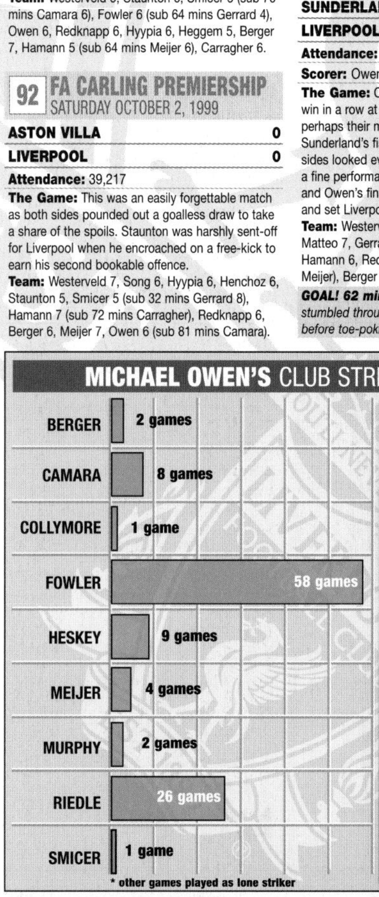

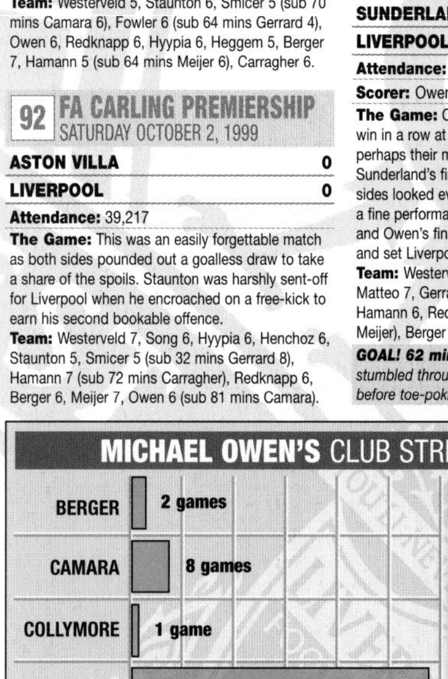
BERGER
2 games
CAMARA
8 games
COLLYMORE
1 game
FOWLER
58 games
HESKEY
9 games
MEIJER
4 games
MURPHY
2 games
RIEDLE
26 games
SMICER
1 game

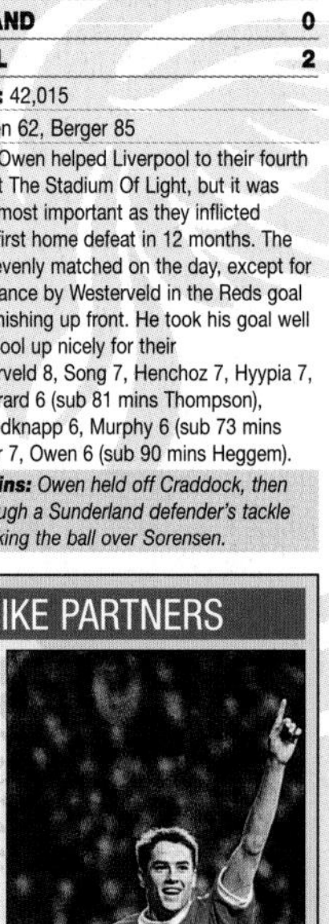

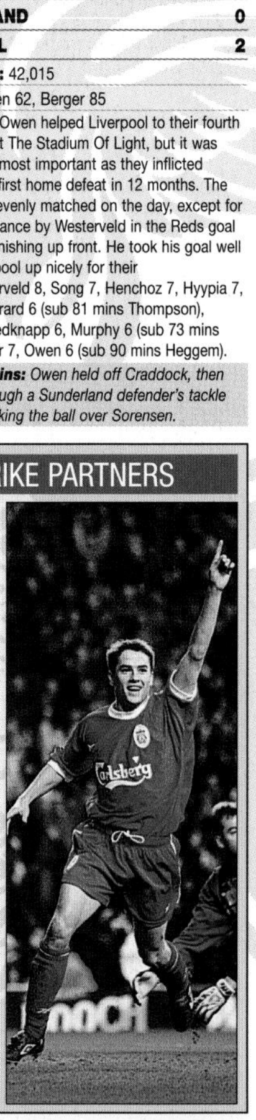

* other games played as lone striker

97 FA CARLING PREMIERSHIP
SATURDAY NOVEMBER 27, 1999

WEST HAM UNITED 1
LIVERPOOL 0

Attendance: 26,043

The Game: It wasn't Michael Owen's day. First he was booked for a theatrical dive in front of goal, which wasted a good chance to put The Reds in front. He had a goal disallowed and then he limped off with a recurrence of his hamstring injury with just 15 minutes left on the clock. It wasn't an enjoyable day for Liverpool either. Despite dominating the second half, they couldn't make their chances count and lost out to a solitary Trevor Sinclair goal.

Team: Westerveld 6, Henchoz 6, Song 6 (sub 69 mins Meijer 5), Owen 5 (sub 74 mins Staunton), Hyypia 7, Heggem 7, Hamann 6, Matteo 6, Murphy 6, Gerrard 6, Berger (sub 18 mins Thompson 7).

98 FA CARLING PREMIERSHIP
SUNDAY DECEMBER 5, 1999

LIVERPOOL 4
SHEFFIELD WEDNESDAY 1

Attendance: 42,517

Scorers: Hyypia 21, Murphy 41, Gerrard 69, Thompson 79

The Game: Wednesday stunned Liverpool at Anfield by going 1-0 up, but The Reds were soon level and romped home comfortably in the end.

Team: Westerveld 7, Henchoz 6, Song 6 (sub 73 mins Carragher), Owen 6 (sub 81 mins Fowler), Hyypia 7, Hamann 6, Camara 7, Murphy 7 (sub 77 mins Staunton), Thompson 8, Gerrard 8.

99 FA CUP THIRD ROUND
SUNDAY DECEMBER 12, 1999

HUDDERSFIELD TOWN 0
LIVERPOOL 2

Attendance: 23,678

Scorers: Camara 36, Matteo 59

The Game: Huddersfield took the game to The Reds in the first half and Camara's goal came against the run of play. But The Reds looked more composed in the second half and made sure of progression to the next round with Matteo's strike.

Team: Westerveld 7, Henchoz 7, Staunton 6 (sub 35 mins Matteo 7), Smicer 7 (sub 72 mins Song), Owen 7, Hyypia 8, Hamann 7, Camara 8, Carragher 7, Murphy 8, Gerrard 8 (sub 88 mins Newby).

100 FA CARLING PREMIERSHIP
SATURDAY DECEMBER 18, 1999

LIVERPOOL 2
COVENTRY CITY 0

Attendance: 44,024

Scorers: Owen 45, Camara 74

The Game: England manager Kevin Keegan turned up to watch and Owen turned on the style to produce his best display since returning from injury. He deserved his goal, but Liverpool had to work hard to secure a second through Camara.

Team: Westerveld 6, Gerrard 7, Henchoz 5, Hyypia 7, Matteo 6, Thompson 6 (sub 36 mins Smicer 7), Hamann 6, Carragher 5, Berger 5, Owen 7, Camara 8 (sub 86 mins Heggem).

***OWEN GOAL! 45 mins:** Owen received the ball from Matteo and turned Breen before poking the ball past the advancing goalkeeper.*

101 FA CARLING PREMIERSHIP
SUNDAY DECEMBER 26, 1999

NEWCASTLE UNITED 2
LIVERPOOL 2

Attendance: 36,445

Scorer: Owen 31, 53

The Game: Owen put in another outstanding performance to answer his critics, but it took two defensive errors to help him score. Newcastle had gone ahead early on, but Owen steered Liverpool into the lead with two well-taken goals. Newcastle equalised on 66 minutes to spoil the striker's party.

Team: Westerveld 6, Song 7, Matteo 7, Hyypia 7, Carragher 7, Hamann 6, Gerrard 7, Murphy 6 (sub 82 mins Fowler), Camara 7 (sub 69 mins Heggem 6), Owen 9, Berger 6.

***OWEN GOAL! 32 mins:** Rifled in from eight yards after Pistone had failed to cut out a throughball from Hamann in Liverpool's midfield.*
***OWEN GOAL! 53 mins:** Slid the ball into the goal after a terrible backpass from Dabizas.*

102 FA CARLING PREMIERSHIP
TUESDAY DECEMBER 28, 1999

LIVERPOOL 3
WIMBLEDON 1

Attendance: 44,107

Scorers: Owen 58, Berger 68, Fowler 79

The Game: Owen made it a very happy Christmas at Anfield with another goal over the festive period. His goal livened up what was proving to be a very dull game and he gave Liverpool the kick-start they needed. Both teams went all-out in attack after Owen's goal and it proved to be an exciting game.

Team: Westerveld 7, Heggem 7, Hyypia 8, Henchoz 7, Matteo 7, Murphy 6 (sub 59 mins Fowler 7), Gerrard 8, Carragher 7, Berger 7, Owen 8 (sub 65 mins Smicer 7), Camara 6 (sub 90 mins Song).

***OWEN GOAL! 58 mins:** A Murphy cross from the left was inexplicably missed by the Wimbledon defence. It fell to Owen one yard out and he made no mistake, lashing the ball into the roof of the net.*

103 FA CARLING PREMIERSHIP
SATURDAY JANUARY 15, 2000

WATFORD 2
LIVERPOOL 3

Attendance: 21,367

Scorers: Berger 10, Thompson 41, Smicer 71

The Game: Owen helped The Reds gain revenge on Watford after the 1-0 defeat at Anfield earlier in the season. The striker was pleased to be back after missing the last two games for Liverpool.

Team: Westerveld 6, Carragher 7, Henchoz 7, Hyypia 7, Matteo 6, Thompson 7, Hamann 7 (sub 62 mins Smicer), Berger 8, Gerrard 9, Owen 7 (sub 73 mins Murphy), Camara 6 (sub 74 mins Staunton).

104 FA CARLING PREMIERSHIP
SATURDAY JANUARY 22, 2000

LIVERPOOL 0
MIDDLESBROUGH 0

Attendance: 44,324

The Game: Owen was taken off after just 28 minutes when he fell awkwardly while crossing a ball. Liverpool failed to get over that loss and their young side couldn't pull themselves out of their bad run of form. Boro packed their defence and without Owen, The Reds found it hard to break through.

Team: Westerveld 6, Matteo 7, Hyypia 7, Henchoz 6, Carragher 5, Berger 6, Gerrard 7, Hamann 7, Thompson 6 (sub 57 mins Murphy 5), Owen 7 (sub 28 mins Meijer 5), Smicer 5 (sub 76 mins Newby).

105 FA CARLING PREMIERSHIP
SATURDAY MARCH 4, 2000

MANCHESTER UNITED 1
LIVERPOOL 1

Attendance: 61,592

Scorer: Berger 27

The Game: Although Owen was fit enough to be considered, Houllier opted for the strike partnership of Meijer and Camara and left him on the bench. Owen did get on the field for the last 13 minutes, replacing Camara. But while Liverpool had a good first half, they failed to convert possession to goals.

Team: Westerveld 7, Henchoz 7, Smicer 7, Hyypia 6 (sub 46 mins Murphy 7), Heggem 6 (sub 18 mins Song 6), Berger 7, Hamann 7, Meijer 6, Matteo 6, Camara 6 (sub 77 mins Owen).

106 FA CARLING PREMIERSHIP
SATURDAY MARCH 11, 2000

LIVERPOOL 1
SUNDERLAND 1

Attendance: 44,693

Scorer: Berger (pen) 2

The Game: Owen was again left on the subs' bench as Meijer partnered new signing Heskey in the Liverpool attack. But the crowd at Anfield got a glimpse of what is to come, for Liverpool and England, when Owen partnered Heskey up front after replacing the hard-working Meijer.

Team: Westerveld 6, Matteo 7, Hyypia 6, Henchoz 6, Song 5 (sub 82 mins Camara), Berger 7, Hamann 7, Carragher 7, Gerrard 7 (sub 46 mins Murphy 5), Meijer 6 (sub 76 mins Owen), Heskey 8.

107 FA CARLING PREMIERSHIP
WEDNESDAY MARCH 15, 2000

LIVERPOOL 0
ASTON VILLA 0

Attendance: 43,615

The Game: Much was expected in the first game of the new strike partnership of Heskey and Owen, but Owen had a nightmare and was taken off after 66 minutes. Earlier in the game Owen stepped up to take a penalty after Berger had been fouled in the area but missed. He was replaced by Camara after failing to make an impact, but even the Guinean striker couldn't provide the inspiration for victory.

Team: Westerveld 6, Henchoz 7, Heskey 6, Hyypia 7, Berger 6, Hamann 6, Carragher 6, Thompson 6 (sub 82 mins Meijer), Gerrard 6 (sub 78 mins Redknapp), Owen 5 (sub 66 mins Camara 5).

108 FA CARLING PREMIERSHIP
SATURDAY MARCH 18, 2000

DERBY COUNTY 0
LIVERPOOL 2

Attendance: 33,378

Scorer: Owen 17, Camara 86

With Owen spearheading the Reds attack, Liverpool looked a constant threat against struggling Derby. It was a much better display from Heskey and Owen, but they should have inflicted a heavier defeat on The Rams. Owen put Liverpool in front early on in the game with a good finish, and the second goal came from Camara in the dying minutes.

Team: Westerveld 6, Henchoz 7, Heskey 6 (sub 88 mins Redknapp), Hyypia 8, Owen 7 (sub 72 mins Camara), Berger 7, Hamann 7, Matteo 6, Carragher 6, Thompson 7, Gerrard 7.

***OWEN GOAL! 17 mins:** Hyypia played a long ball upfield to Owen, who was allowed the space to send a right-footed shot into the bottom corner.*

109 FA CARLING PREMIERSHIP
SATURDAY APRIL 1, 2000

COVENTRY CITY 0
LIVERPOOL 3

Attendance: 23,098

Scorer: Owen 23, 37, Heskey 78

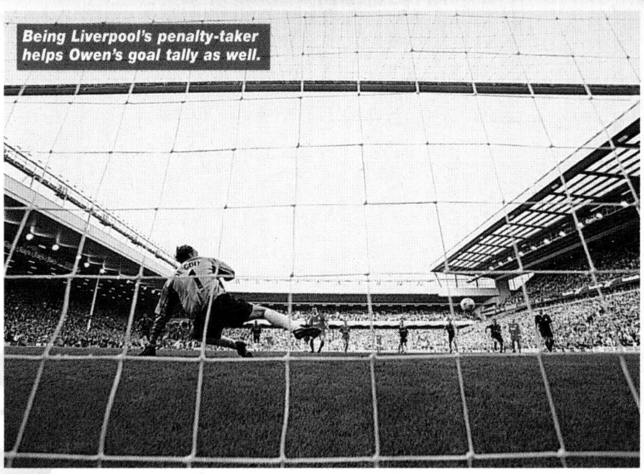
Being Liverpool's penalty-taker helps Owen's goal tally as well.

The Game: Liverpool striker Owen was back to his best as The Reds stretched their unbeaten run to 11 games. Owen very nearly had the hat-trick his performance deserved, but his third effort was saved well by veteran Coventry 'keeper Ogrizovic. Manager Houllier was afforded the luxury of resting his star striker near the end of the game.

Team: Westerveld 7, Henchoz 7, Matteo 8, Hyypia 8, Carragher 8, Gerrard 7 (sub 70 mins Murphy 6), Hamann 7, Thompson 8, Berger 8, Heskey 8, Owen 9 (sub 80 mins Camara).

***OWEN GOAL! 23 mins:** Gerrard opened up the defence with a perfect pass to Owen, who finished off with a fierce right-foot shot from 15 yards out.*
***OWEN GOAL! 37 mins:** Matteo made the goal with a cross to Owen, and the move ended with the England striker shrugging off two defenders before steering the ball past Ogrizovic.*

110 FA CARLING PREMIERSHIP
SUNDAY APRIL 9, 2000

LIVERPOOL 2
TOTTENHAM HOTSPUR 0

Attendance: 44,536

Scorer: Berger 34, Owen 61

The Game: Owen helped Liverpool move into second place with a simple tap-in to make it 2-0 after Berger's earlier effort. Spurs hadn't proved strong opposition apart from the odd moment of magic from on the left-wing from Ginola. Liverpool dominated the entire game and in the end The Reds were well worth their 2-0 victory, and were looking good for a high finish in the Premiership.

Team: Westerveld 6, Henchoz 7, Heskey 8, Owen 7 (sub 87 mins Camara), Hyypia 7, Berger 7, Hamann 6, Matteo 7, Carragher 7, Murphy 7 (sub 82 mins Heggem), Thompson 7 (sub 72 mins Smicer).

***OWEN GOAL! 61 mins:** Heskey showed good work on the wing and his dangerous cross flew in to the edge of the six-yard box, where Owen was lurking with intent for a simple tap-in.*

111 FA CARLING PREMIERSHIP
SUNDAY APRIL 16, 2000

WIMBLEDON 1
LIVERPOOL 2

Attendance: 26,102

Scorer: Heskey 36, 62

The Game: Owen set up the first goal for Heskey, in what was a much better showing than in recent games from the pair up front. Owen should have got his name on the scoresheet as well, with Liverpool dominant in the first half. Relegation-threatened Wimbledon fought back late on in a vain search for a point, but Liverpool held on for a vital away win in their quest to finish in third place in the Premiership and secure qualification for the Champions League in the 2001-2002 season.

Team: Westerveld 7, Henchoz 7, Heskey 7 (sub 78 mins Camara), Owen 7 (sub 83 mins Murphy), Hyypia 8, Berger 8, Hamann 8, Matteo 7, Carragher 8, Thompson 8 (sub 61 mins Smicer 7), Gerrard 7.

112 FA CARLING PREMIERSHIP
FRIDAY APRIL 21, 2000

EVERTON 0
LIVERPOOL 0

Attendance: 40,052

The Game: Even the dream team partnership of Owen and the fit-again Fowler in the second half couldn't resuscitate Liverpool's hopes of a derby victory. The chances were few and far between, as the game soon turned into a battle for supremacy in midfield and with both sides making silly mistakes. The game, just like the first derby of the season at Anfield, was shrouded in controversy because the referee disallowed a late Everton goal. Westerveld, in the Liverpool goal, hit Hutchison's back while he was taking a free-kick and the ball rebounded into the empty net. The home fans were absolutely furious with the decision to disallow the goal and Liverpool were lucky to go home with a point.

Team: Westerveld 6, Carragher 6, Henchoz 6, Hyypia 6, Matteo 7, Thompson 5 (sub 55 mins Heggem 6), Hamann 6, Gerrard 6, Berger 7, Heskey 6 (sub 46 mins Fowler 5), Owen 6.

113 FA CARLING PREMIERSHIP
SATURDAY APRIL 29, 2000

CHELSEA 2
LIVERPOOL 0

Attendance: 34,957

The Game: Liverpool were totally outplayed by a Chelsea side which had been challenged to play for their futures by Vialli after some poor recent showings. Even though Owen was one of four Reds strikers on the pitch for the last 15 minutes, they failed to find a way past Man Of The Match Desailly or even pull back the deficit at Stamford Bridge.

Team: Westerveld 7, Henchoz 7, Heskey 6, Matteo 6, Owen 6, Hyypia 7, Berger 6, Hamann 8 (sub 65 mins Camara 5), Carragher 5, Murphy 6 (sub 75 mins Fowler), Gerrard 6 (sub 51 mins Redknapp 6).

114 FA CARLING PREMIERSHIP
SUNDAY MAY 14, 2000

BRADFORD CITY 1
LIVERPOOL 0

Attendance: 18,276

The Game: Houllier had rested his star striker for the previous game against Southampton, but Owen returned to the starting line-up to partner Heskey against Bradford. Liverpool had good chances, but failed to score despite winning 10 corners. A single Wetherall goal was enough to separate the sides in what was an end-of-season decider. Bradford's win meant they stayed in the Premiership, while defeat for Liverpool meant they finished fourth in the table, and would play in the UEFA Cup rather than the Champions League in the 2000-2001 season.

Team: Westerveld 7, Henchoz 7, Heskey 6, Owen 6, Redknapp 6, Hyypia 7, Hamann 6, Berger 6 (sub 61 mins Camara 7), Matteo 6 (sub 82 mins Meijer), Carragher 7, Gerrard 6 (sub 61 mins Smicer 6).

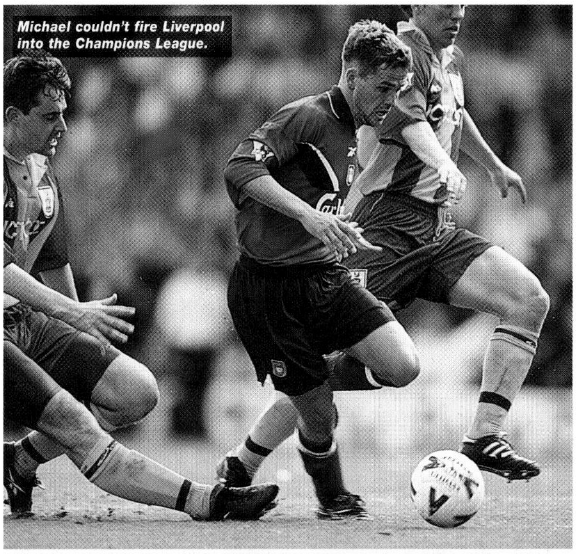
Michael couldn't fire Liverpool into the Champions League.

MIKE'S STRIKES!

The sign of any great striker is netting loads of goals, but Michael Owen's gone one further than that by scoring his share of classic strikes. Here's Michael's top five!

LIVERPOOL v BLACKBURN
August 23, 1997 Premiership

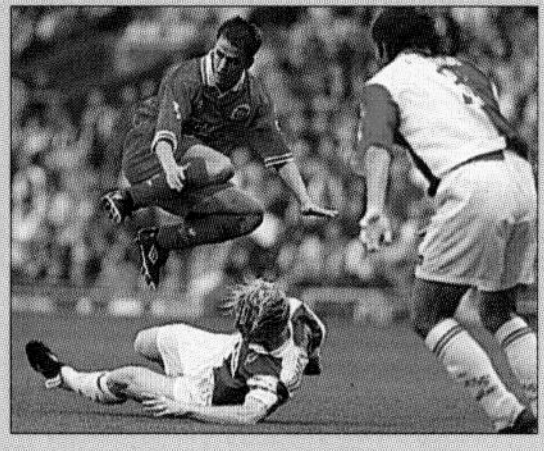

Keen tackling won Michael the ball from Jason Wilcox and he ran a full 50 yards before finishing with a beautifully placed shot low past Rovers 'keeper Tim Flowers.

ENGLAND v ARGENTINA
June 30, 1998 World Cup Finals

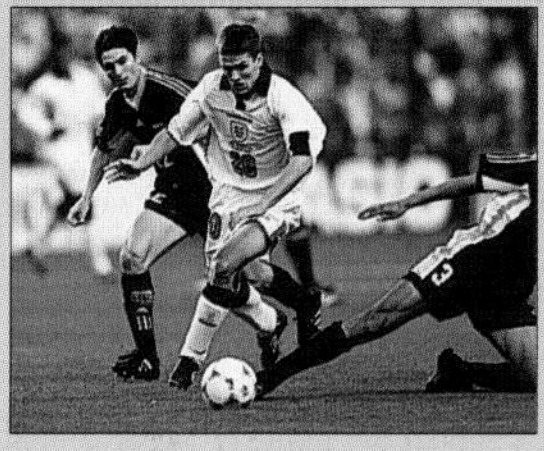

One of the all-time classic international goals, Michael picked up the ball on the halfway line, made fools of Chamot and Ayala before placing an unstoppable shot past Carlos Roa into the top corner.

NEWCASTLE v LIVERPOOL
August 30, 1998 Premiership

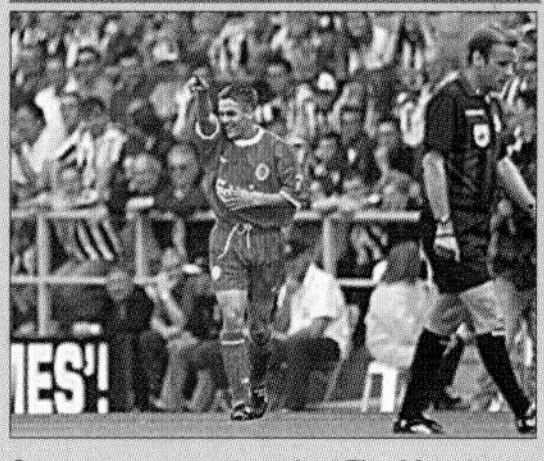

Owen was rampant against The Magpies as he stole the ball from Charvet, raced down the left, shrugged off Albert and – as Given came out – shot past the 'keeper with the outside of his foot for a memorable goal.

LIVERPOOL v NOTT'M FOREST
November 10, 1998 League Cup

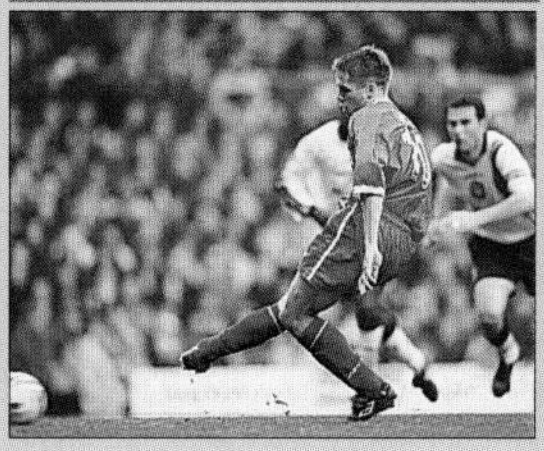

Patrik Berger hit a throughball for Owen to chase and the young striker showed great composure and skill to coolly send a curled right-footer over stranded 'keeper Beasant.

COVENTRY v LIVERPOOL
April 1, 2000 Premiership

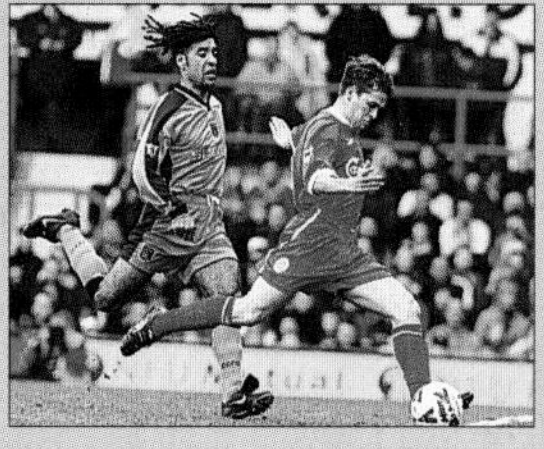

Receiving the ball from the left, Owen freed himself from Richard Shaw to make a yard of space before disposing of Colin Hendry and burying a crisp, low shot into the net.

MICHAEL OWEN STORY
TAKEN FROM THE PAGES OF MATCHfacts

Who will ever forget Owen's goal against Argentina?

Michael did everything he could in the European Championships, but it just didn't go right for England.

MICHAEL OWEN BURST ON TO THE INTERNATIONAL SCENE IN FEBRUARY 1998 becoming the youngest ever England player to pull on the Three Lions shirt. He nearly scored within a few minutes of taking to the pitch and walked off it with the Man Of The Match award, despite a 2-0 defeat against Chile. A few months later, Owen had established himself in the team and made his mark on football's highest stage by scoring a spectacular solo effort against Argentina in the World Cup. Although he couldn't help England to success at Euro 2000, he has become England's first-choice striker after Alan Shearer's retirement from international football. MATCH gives you the definitive guide to his brief, but already memorable England career match-by-match.

1 INTERNATIONAL FRIENDLY
WEDNESDAY FEBRUARY 11, 1998

ENGLAND 0
CHILE 2

Attendance: 65,228
The Game: Michael Owen was handed his full international debut against Chile, which meant he broke the record as the youngest player to wear an England senior shirt. With only six minutes on the clock, Owen nearly maintained his record of scoring on every debut in an England shirt but 'keeper Tapia pushed the ball away after the Liverpool striker shot from ten yards. Despite failing to score, Owen was named Man Of The Match in his first England game.
Team: Martyn 6, Neville, P 6 (sub 46 mins Le Saux 6), Campbell 6, Batty 6 (sub 62 mins Ince 6), Adams 7, Neville, G 7, Lee 6, Butt 7, Dublin 8, Sheringham 5 (sub 62 mins Shearer 6), Owen 9.

2 INTERNATIONAL FRIENDLY
WEDNESDAY MARCH 25, 1998

SWITZERLAND 1
ENGLAND 1

Attendance: 17,000
Scorers: Merson 70
After making a number of changes to the line-up, England struggled through the first-half of this game against Switzerland. Owen partnered Shearer up front for the first time, but the Liverpool youngster was kept out of the game for much of the opening period. With little to play for, Hoddle replaced Owen with Sheringham with just over 20 minutes to go.
Team: Flowers 7, Keown 8, Hinchcliffe 6, Ince 8, Southgate 6, Ferdinand, R 7, McManaman 6, Merson 8 (sub 81 mins Batty), Shearer 7, Owen 6 (sub 69 mins Sheringham 6), Lee 6.

3 INTERNATIONAL FRIENDLY
WEDNESDAY APRIL 22, 1998

ENGLAND 3
PORTUGAL 0

Attendance: 63,463
Scorers: Shearer 5, 65, Sheringham 46
The Game: Owen came on for Sheringham in the 77th minute and he was close to scoring straight away, but the ball thundered into the side netting. In trying to score his first goal for England, Owen was brought down in the penalty area by 'keeper Baia, although the referee did not award a penalty.
Team: Seaman 9, Neville, G 7 (sub 81 mins Neville, P), Le Saux 9, Ince 7, Adams 8, Campbell 7, Beckham 5 (sub 45 mins Merson 7), Batty, Shearer 9, Sheringham 7 (sub 77 mins Owen), Scholes 7.

4 KING HASSAN II TOURNAMENT
WEDNESDAY MAY 27, 1998

ENGLAND 1
MOROCCO 0

Attendance: 80,000
Scorers: Owen 59
The Game: Owen came on at Wembley in the 25th minute after Ian Wright suffered a hamstring injury. Only eight minutes after coming on, Owen was also taken off the pitch after an accidental clash with the Moroccan goalkeeper. The striker's first chance, after he returned to the field, came when McManaman played a superb ball through the defence, but Owen was ruled offside. His moment finally arrived in the 59th minute when he burst through to score the only goal of the game.

Team: Flowers, Keown, Le Saux, Ince, Campbell, Southgate, Anderton, Gascoigne, Dublin (sub 79 mins L Ferdinand, Wright (sub 26 mins Owen), McManaman.
NB. No MATCHfacts ratings for the King Hassan II tournament.

OWEN GOAL! 59 mins: *Running past Rossi on to Steve McManaman's throughball, Owen closed in on goal from 40 yards and placed the ball past the 'keeper into the corner of the net to become the youngest player ever to score for England.*

5 KING HASSAN II TOURNAMENT
FRIDAY MAY 29, 1998

BELGIUM Belgium won 4-3 on pens 0
ENGLAND 0

Attendance: 25,000.
The Game: With little going in England's favour, Glenn Hoddle made a few changes at half-time. Owen and Rio Ferdinand replaced the two Neville brothers and the squad changed to a 3-5-2 system. With time running out, Scifo almost stole victory for Belgium in normal time, but it was not to be. Owen had few opportunities to stamp his authority on the game and the game was settled on penalties, with Belgium coming out on top.
Team: Martyn, Neville, G (Sub 45 mins Ferdinand, R), Neville, P (sub 45 mins Owen), Butt, Campbell (sub 76 mins Dublin), Keown, Lee, Gascoigne (sub 50 mins Beckham), Ferdinand, L , Merson, Le Saux.
NB. No MATCHfacts ratings for the King Hassan II tournament.

6 WORLD CUP FINALS
MONDAY JUNE 15, 1998

ENGLAND 2
TUNISIA 0

Attendance: 54,587
Scorers: Shearer 42, Scholes 90
The Game: As soon as the World Cup squad was announced people were called for Owen's inclusion in the starting line-up, but Hoddle elected to go with experience and chose to start with Sheringham for England's opening game. Alan Shearer opened the scoring just before half-time with a header, but England failed to capitalise on their lead until Owen, the third youngest player to participate in the World Cup Finals, was introduced with five minutes to go. Scholes grabbed a classy second goal from the edge of the box in the last minute of the game.
Team: Seaman 7, Campbell 8, Adams 8, Southgate 7, Le Saux 7, Anderton 8, Ince 8, Batty 8, Shearer 8, Sheringham 7 (sub 85 mins Owen), Scholes 9.

7 WORLD CUP FINALS
MONDAY JUNE 22, 1998

ROMANIA 2
ENGLAND 1

Attendance: 36,500
Scorers: Owen 83
The Game: This game only really came to life in the second-half, when Romanian striker Moldovan put his side ahead. It looked all over for England until Owen came on as a lively substitute after 73 minutes. Within ten minutes the Liverpool striker had equalised, scoring from close range following a good passing move. But things turned sour when Petrescu scored the winner for Romania. He broke free down the left, beat Chelsea team-mate Le Saux to a loose ball and fired a weak shot through the legs of Seaman. Owen had a late chance to get an equaliser, but was denied by the post at the death.

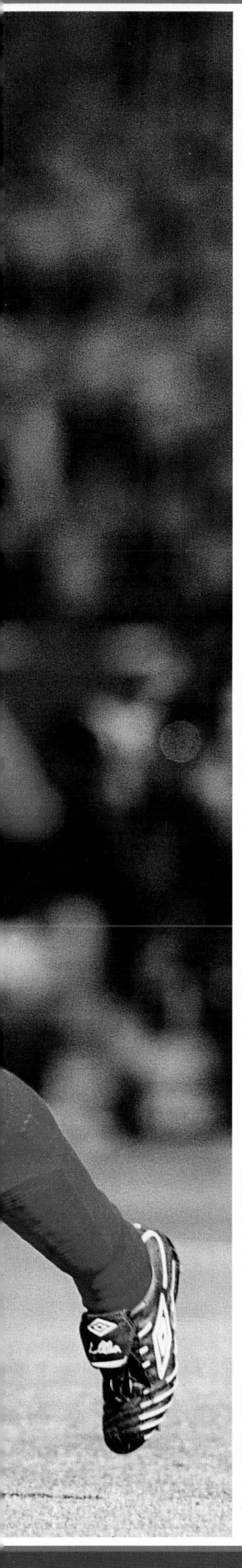

Team: Seaman 7, Campbell 8, Adams 7, Neville, G 7, Le Saux 8, Anderton 7, Ince 6 (sub 33 mins Beckham 8), Batty 8, Shearer 7, Sheringham 6 (sub Owen 73 mins), Scholes 7.

OWEN GOAL! 83 mins: *Scholes, Shearer and Beckham combined to create the chance for Owen. The Liverpool striker picked the ball up on the edge of the area and fired the ball into the far corner of the net, beating the stranded Romanian 'keeper.*

8 WORLD CUP FINALS
FRIDAY JUNE 26, 1998

COLOMBIA	**0**
ENGLAND	**2**

Attendance: 41,275

Scorers: Anderton 20, Beckham 30

The Game: England fans had been hoping and praying for Beckham and Owen to start the final group game – and they got their wish. Owen had an early chance, but he failed to hit the target after Anderton had delivered a perfect cross. England went two up and with the game won, Campbell made a great run from deep. The defender was tackled, but the ball fell to Owen, who just missed.

Team: Seaman 7, Campbell 8, Adams 8, G Neville 8, Le Saux 6, Anderton 8 (Sub 80 mins Lee), Ince 9 (Sub 83 mins Batty), Beckham 9, Scholes 9 (Sub 74 mins McManaman), Shearer 8, Owen 8.

9 WORLD CUP FINALS
TUESDAY JUNE 30, 1998

ARGENTINA	**2**
ENGLAND	**2**

Attendance: 30,600

Scorers: Shearer 10, Owen 16

The Game: Within five minutes of the big kick-off England were a goal behind after Seaman brought down Simeone, and Batistuta put away the penalty. But Owen went down in the Argentinian area five minutes later and Shearer levelled the scores from the spot. Owen then showed a touch of class as he created and scored a beautiful goal to put his side ahead. After the break Beckham was sent-off and the game headed for a penalty shoot-out. Owen may have put his spot-kick away, but he could only watch as Batty's miss put the Argentinians through.

Team: Seaman 8, Campbell 9, Adams 9, Neville, G 8, Le Saux 7 (sub 71 mins Southgate 7), Anderton 7 (sub 97 mins Batty 8), Ince 9, Beckham 7, Scholes 7 (sub 79 mins Merson 7), Shearer 7, Owen 8.

OWEN GOAL! 16 mins: *Beckham played the ball to Owen who sprinted towards the Argentinan goal. The striker got past Chamot and then pushed the ball to the left of Ayala before lashing it past Roa and into the net to put England 2-1 ahead.*

10 EURO 2000 QUALIFIER
SATURDAY SEPTEMBER 5, 1998

SWEDEN	**2**
ENGLAND	**1**

Attendance: 35,000

Scorers: Shearer 2

The Game: Michael Owen had a goal disallowed for offside and caused problems for the Swedes, being brought down while straight through on goal, but his appeal failed to interest the referee. Ince was sent-off as England crashed to defeat in Stockholm.

Team: Seaman 6, Campbell 8 (sub 75 mins Merson), Le Saux 6, Ince 7, Adams 6, Southgate 5, Anderton 6 (sub 42 mins Lee 5), Redknapp 6, Owen 5, Shearer 6, Scholes 5 (sub 86 mins Sheringham).

11 EURO 2000 QUALIFIER
SATURDAY OCTOBER 10, 1998

ENGLAND	**0**
BULGARIA	**0**

Attendance: 72,974

The Game: Little heart was shown in a game that England really had to win. Shearer and Owen were paired together again but had little opportunity to show off their finishing skills due to poor service.

Team: Seaman 6, Neville, G 7, Hinchcliffe 6 (sub 34 mins Le Saux 7), Lee 5, Campbell 7, Southgate 6, Anderton 5 (sub 67 mins Batty 6), Redknapp 7, Shearer 6, Owen 5, Scholes 6 (sub 76 mins Sheringham).

12 EURO 2000 QUALIFIER
WEDNESDAY OCTOBER 14, 1998

LUXEMBOURG	**0**
ENGLAND	**3**

Attendance: 8,000

Scorers: Owen 19, Shearer 40, Southgate 90

The Game: Owen opened the scoring for England and watched as Shearer made it 2-0 minutes before half-time. The striking partnership caused no end of problems for the part-timers and Owen, in particular, should have added to his goals tally.

Team: Seaman 6, Ferdinand, R 9, Neville, P 8, Batty 8, Campbell 6, Southgate 6, Beckham 7, Anderton 5 (sub 63 mins Lee 5), Shearer 6, Owen 5, Scholes 5 (sub 76 mins Wright).

OWEN GOAL! 19 mins: *Owen ran through the Luxembourg defence, on to Anderton's throughball, and drove a shot past Strasser inside the far post.*

13 INTERNATIONAL FRIENDLY
WEDNESDAY FEBRUARY 10, 1999

ENGLAND	**0**
FRANCE	**2**

Attendance: 74,111

The Game: For the first time in his career, Owen was overshadowed by another youngster as Anelka scored twice for France. The Arsenal star looked a genuine class act as England were easily beaten at Wembley. Looking jaded, Owen was replaced by Cole for the final 25 minutes.

Team: Seaman 7 (sub 46 mins Martyn 6), Dixon 6 (sub 72 mins Ferdinand, R), Le Saux 7, Ince 5, Adams 6, Keown 6 (sub 85 mins Wilcox), Beckham 7, Redknapp 5, Shearer 5, Owen 6 (sub 66 mins Cole), Anderton 5.

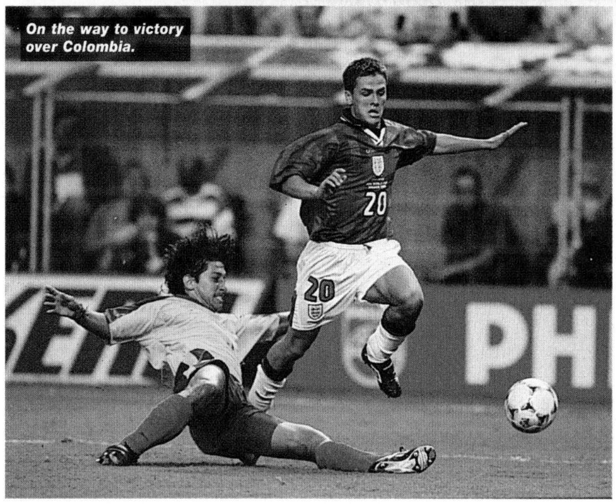

On the way to victory over Colombia.

14 EURO 2000 QUALIFIER
SATURDAY SEPTEMBER 4, 1999

ENGLAND	**6**
LUXEMBOURG	**0**

Attendance: 68,772

Scorers: Shearer 11 (pen), 27, 34, McManaman 30, 43, Owen 89

The Game: Owen came off the bench to make his first international appearance in over six months and he made it a memorable return to action by scoring England's sixth and best goal of the day. His usual striking partner Alan Shearer had earlier scored an impressive hat-trick as England played their penultimate Euro 2000 qualifying game.

Team: Martyn 6, Dyer 8 (sub 46 mins Neville, G 7), Keown 6, Adams 6 (sub 65 mins Neville, P 7), Pearce 7, McManaman 8, Beckham 8 (sub 65 mins Owen 7), Batty 8, Parlour 7, Shearer 9, Fowler 8.

OWEN GOAL! 89 mins: *Added the icing on the cake to a professional 6-0 victory with a fantastic curling shot from the edge of the area, which gave Luxembourg 'keeper Felgen absolutely no chance.*

15 EURO 2000 PLAY-OFF
SATURDAY NOVEMBER 13, 1999

SCOTLAND	**0**
ENGLAND	**2**

Attendance: 50,132

Scorers: Scholes 20, 41

The Game: Owen had an outstanding game for England, before being replaced by Cole, although he didn't play any part in England's goals, which were both scored by Scholes to put England in an excellent position for the return leg at Wembley.

Team: Seaman 7, Neville, P 7, Campbell 6, Ince 6, Adams 7, Keown 6, Beckham 7, Scholes 8, Shearer 7, Owen 8 (sub 67 mins Cole 5), Redknapp 7.

16 EURO 2000 PLAY-OFF
WEDNESDAY NOVEMBER 17, 1999

ENGLAND	**0**
SCOTLAND	**1**

Attendance: 75,848

The Game: Owen and the England forwards didn't have a single shot on Scotland's goal in this crucial play-off match. Kevin Keegan's team looked poor in attack and after Owen had run out of ideas, he was replaced by Heskey. Scotland always looked the stronger side and Owen left Wembley knowing that he still has a lot to learn on the international stage.

Team: Seaman 7, Neville, P 6, Campbell 6, Adams 6, Southgate 6, Ince 5, Redknapp 5, Beckham 7, Scholes 5 (sub 90 mins Parlour), Shearer 5, Owen 5 (sub 63 mins Heskey 6).

17 INTERNATIONAL FRIENDLY
SATURDAY MAY 27, 2000

ENGLAND	**1**
BRAZIL	**1**

Attendance: 73,956

Scorers: Owen 38

The Game: Owen looked lively on his return to the England fold after injury and he cemented his claims for a starting place at Euro 2000 with a well-taken goal against visitors Brazil. Owen again formed an exciting partnership with Alan Shearer, who worked more as a provider. Owen was replaced with a few minutes left on the clock so that Keegan could take a look at Phillips in the England attack.

Team: Seaman 7, Neville, G 8, Neville, P 7, Ince 7 (sub 59 mins Parlour 6 (sub 90 mins Barmby), Campbell 8, Keown 8, Beckham 8, Scholes 7, Shearer 8 (sub 84 mins Fowler), Owen 9 (sub 84 mins Phillips), Wise 7.

OWEN GOAL! 38 mins: *A long throw from Gary Neville found its way to Shearer, who put through Owen to slip the ball past 'keeper Dida to score.*

18 EURO 2000 GROUP STAGE
MONDAY JUNE 12, 2000

ENGLAND	**2**
PORTUGAL	**3**

Attendance: 30,000

Scorers: Scholes 3, McManaman 19

The Game: Owen played a vital part in England's second goal against Portugal in the first game of Euro 2000, but he didn't get much of the ball in the first half. He played a short pass to Beckham on the right, whose cross led to McManaman's goal, but Owen generally found himself marked out of the game. He appeared to be constantly fouled by the Portuguese defence, but found little favour with the referee before being substituted at half-time to make way for the physically stronger Heskey.

Team: Seaman 6, Neville, G 6, Neville, P 6, Campbell 7, Adams 6 (sub 82 mins Keown), Ince 7, Scholes 7, Beckham 8, McManaman 7 (sub 58 mins Wise 7), Shearer 6, Owen 6 (sub 46 mins Heskey 6).

19 EURO 2000 GROUP STAGE
SATURDAY JUNE 17, 2000

ENGLAND	**1**
GERMANY	**0**

Attendance: 30,000

Scorers: Shearer 53

The Game: Despite rumours that he'd be dropped after struggling in his first game, Owen made the starting line-up alongside Alan Shearer for the clash against Germany. Owen had an excellent chance to put England ahead early on, but 'keeper Kahn tipped his header on to the post. Owen had a good game up front with Shearer, who scored the only goal of the game, but the team didn't create enough opportunities to increase the scoreline.

Team: Seaman 8, Neville, G 7, Keown 8, Campbell 8, Neville, P 7, Beckham 7, Ince 7, Scholes 7 (sub 73 mins Barmby), Wise 7, Shearer 8, Owen 7 (sub 61 mins Gerrard 8).

20 EURO 2000 GROUP STAGE
TUESDAY JUNE 20, 2000

ENGLAND	**2**
ROMANIA	**3**

Attendance: 30,000

Scorers: Shearer 41 (pen), Owen 45

The Game: Owen and his team-mates were so close to a place in the second round, but Romania scored a winning penalty in the dying moments of the game and consigned England to an early plane home. Owen scored his first goal of the tournament to put England 2-1 ahead on the stroke of half-time, but Romania came back to win 3-2. Owen had done well in his last international match with Shearer, but it wasn't enough and England were out.

Team: Martyn 6, Neville, G 6, Campbell 7, Keown 7, Neville, P 6, Beckham 7, Ince 7, Scholes 7 (sub 80 mins Southgate), Wise 6 (sub 75 mins Barmby), Shearer 7, Owen 7 (sub 67 mins Heskey 6).

OWEN GOAL! 45 mins: *Scholes played a lofted pass over the Romanian back line and Owen ran the ball past the 'keeper and side-footed home.*

MICHAEL OWEN'S INTERNATIONAL STATISTICS

STRIKE RATIO	20 games/6 goals	30%
TOTAL MINS PLAYED	1231 minutes	
AVE MINS PLAYED	61.5 minutes	

OWEN'S ENGLAND

Even though Michael only made his international debut in 1998, he's already experienced some fantastic highs and depressing lows in his senior England career.

FEBRUARY 1998

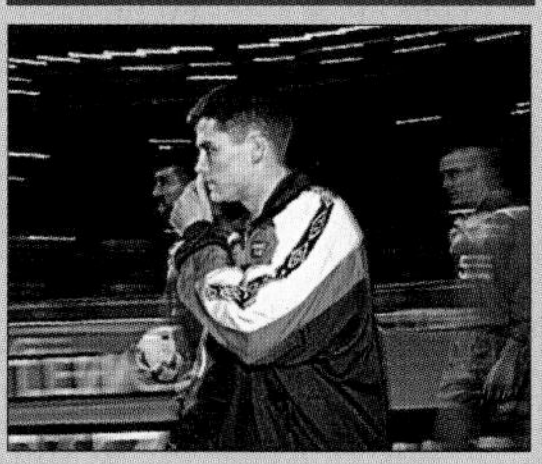

After much hype in the Press, Glenn Hoddle includes Owen in his England squad for the home friendly against Chile. He becomes the youngest player to pull on a senior shirt when he starts the game at the age of 17 years and 59 days, but the team loses 2-0.

JUNE 1998

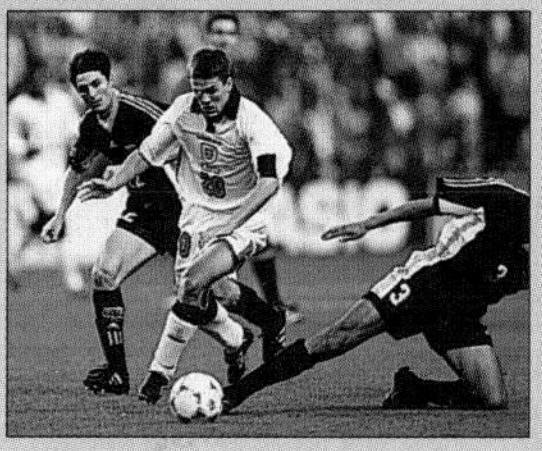

Owen proves his worth to Hoddle and is picked in the manager's 22-man squad for the World Cup. He makes a telling impact when he scores a spectacular goal during the enthralling clash with Argentina, which the South Americans win on penalties.

SEPTEMBER 1998

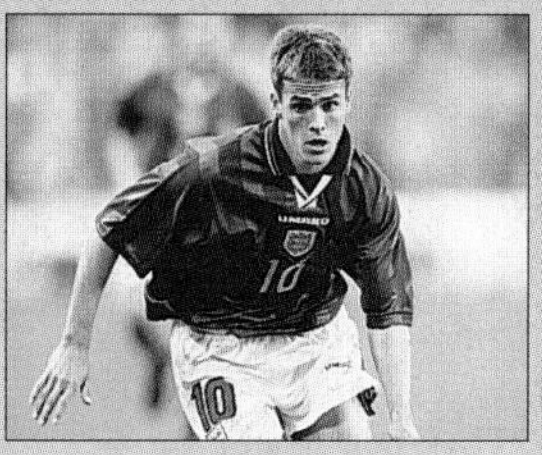

After the goal which made him a star, Owen gets back to the mundane as England start their Euro 2000 qualifying campaign. But he has a goal disallowed and doesn't play well in the 2-1 away defeat in Sweden.

NOVEMBER 1999

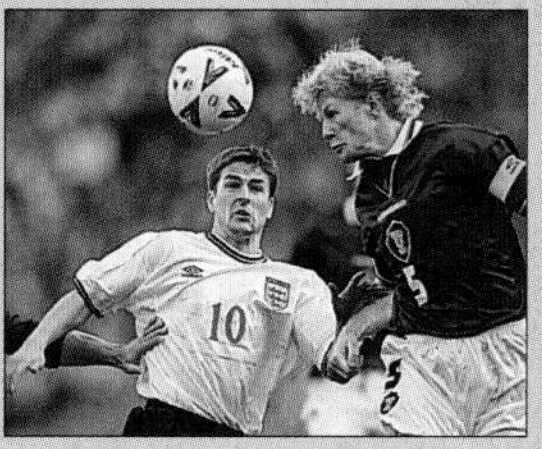

Owen has a disappointing game and is criticised by the Press after a lacklustre performance in the home leg of the Euro 2000 qualifying play-off against Scotland. England lose 1-0, but the result is enough after a 2-0 first-leg win at Hampden Park.

JUNE 2000

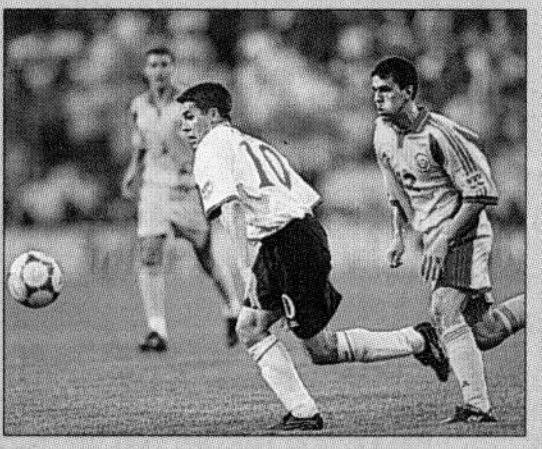

Michael partners Alan Shearer up front in every starting line-up at Euro 2000 and he nets a goal against Romania. Although England beat Germany, two defeats mean they don't even get past the group stages.

HOW DID YOU SCORE?
This is your final chance to rack up some points to see how good your football knowledge really is. Remember to fill in your answers in the boxes on page 108.

Tony Cottee lifts the Worthington Cup.

fifth XI

The League Cup may not be as big as the FA Cup, but it's still an exciting competition. Test your knowledge here.

1 The League Cup has not been running as long as the FA Cup, but in which year was the first League Cup held in England?

2 And which team were the first ever winners of the new competition?

3 Which two clubs hold the record for having won the most League Cups?

4 The competition has had many different sponsors in its history, but can you remember when the League Cup became the Milk Cup?

5 The first five League Cup Finals were all played over home and away legs. True or false?

6 One club, now stuck in the Third Division, once appeared in the final of the League Cup. They lost the match, but who was it that came so close to glory?

7 In which year did Arsenal win the League Cup and the FA Cup in the same season, beating the same opposition in both finals?

8 Which drinks company sponsored the League Cup from 1993 to 1998?

9 The League Cup became the Worthington Cup in July 1998. Which team won the trophy at the end of the 1998-99 season?

10 And which player went mad when he scored the only goal of that final?

11 In the last League Cup Final to be played at Wembley before it is rebuilt, Leicester City beat First Division Tranmere Rovers. Who scored both Leicester's goals in their 2-1 win?

THE MEGA WORD SPOT

Can you find these top Premiership defenders in the grid below?

```
G T G K R G C E P N Z U G P C S U K K
J L P E H P A L L I S T E R K E L L Y
W D S C H N O O R Y I M F E R R E R C
B O U L D G P V X Q N B A R T O N B V
Q I K P Y Z H E E K E O W N D O M I M
N I H E B J O C T C Y Y O V D N Q I D
R Y E O D H H P W R I R O X L Q L R A
C A N Y G Y N Q Y T A G G A R T B A B
H R D Y L Y I S O U T H G A T E E N I
Z G R R I P V F K S F H W A L Z N O Z
R Z Y R X I L C S W W C X E O V A B A
G O D E S A I L L Y M E B F R S L R S
O H Y P Y S S H C E G B L Q K G I A G
R C R L H U Y A L O A B X L O F Y C A
D N R V J N R C G B S N E V I L L E S
O E A S H R H F E S T A D M U O S I M
N H B Z T I R U D D O C K J T W T A A
J K U A O A R V Z F T H O M E J E T D
C L P T M T M O E Q C A M P B E L L A
```

- ADAMS
- BABBEL
- BARRY
- BARTON
- BENALI
- BOULD
- CAMPBELL
- CARBONARI
- CARR
- DABIZAS
- DESAILLY
- DOMI
- ELLIOTT
- FERRER
- FESTA
- GORDON
- GRAY
- HARTE
- HENCHOZ
- HENDRY
- HYYPIA
- KELLY
- KEOWN
- LUZHNY
- MELCHIOT
- NEVILLE
- PALLISTER
- PERRY
- RUDDOCK
- SCHNOOR
- SILVINHO
- SOUTHGATE
- STAM
- TAGGART
- THOME

paolo di canio quiz

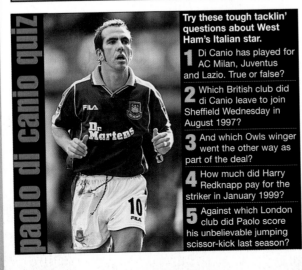

Try these tough tacklin' questions about West Ham's Italian star.

1 Di Canio has played for AC Milan, Juventus and Lazio. True or false?

2 Which British club did di Canio leave to join Sheffield Wednesday in August 1997?

3 And which Owls winger went the other way as part of the deal?

4 How much did Harry Redknapp pay for the striker in January 1999?

5 Against which London club did Paolo score his unbelievable jumping scissor-kick last season?

former clubs

Who did these stars play for before their current club?

1 Kevin Phillips — Sunderland

2 Dion Dublin — Aston Villa

3 Christian Ziege — Middlesbrough

4 Mark Kennedy — Manchester City

MATCH facts
CODE BREAKER

CRACK THE CODE!

3	6	19	19	12	16
10	16	20	7	16	

connections...

What links Man. United's Roy Keane and Celtic manager Martin O'Neill?

club nicknames

Can you match these teams with their nicknames?

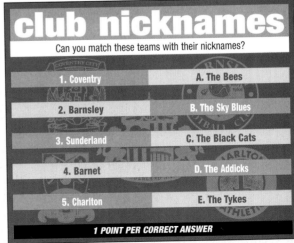

1. Coventry	A. The Bees
2. Barnsley	B. The Sky Blues
3. Sunderland	C. The Black Cats
4. Barnet	D. The Addicks
5. Charlton	E. The Tykes

1 POINT PER CORRECT ANSWER

ROBBIE KEANE
Coventry City

MATCH
YOUNG GUNS

Chants Chants Chants

ARSENE WENGER'S MAGIC

♫ (To The Tune Of 'My Old Man's A Dustman')
Arsene Wenger's magic
He wears a magic hat
And when he saw the FA Cup
He said, 'I'm having that'
Ohhhhh (repeat)
Johnny, Pinner

PRIDE OF MANCHESTER

One 's' in Manchester
There's only one 's' in Manchester
One 's' in Manchester
And that's Stockport County…
Craig Cheetham, Stockport

BALD CHOICE

Stevie Stone
Stevie Stone
Stevie, Stevie Stone
He's got no hair, but we don't care
Stevie, Stevie Stone
Geoff Wilkins, Bromsgrove

REDS SONG

He's big, he's cool
He plays for Liverpool
His name is Song
Rigobert Song
Adam Field, Somerset

SEXY QUINN

♫ (To The Tune Of 'You Sexy Thing')
I believe in miracles
Niall Quinn, you sexy thing
I believe in good goals
Niall Quinn, you sexy thing
Ryan O'Neill, Newcastle

Danielle walked out at the Euro 2000 game against Portugal with her hero David Beckham. What did Posh say?

MY BIG DAY OUT!

MATCH follows a lucky competition winner on her big day out in Holland!

DANIELLE AT HER HOME IN JERSEY WHEN SHE FOUND OUT SHE HAD WON.

LINING UP IN FRONT OF BECKS AND PAUL SCHOLES FOR THE NATIONAL ANTHEM.

DESTINATION: Philips Stadion, Eindhoven

EVENT: England v Portugal

How many people have dreamed that they could walk out beside David Beckham onto the pitch for an England game? Thousands probably, but the dream came true for one lucky girl last summer.

Danielle Ward, from Jersey, was the winner of a Coca-Cola competition to be an official player escort at the England v Portugal game at Euro 2000. She wore a Portugal shirt and walked out with the England team. **"Danielle found out on the Thursday before the game that she had won and she was really over the moon. She kept on jumping around the kitchen!"** explained her mum Alison.

Danielle flew to Holland with her dad for the game. **"I was supposed to walk out with Paul Scholes, but David Beckham grabbed my hand,"** she explained. **"He asked me if I was nervous and said, 'Don't worry, there's only millions of people watching!',** Danielle told MATCH. **"He asked me what I thought the score was going to be and I wished him good luck. My friends are all really jealous that I met David Beckham and some people have even asked me for my autograph!"**

Danielle has become a celebrity in Jersey and even gets recognised when she's out!

AFTER CHANGING, DANIELLE WATCHED THE GAME FROM THE STAND WITH HER DAD.

DANIELLE WASN'T HAPPY WITH THE 3-2 LOSS, BUT SHE ENJOYED HER DAY OUT.

OUT & ABOUT!

Footy stars pictured with **MATCH** readers!

MATCH reader **MARTIN SIDNEY** of Lincoln had his photograph taken with team captain **Jamie Redknapp** when he went to see Liverpool play.

ALAN PURCELL and **EOIN O'CARROLL** were lucky enough to get a top photo with Man. United legend **George Best** in their hometown of Dublin.

Middlesbrough supporter **AMY COLEMAN** had her picture taken with manager **Bryan Robson** at Boro's Rockcliffe training ground in Hurworth.

WHO DO YOU SUPPORT?

Take the Extra Time quiz challenge to work out which international side you should support.

1 **What odds would you get on your chosen team winning the World Cup in 2002?**
a. 2-1 The bookies rate you as probably the best side in the tournament.
b. 15-1 You've got a chance, but it'd be a major shock if your country won it.
c. 25-1 You've done well just to qualify, so go out there and enjoy yourselves.

2 **What statement would best describe your favoured country's Euro 2000 captain?**
a. He's under criticism from the fans, but he's still playing well.
b. He is an experienced player, playing some excellent football in Serie A.
c. He has now retired from international football to concentrate on chilling out.

3 **Your team step up to take penalties at the next World Cup, do they...**
a. Scrape through on luck, because everything seems to go their way.
b. Always win on spot-kicks, because that's how it's always been.
c. Typically lose on penalties, with a few players missing abysmally.

4 **How does your team qualify for tournaments?**
a. It's been shaky of late, but once they get to the tournament they are good.
b. The team often looks shaky, but they always do well.
c. They usually leave it until the last minute, then qualify by finishing in second place.

5 **Which of these statements best describes your team's style?**
a. They have plenty of flair in midfield, as well as in defence and now attack!
b. Strong, dominant and threatening. They are usually efficient in defence.
c. More attacking than they sometimes should be, but it makes them exciting to watch.

6 **What is the usual score when they win a game?**
a. They usually keep a clean sheet and manage to score more than once.
b. They usually keep a clean sheet, so the score would be 1-0.
c. Almost always 2-1, because the dodgy defence will always leak goals.

HOW DID YOU SCORE?

A = 10 points, **B = 0** points and **C = 5** points.

Below 20 ...YOU SUPPORT THE GERMAN TEAM! THEY HAVE A GLORIOUS HISTORY, BUT THEY'RE STRUGGLING TO KEEP UP THEIR FINE WINNING TRADITIONS!

25-65 ...YOU'RE ENGLAND! STILL CLINGING ON TO STORIES OF 1966 AND STILL STRUGGLING!

70-90 ...YOU'RE FRANCE! YOU LIKE TO SUPPORT THE BEST TEAM IN THE WORLD – FANTASTIQUE!

MY SCORE

CLUB WATCH!

MATCH tells you how to contact your fave club.

Manchester United FC

Club address: Sir Matt Busby Way, Old Trafford, Manchester, M16 0RA.
Official website: www.manutd.com

Help!

MATCHMAN is always ready to answer all your footy queries...

Dear MATCHMAN,
Can you give me some information about last season's Serie A winners Lazio?
Joby Mullins, Newbury

MATCHMAN SAYS: As you said Joby, Lazio won the title last season after narrowly missing out to AC Milan on the final day of the 1998-99 campaign. It was the second time the club had won the league championship after their first success in 1974. They have won the Italian Cup twice, in 1958 and 1998, and they lifted the Cup-Winners' Cup in 1999, beating Real Mallorca (who had beaten Chelsea in the semis) in the Final at Villa Park. Their star players include Alessandro Nesta, Fernando Couto and Pavel Nedved. Gazza played for Lazio between 1992 and 1995.

Lazio won only their second Serie A championship last season.

Young Sunderland fan **DAVID RAY** had his photo taken with Sunderland mascot **Delilah** before the last home game of last season against West Ham.

This Liverpool fan from Bristol was lucky enough to meet **Phil Thompson**, the assistant manager of The Reds, while he was on a school trip to Anfield!

MATCH reader **DEAN TURNER** of Basingstoke sent in this photograph he had taken with Fulham and Northern Ireland goalkeeper **Maik Taylor**.

the JOKE'S on You!

Check out this bunch of footy jokes sent in by **MATCH** readers!

HEAVEN'S ABOVE!

Three kids are playing in the street and get tragically hit by a speeding car. All three of them go to heaven and at the gates God says to them:

"You weren't supposed to die kids, you were all supposed to live long lives. This was not your time. To make it up to you, I'll let you choose whatever you want to do with your future. Take a run and jump off that cloud over there. But as you are flying back down to Earth, shout out what you want to do in the future and it'll happen."

The first kid takes a running leap off the cloud and shouts: **"I want to be a lawyer."** And so, 20 years later, he is a highly respected and very successful lawyer, making lots of money, and sitting in a huge office with all the latest gadgets.

The second kid takes his turn and shouts: **"I want to be a brain surgeon."** And so, 20 years later, he is the most admired man in his field of medicine and is making a lot of money saving lives.

The third kid goes to take his turn but as he runs, he trips over his own feet and stumbles off the cloud, muttering: **"Clumsy great oaf!"** And so, 20 years later…
…he's still playing at left-back for Manchester United and England!
★ *Lee Daffern, Manchester*

KEEGAN'S GAFFS!

Look at these funny quotes from Kevin Keegan, they're great!

"Argentina are the second-best team in the world and there is no higher praise than that."

"England have the best fans in the world and Scotland's fans are second to none."

"Gary has weighed up his options, especially when he had no choice."

"The tide is very much in our court now."

"I'd love to be a mole on the wall in the Liverpool dressing room now."

"The 33 or 34-year-olds will be 36 or 37 by the next World Cup, if they're not careful."

"I came to Nantes two years ago and it's much the same today, except that it's totally different."
★ *Shaun White, London*

SEND YOUR JOKES OR PUNS TO: The Joke's On You, MATCH Magazine, Bretton Court, Bretton, Peterborough, PE3 8DZ.

Side-parting, round face and good at dribbling. There's quite a likeness, don't you think?

Sam adds another United legend to his photo collection.

Roy Keane was lucky enough to have his photo taken with Sam and printed in MATCH.

Sam admires another trophy in the Man. United museum.

Sam met up with Becks on the way to the hairdresser.

Does anyone think this lad supports Manchester United?

MATCH SUPERFAN!

MATCH goes in search of the most footy mad readers on the planet!

Name: Sam Cale

Age: Ten

Sam thinks he is Man. United's No.1 fan. Now there may be at least a million people all over the world who think that they are the No.1 fan, but here are a few reasons why Sam is different from most of the rest. First, he lives in Middleton in Manchester, which puts him a darn sight nearer to Old Trafford than most Red Devils. Second, Sam's mum has been taking him to matches since he was six-years-old and third, he even has some 'treble-winning' turf potted in his back garden! Do you really need any more evidence?

Okay, well Sam's bedroom is covered in Man. United memorabilia and he's met several United players, including David Beckham, Paul Scholes, Ole Gunnar Solskjaer and his personal favourite, Dwight Yorke. If he gets bored when the team isn't playing, he watches one of over 100 United videos he has in his collection! **"My mum said I could name the team before I knew my alphabet and I used to sit on the potty and watch football!"** explains Sam. **"I have the Man. United television channel on my TV and they even came to film me in my bedroom. They asked me questions on Man. United – I can answer questions going back to 1968."** So that would be: who won the European Cup in 1968? Any ideas? Yes, you guessed it, Man. United.

Sam has been lucky enough to watch United play at Wembley four times and he has a collection of programmes from the last three seasons. No doubt he'll also get to see them in numerous other cup finals and charity shields. Mind you, he's one Man. United fan that other supporters can't have a go at!

Green pyjamas, they won't do. Where's the red of Man. United?

SAM MET THE GREAT PETER SCHMEICHEL BEFORE HE LEFT

All around the WORLD

Check out these **MATCH** readers in exotic places.

Blackpool fan **Tom Dunderdale** of Leicestershire is pictured with a 'friend' reading MATCH over his shoulder while on holiday in **GRAN CANARIA**!

Richard Bates went to **MALTA** on holiday with his parents, but he couldn't go all that way without taking along a copy of his favourite football mag!

Daniel Wallwork, a ten-year-old Bolton fan, went to Lineker's Bar in **TENERIFE**. He only just missed Gary Lineker, who was visiting the bar he owns!

FOOTY DAYS OUT!

MATCH looks at the best way to spend your holidays – enjoying football!

Arsenal Museum

WHAT IS IT? Basically, if you understand it from the name, it's a football museum that traces the history of Arsenal and their glory years. It's not the biggest football museum, but it's comprehensive.

WHERE IS IT? The museum is situated on the second floor of the North Bank stand at Highbury in north London.

PRICES: If you're an adult, entry will cost you £4, but it's only £2 for under-16s and senior citizens are admitted for £1. That's a bargain if you're an old Gunners fan!

ANY GOOD? There's loads of Arsenal memorabilia, replicas of the trophies that The Gunners have won and stories of the team's triumphs and losses. There are loads of quizzes to try and a film on the club's history to watch, so you'll love the museum if you're an Arsenal nut. If you're not, then you probably shouldn't go at all!

OPENING HOURS: Plan ahead because at the moment the museum is only open to the public on Fridays from 9.30am until 4.00pm. The museum is no longer open on matchdays for security reasons.

CONTACT: 0171 704 4100

Liverpool Training

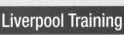

WHAT IS IT? It's your chance to check out the size of Sami Hyypia in real life, see how competitive Steven Gerrard is and watch Michael Owen taking shots on the training field. Owen and co practise their skills every weekday morning.

WHERE IS IT? The famous Melwood training ground in Liverpool and, very occasionally, at the Liverpool Academy.

PRICES: Nothing (other than your bus fare to Melwood), if you get in that is…

ANY GOOD? Well, there's just one slight problem. Training is usually behind closed doors because manager Gerard Houllier doesn't want other teams to know his tactics ahead of Liverpool's next game.

OPENING HOURS? Occasionally Houllier will let some fans in, but this will be done on the spur of the moment and nothing will be arranged beforehand. It's a long shot, but hang around outside the ground every day during half-term, just in case.

CONTACT: It may not work, but try writing to the club and ask if you can watch one of their rare open training sessions, then you'll have to keep your fingers crossed!

Manchester United Museum

WHAT IS IT? It's basically a shrine to United and tells the history of the team, from when the club was founded in 1902 right up to the magnificent treble triumph.

WHERE IS IT? You'll find the museum at Manchester United's home, Old Trafford.

PRICES: It will cost you £8 to get in if you're an adult, but kids and oldies get in for £5.50. You could save some money by getting a family ticket (for two adults and three children) which costs £22.

ANY GOOD? You should definitely check out the Hall Of Fame and a virtual reality tour of the stadium. You can even see the Premiership trophy close-up, as well as other exciting memorabilia from magic occasions, so it's well worth a look. Get yourself down to the ground now!

OPENING HOURS? The museum is open seven days a week, between 9.30am and 5.00pm, but make sure you leave yourself plenty of time to have a good look around because there's a lot to see. The club also runs tours of the stadium. Book tickets in advance to avoid any disappointment.

CONTACT: 0161 868 8000 (switchboard)

Newcastle United Training

WHAT IS IT? Check out Bobby Robson's team in action as they're taken through their paces before the next game.

WHERE IS IT? The Newcastle squad train in Chester-le-Street on the pitches which are behind Durham County Cricket Club. The nearest train station to their training ground is Durham, which is on the main railway line from London to Scotland.

PRICES: You don't have to pay to attend any of Newcastle's training sessions, but you'll have to find your own transport to get yourself to Chester-le-Street.

ANY GOOD? Are you kidding? You get to see stars like Alan Shearer, Carl Cort and Kieron Dyer in training! Can you think of a better way to spend your holidays? No, neither can we, so get down there.

OPENING HOURS? Newcastle usually train for two hours from 10.30am until 12.30pm, Monday to Friday. Wednesday is sometimes a day off, though. You should watch out around the Christmas holidays because training times may differ.

CONTACT: You don't need to call the club, just turn up for training with the players!

The Caen football stadium in **FRANCE** was the impressive setting when **Robert Williams** from Stoke was pictured with his fave football magazine!

Avid reader **Josh Reynard** and friend had a quick read of **MATCH** before they went snorkelling off the Great Barrier Reef in **AUSTRALIA**!

Philip Whitby from Merseyside is pictured with his copy of **MATCH** in the Dachstein mountains of **AUSTRIA**, with a drop of 2055 metres behind him!

THE FINAL WHISTLE
ANSWERS

There are a grand total of 300 points available if, by some miracle, you managed to answer every quiz question on all five Final Whistle pages correctly. Check out all the answers to the quizzes here and see how many you got right, and then find out in the guide below just what type of footballer you are!

261-300
YOU'RE WORLD FOOTBALLER OF THE YEAR!

Congratulations! Your knowledge knows no bounds and your friends always come to you when they want to know any footballing fact. You understand the technical side and can reel off results.

221-260
YOU'RE PLAYER OF THE YEAR!

Well done! You're knowledge may not be world-class, but you certainly know your stuff. Definitely a fan who keeps up with the latest news, you've also got respect for the football from before you were born. Impressive!

176-220
YOU'RE A MILLION POUND MAN

An impressive score. You have a steady knowledge of the game and can still beat a lot of your mates on who played where, when and what the score was. Although you are not quite a Statto, you do know your footy.

131-175
YOU'RE A REGULAR STARTER

That's not bad. You get most of the answers right, but you slip up and make the odd mistake. If you want to improve you should listen out every day for football news and speak to your dad about 'the good old days'.

86-130
YOU'RE ON A WEEKLY CONTRACT

You're okay, for a part-time fan, but you could be doing a lot better. Less than half marks is a pretty dismal showing, but there is still time to make a fan out of you yet. Read the annual and start learning about football!

41-85
YOU'RE AVAILABLE ON A FREE TRANSFER

Hmmm. Do you read MATCH or not? It looks like you need to order a subscription right away because you don't know much about the game. But don't worry, you're not a lost cause… yet! Get yourself to some games!

under 40
YOU'D BETTER TAKE EARLY RETIREMENT MATE!

Oh dear. Do you even like football? Unless you're under the age of five, we hope you're feeling totally and utterly embarrassed at your pathetic knowledge. In fact, why don't you try teaching cricket instead?

NAME THE CLUB
1.
1. Ipswich.

CONNECTIONS
1.
1. Their dads are both Premiership managers.

Final Whistle One page 32

FIRST XI
1.
2.
3.
4.
5.
6.
7.
8.
9.
10.
11.

1. Phillips, Shearer, Cole; 2. False; 3. Leeds, 28 goals; 4. Arsenal; 5. 10 (Barnsley, Bolton, Crystal Palace, Charlton, Leicester, Nottingham Forest, Middlesbrough, Sunderland, Swindon, Watford); 6. Thomas Brolin; 7. None; 8. Attilio Lombardo; 9. Carlton Palmer (Leeds, Southampton, Nottingham Forest, Coventry); 10. No Englishmen in starting kit; 11. Three (Steve Bruce, Tony Adams, Tim Sherwood).

WHO WON IT?
1.
1. Everton.

1-0
1.
2.
3.
4.
5.
1. Frank Lebeouf; 2. Ian Harte; 3. Matt Elliott; 4. Gary McAllister; 5. David Ginola.

CODE BREAKER
1.
1. Steven Gerrard.

CIVVY STREET
1.
1. Francis Jeffers.

Final Whistle Two page 50

SECOND XI
1.
2.
3.
4.
5.
6.
7.
8.
9.
10.
11.

1. 1956; 2. Real Madrid; 3. Celtic, 1967; 4. Benfica; 5. Red Star won 5-4 on penalties; 6. Phillip Don; 7. 1995; 8. AC Milan and Juventus; 9. Inter Milan and Juventus; 10. Ole Gunnar Solskjaer; 11. Raul.

CROSSWORD
1. Out of 34 points I scored…
*22. Morris; 23. Mills; 24. Halle; 26. Blake; 27. Dyer.
16. Neville; 17. Toshack; 18. Rio; 19. Saunders;
5. Durie; 6. Nolan; 8. Emerson; 10. Arsenal; 13. Rae;
DOWN: 1. Campbell; 2. Lomas; 3. Song; 4. Hughes;
28. Elleray; 29. Keane; 30. Souness; 31. Rangers.
20. Evans; 21. Kinsella; 23. Melchiot; 25. Carbon;
11. Bosses; 12. Pedersen; 14. Linesman; 16. Stone;
ACROSS: 1. Collins; 4. Hodgson; 7. Moore; 9. Nigeria;
ONE POINT FOR EACH CORRECT ANSWER.*

WHO AM I?
1.
1. David Johnson.

CODE BREAKER
1.
1. Luc Nilis.

FORMER CLUBS
1.
2.
3.
4.
1. Wimbledon; 2. Wimbledon; 3. Oxford; 4. Ipswich.

AND SEE HOW YOU SCORED!

MY TOTAL OUT OF 300

WHO WON IT?
1

1. Bayern Munich.

DATING AGENCY
1

1. Steven Gerrard.

WHAT POSITION?
1 | 4
2 | 5
3

1. B. 2. D. 3. A. 4. C. 5. E.

Final Whistle Three — page 64

THIRD XI
1
2
3
4
5
6
7
8
9
10
11

1. 1872. 2. Wanderers and Blackburn. 3. 1923. 4. 4-3.
1953 Final 5. Portsmouth. 6. Ian Porterfield;
7. Tottenham, 1981. 8. Arsenal, 1993; 9. Man. United, 10.
10. Man. United. 11. Roberto Di Matteo.

2-1
1
2
3
4

1. Alan Shearer. 2. Tim Sherwood. 3. Dean Saunders.
4. Kevin Phillips.

WHO AM I?
1

1. Michael Bridges.

CODE BREAKER
1

1. Thierry Henry.

GAFFERS
1
2
3
4
5

1. Chris Turner. 2. Sir Alex Ferguson. 3. David Moyes;
4. Egil Olsen. 5. Vicente Del Bosque.

STEVEN GERRARD QUIZ
1
2
3
4
5

1. Tottenham. 2. True. 3. Central midfield. 4. Ukraine;
5. Adidas.

Final Whistle Four — page 84

FOURTH XI
1
2
3
4
5
6
7
8
9
10
11

1. Inter-Cities Fairs' Cup. 2. 1972. 3. True. 4. Tottenham;
5. Bobby Robson. 6. Real Madrid - 1985, 1986. 7. Inter
Milan. 8. Tottenham; 9. Schalke 04, 10. Moscow;
11. Galatasaray.

CROSSWORD
1 Out of 33 points I scored...

ONE POINT FOR EACH CORRECT ANSWER:
ACROSS: 1. Malta; 3. Silvinho; 7. Schmeca; 9. Austria;
11. Rodney; 12. Barton; 14. Sweden; 15. Crossbar;
18. Phillips; 20. McCall; 24. Accles; 26. Orient;
28. Chelsea; 29. Shakers; 30. Desailly; 31. Dixon.
DOWN: 1. Mascots; 2. Arendse; 3. Scales; 4. Loan;
5. Hurst. 6. Warner; 8. Israeli; 10. Stags; 13. Fry;
16. Beattie; 18. Pearce; 19. Leeds; 21. Cleland;
22. Larsson; 23. Gresty; 25. Crewe; 27. Ball.

WHO WON IT?
1

1. Blackburn Rovers.

CIVVY STREET
1

1. Dean Richards.

CODE BREAKER
1

1. Paul Scholes.

FORMER CLUBS
1
2
3
4

1. Leeds; 2. Benfica; 3. Blackburn; 4. Man. United.

WHO PLAYS WHERE?
1 | 4
2 | 5
3

1. C. 2. E. 3. A. 4. B. 5. D.

CONNECTIONS
1

1. They have both played for QPR.

Final Whistle Five — page 102

FIFTH XI
1
2
3
4
5
6
7
8
9
10
11

1. 1961. 2. Aston Villa. 3. Aston Villa and Liverpool;
4. 1982. 5. False, it was the first six finals. 6. Rochdale;
7. 1993. 8. Coca-Cola; 9. Tottenham; 10. Allan Nielsen;
11. Matt Elliott.

FORMER CLUBS
1
2
3
4

1. Watford; 2. Coventry; 3. AC Milan; 4. Wimbledon.

CODE BREAKER
1

1. Robbie Keane.

CLUB NICKNAMES
1 | 4
2 | 5
3

1. B. 2. E. 3. C. 4. A. 5. D.

PAOLO DI CANIO
1
2
3
4
5

1. True. 2. Celtic; 3. Regi Blinker; 4. £1.7 million;
5. Wimbledon.

CONNECTIONS
1

1. They have both played for Nottingham Forest.

MEGA WORDSPOT – FINAL WHISTLE 1
Out of 35 points I scored...

MEGA WORDSPOT – FINAL WHISTLE 3
Out of 35 points I scored...

MEGA WORDSPOT – FINAL WHISTLE 5
Out of 35 points I scored...

M 109

FOOTBALL'S BEST ENTERTAINER

The MATCH award for the best entertainer of the year goes to West Ham forward Paolo di Canio. That volley he scored against Wimbledon last season was pure magic.

FANZINES ON THE NET

MATCH takes a look at the best fanzines on the world wide web.

Website: 'Hob Nob Anyone?'

Club: Reading FC

Web address: www.royals.cx

What's it all about? The site is a regularly updated fanzine which tells you everything you need to know about The Royals. **Contents:** Latest news, fixtures, gossip, match reports, archived news articles, links to websites, a supporters' index, a cool away supporters' guide and the chance to buy a Reading car sticker! **Best Features:** The away fans' guide is great for anyone who's planning a trip to Reading. There is advice on whether to buy hot dogs or burgers, detailed maps, a comprehensive list of bus times and even a local pub guide.

Rating: 9/10

Spot on!

Website: 'It's the HOPE I can't stand'

Club: Sunderland AFC

Web address: www.dspace.dial.pipex.com/hope

What's it all about? It's a site that's run by some despairing Sunderland fans and is aimed at anyone who appreciates 'Super' Kevin Phillips! **Contents:** Latest editions of the fanzine on-line, archived editions, match reports, club info, fixture lists and a fun & games section. **Best Features:** Check out the fun and games lookalikes and marvel at the weird resemblance between Temuri Ketsbaia and Bert from Sesame Street!

Rating: 8/10

Loads of Sunderland info!

Website: 'The Dover Athletic Prime Web Site'

Club: Dover Athletic

Web address: www.doverathletic.co.uk

What's it all about? The site is one fan's attempt at telling the rest of the world about the club that they've obviously become so devoted to. **Contents:** Updated news, a chat room, editorial and information on the Dover supporters' club. **Best features:** The website is fully interactive, so as well as the chat room you get to vote for Dover Athletic's Player Of The Season. Pretty impressive, eh? You decide who wins the award!

Rating: 6/10

Put a lot of work into it!

10 ESSENTIAL THINGS
...to make you a football statto!

1 A good memory. You will need to remember hundreds of names, match results, goalscorers and cup winners if you are to be taken seriously.

2 A frown. Football stattos are only taken seriously if they look very serious. Develop a frown and if people start taking the mickey, quote some statistics at them so they'll feel inferior.

3 A library, filled with football books. Not only do you need player factfiles, but every Rothmans yearbook since time began. And, of course, you need to have read them all. Twice.

4 Hundreds of football quiz books. What a statto really likes to do is to test his or her football knowledge through crosswords, puzzles and riddles.

5 Technical knowledge. As well as being able to name the scorers from the 1923 FA Cup Final, you need to know the technical side, like analysing Holland's total football of the '70s.

6 Cut out and keep MATCHfacts sections. You should be able to memorise each player's ratings in your team from the last match they played.

7 A collection of memorabilia. This should include items to read such as rare programmes, old newspapers with match reports and the first issues of magazines. Footy stamps are a must.

8 A lot of money. Stattos don't gain their knowledge by just sitting at home sifting through books and MATCH, you'll need to go to as many matches as possible. Then you can boast, "Oh yes, I remember that well. I was there…"

9 A television. If you're a real statto you'll be able to watch football quiz shows and impress your friends by always knowing 'what happens next'. Watch every week and make sure you always improve on last week's score.

10 A membership with the highly respected Association Of Football Statisticians. This is the official body which people phone up when they want to know hard-to-find stats. So if you're serious, you should become a member.

11 A pair of glasses and a sheepskin coat, à la John Motson. You'll only be taken seriously as a statto if you really look the part as well.

That's it. Another year gone and you've come to the end of yet another fab MATCH annual, but don't worry because the MATCH team will soon be working on a new one and you could be part of the fun! We want photographs of you to be included in the MATCH Annual 2002. All you have to do is get your picture taken with the annual or with a well-known football player. If you're a bit camera-shy, you can also send in your football jokes or your stories of footy days out. Send your entries to: MATCH, Bretton Court, Bretton, Peterborough, PE3 8DZ. And you could be reading your story! **We hope you enjoyed the annual and wish you a great 2001!**